EDINBURGH BIBLIOGRAPHICAL SOCIETY
OCCASIONAL PUBLICATION

Books, Borrowers, and Shareholders

By K. A. Manley

Edinburgh Bibliographical Society

Founded in 1890, the Edinburgh Bibliographical Society promotes the study of books and manuscripts of any date, particularly Scottish, and prints articles in the annual *Journal* and monographs in *Occasional Publications*.

A programme of six to eight meetings (including visits to private and other libraries) is organized every year, and members receive the *Journal* at no extra cost as well as being eligible to purchase any other publications by the Society at a substantial discount. The annual subscription is £15 for individuals, £10 for students and £20 for corporate entities. Enquiries should be directed to the Treasurer, c/o The National Library of Scotland, George IV Bridge, Edinburgh EH1 1EW.

Contributions for the *Journal* are invited in the fields of bibliography (in its widest sense), the book trade, the history of scholarship libraries, and book collecting. They should be submitted for consideration to the Society, c/o The National Library of Scotland.

The society is grateful for the generous support of the Marc Fitch Fund towards the publication of this volume.

Books, Borrowers, and Shareholders

Scottish Circulating and
Subscription Libraries before 1825

A survey and listing

By K. A. Manley

EDINBURGH
EDINBURGH BIBLIOGRAPHICAL SOCIETY
IN ASSOCIATION WITH
THE NATIONAL LIBRARY OF SCOTLAND

2012

© Edinburgh Bibliographical Society & K. A. Manley 2012.
Published by the Edinburgh Bibliographical Society.
First published 2012.

All rights reserved. No part of this publication may be reproduced, stored in a retrieval system, or transmitted in any form or by any means electronic, mechanical, photocopying, recording or otherwise, without the prior permission of the Edinburgh Bibliographical Society, c/o The National Library of Scotland, Edinburgh EH1 1EW.

British Library Cataloguing-in-Publication Data
A catalogue record for this book is available from the British Library.

ISBN 978-0-9573359-0-5

Cover design by Kamillea Aghtan: front cover title image from the trade card of Alexander Brown's Circulating Library, Aberdeen, c.1795; image of marbled boards and spine from Adam Smith's *Wealth of Nations*, 6th edition, 1791, a copy once in Donaldson's Circulating Library, Portsmouth. Both items from the collection of William Zachs.

Typeset by Kamillea Aghtan
in Adobe Garamond Pro.

Printed and bound by 4edge Ltd,
Hockley, Essex.

Contents

Abbreviations	VII
Preface	IX
Acknowledgements	XI
Survey	
Introduction and Background	1
The Beginnings of Circulating Libraries: Allan Ramsay	9
The Variety of 'Community' Libraries	11
The Earliest Subscription Libraries: Leadhills and Other Miners' Libraries	17
Kelso and the Borders: the First Proprietary Subscription Libraries	28
Subscription Libraries and Shares	36
The Growth of Circulating Libraries: the Capital City	45
The Spread of Circulating Libraries: Glasgow, the Provinces, and Overseas	53
The Business of Circulating Libraries	65
Workers' Libraries	69
Rules and Regulations	84
Stock Selection and Ordering	90
The Work of the Librarian	106
The Physical Form of Libraries	109
Religious and Children's Libraries	111
Special Libraries: Law, Foreign Books, Music	116
The Question of Book Clubs	119
Later History	123

Appendix I: Rules of the Montrose Library (1785) — 131

Appendix II: Size and Membership of Libraries: Statistical Survey — 133

   Table 1: Number of Volumes in Selected Subscription Libraries 1790-1910 — 133

   Table 2: Number of Members in Selected Subscription Libraries 1790-1910 — 134

   Table 3: Number of Volumes in Selected Circulating Libraries 1770-1825 — 135

   Table 4: Number of Titles in Selected Circulating Libraries 1770-1825 — 136

Listing:

   Scope — 137

   Counties A-Z — 139

   Islands — 228

   Index of Locations in Listing — 231

   Index to Survey — 236

ABBREVIATIONS

AO	Archives Office
BL	British Library, London
edn.	edition
est.	established
Franks clln.	Franks Collection of Bookplates, Department of Prints & Drawings, British Museum, London
G. K. Scott clln.	Collection of library labels formerly owned by the late Graham Scott, Esq., bookseller of Bury St. Edmunds; collection now dispersed
gn(s).	guinea(s)
Holden	*Holden's Triennial Directory* (various dates)
incl.	including
n.d.	no date given
NLS	National Library of Scotland, Edinburgh
NRS	National Records of Scotland, Edinburgh (formerly National Archives of Scotland, and previous to that Scottish Record Office)
NSA	'New Statistical Account', viz. [J. Gordon (ed.)], *The New Statistical Account of Scotland*, 15 vols. (Edinburgh, 1845), available online at www.electricscotland.com/history/statistical, and also by subscription through other sites.
OSA	'Old Statistical Account', viz. Sir John Sinclair (ed.), *The Statistical Account of Scotland*, 21 vols. (Edinburgh, 1791-99), available online at www.electricscotland.com/history/statistical and also by subscription through other sites.

ODNB	*Oxford Dictionary of National Biography* (Oxford, 2004), updated version available online by subscription at www.oxforddnb.com
p.a.	*per annum*
Pigot	Pigot & Co.'s *National Commercial Directory of Scotland* (various dates)
PL	Public Library
SBTI	Scottish Book Trade Index, compiled by John Morris, available online through NLS website at www.nls.uk/catalogues/resources/sbti
ser.	series
supp.	supplement
UL	University Library
vol(s).	volume(s)

Preface

Scottish commercial circulating and proprietary (or private) subscription libraries have not been ignored by historians but have rarely taken centre stage. The pioneer library historian in this area, Paul Kaufman, published, mostly in the 1960s, a series of articles on eighteenth-century British libraries, including Scottish subscription libraries. Particularly important is his 'The rise of community libraries in Scotland'.[i] But Kaufman, an American librarian who lived and worked in Seattle, conducted much of his research in the 1950s and relied heavily on postal enquiries. He uncovered a great deal of material but lacked the opportunity to do field research himself in archives. His efforts have in some respects been overtaken by the discovery of new sources, though many of his conclusions remain valid. In the present work Kaufman's terminus of 1800 has been extended to the year 1825, a far more logical date. After that date local trades directories and newspapers become more common and were published more frequently, and so libraries can more easily be tracked. Moreover, 1825 significantly marks the beginning of the period when mechanics' institutes suddenly became a powerful force in the self-education movement. To include those in the present work would be to distort the development of private subscription libraries, even though the libraries of mechanics' institutes effectively operated along the lines of subscription libraries and, in some places, took over their role. Mechanics' institutes introduced the idea of permanent community libraries for self-improvement and self-education to the working classes, after initial development in proprietary subscription libraries; the latter had, throughout most of the eighteenth century, been the preserve of the gentry and the professional classes. But the history of mechanics' institutes belongs primarily to a later period.

Since Kaufman's time, the only library historian to have researched new angles of the subject has been John C. Crawford, formerly of Glasgow Caledonian University, whose MA thesis[ii] is a detailed examination of Scottish circulating and subscription libraries in the eighteenth and early nineteenth centuries, based on archival sources, and far more of a social history of libraries than Kaufman's. Though unpublished, this thesis spawned a number of significant journal articles by Dr Crawford including several on individual

---

[i] P. Kaufman, 'The Rise of Community Libraries in Scotland', *Proceedings of the Bibliographical Society of America* 59 (1965), 233-94. A selection of his essays, including this, was published in condensed form in his *Libraries and Their Users* (London, 1969).

[ii] John C. Crawford, 'The Origins and Development of Societal Library Activity in Scotland' (unpublished MA thesis, Strathclyde University, 1981).

libraries, namely Fenwick, Leadhills, Wanlockhead, and Paisley, which are cited in the Listing.

The present work is in part intended to present a history of the development of subscription and circulating libraries, with special attention devoted to aspects of their administration, using as many archival and other sources as are available. Although William R. Aitken's useful *History of the Public Library Movement in Scotland to 1955*, published by the Scottish Library Association in 1971, has become the standard secondary reference work in this area, it was researched and written in the 1950s and published without any updating; but many more original sources have become accessible since then. In particular, far more newspapers have been consulted than by previous researchers with the aim of compiling a more detailed identification of libraries, as will be seen in the Listing. For general material on library history in the eighteenth and early nineteenth centuries, Thomas Kelly's *Early Public Libraries* (London, 1966) and *The Cambridge History of Libraries in Britain and Ireland, Vol. 2: 1640 to 1850*, edited by Giles Mandelbrote and K. A. Manley (Cambridge, 2006), should also be consulted.

Essential background reading is *The Edinburgh History of the Book in Scotland*; volumes 3 and 4 were published in 2007, volume 2 in 2012 and volume 1 is forthcoming. Volumes 2 and 3 contain chapters on book production in the period covered here, as well as chapters on subscription and circulating libraries before and after 1800 by, respectively, the present author and John C. Crawford. Volume 2 additionally includes chapters on private and institutional libraries for the pre-1800 period by Murray Simpson. A recent addition to the literature is Mark Towsey's *Reading the Scottish Enlightenment* (Leiden, 2010), which includes chapters on circulating, subscription, and religious and endowed libraries in the period covered by the present book, as seen from the perspective of the Scottish Enlightenment; it includes useful tables of 'popular' books as listed in relevant library catalogues. For Scottish publishing history during the eighteenth century, Richard Sher's *The Enlightenment and the Book* (Chicago, 2006) provides a comprehensive overview, with an up-to-date and exhaustive bibliography.

In the following Survey of subscription and circulating libraries and book clubs, bibliographical references appear in the footnotes. However, not every source to every local library or club will be given here; more references may appear in the Listing.

Acknowledgements

I am particularly grateful to Dr John C. Crawford for his advice and assistance over the twenty-five years or more I have been researching this book, and to Dr Warren McDougall for encouraging me to complete it for the Edinburgh Bibliographical Society and also for sharing his knowledge of Charles Elliot material in the John Murray Archive. I am also indebted to successive directors and librarians of the Institute of Historical Research who allowed me to have study leave at various times. It was on the shelves of the Institute where I first encountered the reports of the National Register of Archives for Scotland which suggested that a visit to Scottish record repositories would reveal more about the history of subscription libraries than was generally known. In 1984 I was awarded a small grant by the British Academy towards travel expenses, which enabled me to complete some very useful research in Scotland.

Several other people deserve to be thanked for their help, though, because of the passage of time, most will have moved on from where I first encountered them. I have visited, or corresponded, with virtually all the local history libraries and record offices in Scotland, and it would be impossible to thank their staff individually. A general acknowledgement must suffice, however imperfect, with a special note of thanks to the staff of the National Library of Scotland and the National Records of Scotland. The latter body was also helpful in securing access to items in the possession of the Marquis of Linlithgow and the Stirling of Garden family, to all of whom I am most grateful.

All the librarians and archivists I have consulted have responded courteously and speedily, and many of them were far more helpful than I could reasonably have expected. I particularly remember one archivist who wrote to report having just discovered a collection of archives at the back of a cupboard and recalled that I had been enquiring about these very documents a few months earlier. The reason these items had not yet been catalogued was because of a particular problem I encountered several times, namely the disruption caused by local government re-organization in the 1970s. Because old counties merged to form larger authorities, many local history collections were dispersed to other towns where they languished unloved until money could be found to integrate them. When I began my researches in the 1980s, the dust had still not settled.

Some archives may even have ended up in still unknown locations. Extracts taken from minute books of the Kelso Library were used by Kaufman in the early 1960s, but the originals had disappeared when I arrived in Kelso twenty years later. However, the copies used by Kaufman did survive, and some of the later records of that library turned up in the National Records of Scotland, as pointed out to me by Dr Tristram Clarke of that body, who happened to attend a talk I gave on the subject. Since then, the spread of online catalogues and digitized books and newspapers has uncovered far more information than I could possibly have anticipated; but to continue to collect material for a further twenty-five years did not seem a wise option. I must also thank Dr Bill Bell, formerly of the Centre for the History of the Book at the University of Edinburgh, for his knowledge of the Oliver & Boyd logbooks, as well as Dr Murray C. T. Simpson and Dr William Zachs for their many suggestions for improving my text.

Survey

Introduction and Background

The idea of borrowing books for knowledge or pleasure hardly seems revolutionary. Not everyone wants to own or can afford to buy every book they might wish to read, whether the latest bestseller or some weighty scientific tome or a monthly journal. Paying to borrow books may seem strange today in a world where books are freely available in a range of public libraries and increasingly so on the internet in digitized form. But before the earliest Public Libraries Acts (1850 for England and Wales, 1853 for Scotland and Ireland), borrowers usually paid for the privilege, thereby restricting access to those who could afford it. Yet the records of such libraries show that the search for knowledge was not confined to an intellectual élite. The desire for reading is found equally amongst the Leadhills miners of the 1740s, the clergy and gentry of the Borders in the 1750s, and the Glasgow weavers of the 1790s; the desire to read spread through all classes. Even so, the middle classes often regarded working class libraries with suspicion because they were perceived as spreading revolutionary ideas; this was also true later of mechanics' institutes.

The present work is intended to describe two related forms of lending organizations – circulating and subscription libraries – which were widespread for much of the second half of the eighteenth and most of the nineteenth centuries when the printed word was a primary medium of communication for transmitting knowledge, whether scientific or cultural. In the realm of lending books for home reading, Scotland played a leading role. Not only was the progenitor of the first Public Libraries Act a Scottish MP (though born in England, William Ewart, MP for Dumfries, was from Scottish stock), but the earliest successful British circulating and subscription libraries originated in Scotland, such as the libraries of Allan Ramsay (1725) in Edinburgh and John Smith (1753) in Glasgow, and the Kelso (1750), Hawick (1762), and Duns (1768) libraries; all lasted for a hundred years or more.

The term 'subscription library' is employed here to indicate a private proprietary library where subscribers paid not only an annual subscription to borrow books but also an entrance fee (often referred to as 'entry money') to possess a share in the library; the shareholders owned the library and chose the books. Buying shares in cultural institutions was common, as in theatres, opera-houses, and similar establishments. To cater for the public's reading needs, a network of libraries grew up in towns, and later cities, around Scotland. They were typically run by the members themselves, who bought shares and thus owned not just a financial interest in their library's success but, in a sense, also a share in the so-called Scottish Enlightenment. The purpose of such proprietary subscription libraries was to provide a permanent collection of books for both current and future benefit.

The term 'circulating library' means a library where a subscription was paid to hire books from the library's owner, usually a bookseller, sometimes a stationer, and sometimes another kind of tradesman altogether. The owner selected and owned the stock with the intention of turning a profit. The phrase 'circulating library' was in all probability coined by Samuel Fancourt, a dissenting minister who was influential in English library history. In 1740 he published a plan intended as a model for a public library, but which in fact was for a proprietary library. His own library in London he called a circulating library, though supported by shareholders with transferable shares, employing himself as their librarian; in other words, a proprietary subscription library.[1] Nevertheless, the phrase became attached to commercial loan collections belonging, often but not always, to booksellers.

In the eighteenth century differences in terminology were hardly appreciated. Many circulating libraries called themselves subscription libraries because, obviously, they charged a subscription. And it sounded more high class, because it implied that circulating libraries which charged an annual or monthly subscription were in some way superior to those which merely charged by the night. On the other hand many private, or proprietary, subscription libraries called themselves circulating libraries. The Leeds Library, the oldest surviving proprietary subscription library in the United Kingdom, is still officially known as the Leeds Circulating Library. In Scotland, proprietary subscription libraries called themselves just 'libraries', or 'public libraries', a fact that in itself points towards the aspirations of such institutions. The key element in these libraries was permanence. Similar libraries existed throughout the British Isles, but communal book provision in Scotland revolved around permanent institutions. In England and Wales book clubs, in which members bought books in common but sold them amongst themselves after a year, were legion, but did not feature in Scotland before the nineteenth century. Furthermore in England the development of private subscription libraries was associated initially with dissenters, a totally different story to the Scottish experience. And the sociable dimension of English book clubs was largely absent in Presbyterian-dominated Scotland, just as the largest Scottish circulating libraries never became social centres in the same way as in English resort towns such as Bath. In Scotland, reading was a more serious business.

Commercial circulating libraries came to be held in low esteem because they became associated with the provision of cheap, romantic fiction. Writing in 1793, Professor James Beattie recalled a visit to Dundee: 'About thirty years

---

[1] K. A. Manley, 'The Road to Camelot: Lotteries, the Circle of Learning, and the "Circulary" Library of Samuel Fancourt', *The Library*, 7th ser., 8 (2007), 398-422.

ago I went into a bookseller's shop, and expressing my surprise at finding it *merely a circulating library of novels*, the man of the shop told me that nothing else was read in Dundee'.[2] By the end of the century the phrase 'circulating library' was virtually synonymous with popular literature. Comparing how the social and cultural life of Edinburgh had changed between 1763 and 1783, the bookseller, publisher, and magistrate William Creech offered his personal, tongue-in-cheek, opinion:

> In 1763 – In the best families in town, the education of daughters was fitted, not only to embellish and improve their minds, but to accomplish them in the useful and necessary arts of domestic economy. The sewing-school, the pastry-school, were then essential branches of female education; nor was a young lady of the best family ashamed to go to market with her mother.
>
> In 1783 – The daughters even of tradesmen consume the mornings at the toilet, (to which *rouge* is now an appendage), or in strolling from the perfumer's to the milliner's, &c. They would blush to be seen in a market. The cares of the family are devolved upon a housekeeper; and Miss employs those heavy hours, when she is disengaged from public or private amusements, in improving her mind from the precious stores of a circulating library.[3]

Circulating libraries were hardly regarded as the panaceas of modern life. Sir Walter Scott, in his novel, *The Monastery* (1820), has his protagonist, Captain Clutterbuck, bemoan the boredom of living in a small Scottish town (based on Melrose):

> Books I tried, both those of the little circulating library, and of the more rational subscription collection maintained by this intellectual people. But neither the light reading of the one, nor the heavy artillery of the other, suited my purpose. I always fell asleep at the fourth or fifth page of history or disquisition; and it took me a month's hard reading to wade through a half-bound trashy novel, during which I was pestered with applications to return the volumes, by every half-bred milliner's miss about the place.

By Scott's time, circulating libraries were perceived as existing primarily to proffer entertainment, while private subscription libraries offered more cerebral fare; in practice this distinction was not always so clear-cut. Subscription libraries increasingly collected novels, but generally the 'better' sort. Works

---

[2] Margaret Forbes, *Beattie and his Friends* (London, 1904), p. 276.

[3] [William Creech], *Letters Reflecting the Mode of Living, Trade, Manners, and Literature, &c. of Edinburgh in 1763, and the Present Period* (Edinburgh, 1788), p. 17; reprinted in: *OSA*, vol. 6 (1793), p. 616.

such as, for instance, Oliver Goldsmith's *Vicar of Wakefield* were seen as presenting moral lessons, while, later, the novels of Scott awakened an intense interest in national history; but cheap, romantic, and formulaic novels were the mainstay of the commercial circulating library.

Susan Mein (1783-1866), later wife of Colonel William Sibbald, provides arguably an all-too-common example of what James Beattie and William Creech deplored. Though born in Cornwall, she came from an educated Scottish background – her father, Dr Thomas Mein, was a naval surgeon and friend of Dr John Wolcott, alias 'Peter Pindar'. The family moved to Eildon Hall, near Melrose, in 1800, where Susan later recalled:

> As my father would not let us read any of the Romances or novels he had in his library, Jane [her elder sister] subscribed to the circulating library at Melrose, and read the books in her own room, and having Mr. [sic] Radcliffe's most horrible Romance of the *Mysteries of Udolpho*, she would read so much of it to me in mine before going to bed and after the maid was dismissed, taking care, however, to leave off before the dreaded hour of 12 when ghosts were supposed to wander abroad till past 1.[4]

Once, inevitably, they read till well after midnight and were terrified by the sound of distant rumbling, causing their dog to howl. Only in the morning did they discover that the servants had been rolling out beer barrels which they had forgotten earlier. The sisters held a well-founded fear of ghosts ever since their butler, Dennis, had woken up one night to see a coach-and-four racing through his bedroom, driven by a headless coachman. His story certainly deterred the sisters from raiding the butler's larder at night.[5]

This story is in sharp contrast with the experience of Willy Carruthers, the shepherd employed by Susan Mein's father. He, too, subscribed to the same library in Melrose, and the sisters would often find him in the fields, reading. At night, after the sheep had returned to the fold, he would read to his wife and son. But his tastes were for more serious fare, putting the girls to shame. Writing of the summer of 1802, Susan recalled meeting him and enquired about two books lying beside him: 'Oh! I'm reading *Josephus* – now, ha' na ye read it?'. 'No, Willy, but I will some day', replied Susan, while Willy expounded on the ancient Jewish historian. The second book was the Bible. In fact many circulating libraries contained large amounts of 'respectable' non-fiction. On a later occasion, she spots Willy putting a book in his pocket: 'That is not *Josephus* you are reading now Willy'. 'Na, when I had read it ... they sent me this ane, 'tis but a navel or nonsense buke as I ca' them. My reading is

---

[4] *The Memoirs of Susan Sibbald*, edited by Francis Paget Hett (London, 1926), p. 176.

[5] *Memoirs of Susan Sibbald*, p. 175.

like the Warld, sometimes grave and sometimes gay ...'. The book was Samuel Richardson's *Sir Charles Grandison*.[6]

If Gothic horror and romantic fiction were the staples of the circulating library, private subscription libraries were for serious fare. If shares could be bought in knowledge, then the latter provided a point of access for people who desired a share in the new ideas of the day. And that is no exaggerated claim: the eighteenth century saw an enormous surge in a desire for self-education and knowledge. By 1800 proprietary subscription libraries were well established in the Scottish Lowlands. So too in England; but few places in England possessed more than one subscription library, and many had none before the 1820s. In Scotland relatively small towns (with a population of 3,000 or less) frequently had at least one by 1800, and several had more. Where there was more than one library, the more recently founded usually catered for a lower class of society; in other words, the 'trickledown effect'. In the Borders, there were three libraries in both Kelso and Jedburgh by 1800, and one in Hawick, with a second there shortly after 1800. They were joined in the neighbourhood by one library each in Coldstream, Morebattle, and Denholm, all very small places. Subscription libraries flourished in rural towns, and so in a very real sense were aiding the spread of knowledge to the countryside.

The Pocklington Public Library, near York, which dissolved in 1749, is the earliest known English subscription library, but its origins are unclear (the presence of a public school was probably influential), and it is impossible to know whether Pocklington was a pioneer or reflecting a trend for which other evidence is simply lacking; at all events, it did not last long, and subscription libraries were flourishing in Scotland before England. In general, their origins are not as clear-cut as may be supposed. Most of the earliest similar English libraries were associated with dissenting clergymen, such as Joseph Priestley, but in Scotland this was not the case. The early Borders libraries were initiated by local leaders; not until the 1790s do Scottish nonconformists play a major role when two dissenting Presbyterians, James Hall and James Peddie, both leading members of the New Light Associated Synod (which refused to accept that civil authorities could have jurisdiction over religious affairs), founded the Edinburgh Subscription Library; another co-founder was Gavin Struthers, minister of the Relief Church.

As with circulating libraries, subscription libraries developed differently in some respects in Scotland compared to England and Wales. Rules concerning libraries were typically far more strict and complex in Scotland, where, for instance, issues of inheritance of shares were strongly fought. And libraries should not be seen as isolated from other aspects of Scottish life. Stricter library rules concerning rights of inheritance, levels of fees, fines for misbehaviour,

---

[6] *Memoirs of Susan Sibbald*, pp. 166-8, 196-7, 200.

even the right to enter houses to see whether its books were being mis-handled or even lent to non-members, have parallels with the regulations found for trade guilds such as the Hammermen and Weavers, and also the Freemasons.[7]

In the proprietary subscription library, the profit motive is no less visible than in the circulating library since the subscribers were also shareholders: they were buying into an asset of increasing value. Since they chose the books, they enjoyed freedom of choice with a commercial edge: they could sell their shares at any time and (hopefully) make a profit. Subscription libraries were intended as a permanent resource for the community, as expressed poetically by Peter Forbes, a member of the Dalkeith Subscription Library, founded in 1798 to provide books 'necessary to inform the judgment and to polish the manners'[8] of its members who:

> hae an orry hour to spare,
> 	In reeky neuks,
> Now, now's ye'r time to get ye'r [shair]
> 	O' readin' beuks.
>
> Some canny lads of o' gleg invention,
> Wi' kindly, honest, guid intention,
> An' that without bribe, fee, or pension,
> 	Or gapin' greed,
> Got a' kin' kind o' Books ye'll mention,
> 	For folk to read.
>
> Now this same Plan, my friends, ye'll find
> For noblest motives was design'd,
> That morals might be more refin'd,
> 	Wi' modest looks,
> An' to improve each studious mind
> 	Wi' wale of Books.[9]

The purpose was to allow people to read 'beuks' in their own 'neuks': home reading without the constraints of an institution, but within a framework of regulations to preserve those books for posterity. Or, as an advertisement for the Caledonian Literary Society in Aberdeen expressed it more succinctly in 1805:

---

[7] For relevant material on the Hammermen, see: Arthur Muir, *Traditions and Customs of the Hammermen of Glasgow*, 2nd edn. (Glasgow, 1939); M. Wood, 'The Hammermen of the Canongate. Pt. 2', *Book of the Old Edinburgh Club* 20 (1935), 78-110; J. H. Jamieson, 'The Incorporation of Hammermen at Haddington', *Transactions of the East Lothian Antiquarian & Field Naturalist's Society* 2 (1934 for 1931/3), 97-111, 182-203.

[8] *Rules for the Regulation of the Dalkeith Subscription Library* (Edinburgh, 1798).

[9] [Peter Forbes], *Poem* (Edinburgh, 1803).

> The silent friends which ever please,
> With them we sit at home, and crack wi' Kings.[10]

The general idea of dispersing libraries throughout a large area can be ascribed to the encouragement of the Englishman, Dr Thomas Bray (1656-1730), whose original plan, published in 1695, was to provide town libraries for the benefit of clergy and gentry in England. In the event, his scheme was taken over by the Society for Promoting Christian Knowledge (SPCK), which he founded in 1699, and led to the establishment of small libraries for local ministers (but not parishioners) in England, Wales, and Maryland.[11] As for Scotland, the idea was extended and prosecuted vigorously by Rev. James Kirkwood (ca. 1650-1709), who had in the 1690s been responsible for a scheme for distributing Irish Bibles to Gaelic-speaking ministers in the Highlands. He had refused to sign the Test Acts in 1681 and fled to England, where he was again deprived of his living in 1702 as a non-juror. Kirkwood's plan was more ambitious than Bray's in proposing that libraries be sent to parishes and presbyteries for the use not just of ministers, but also of heritors and other residents; stringent rules were drawn up. But the (Presbyterian) General Assembly of the Church of Scotland failed to support Kirkwood, being suspicious of Episcopalians.[12] A less ambitious plan to distribute libraries to ministers in the Highlands and Islands did find favour, not least because much of the money to provide the books came from SPCK members in England. By Kirkwood's death around 80 libraries had been distributed, and the General Assembly was keen to encourage their use. By the end of the eighteenth century, most of these collections had disappeared, but in their heyday, they provided a model of how books could be brought to small communities. But their significance towards the history of subscription libraries revolves around the Kirkwood library sent in 1706 to Dumfries, a place not noticeably in the Highlands, but a beneficiary nonetheless. Kirkwood in fact attempted to found other libraries in the Lowlands.[13]

The Dumfries Presbytery Library, enlarged by a bequest from its Member of Parliament in 1712, was not exclusively a collection of religious books, but contained many volumes on history and other subjects. The library was said to have been 'purged' in 1730, when presumably any religious books obnoxious to presbytery members were removed. In 1736 the Presbytery

---

[10] *Aberdeen Journal*, 20 November 1805.

[11] Thomas Kelly, *Early Public Libraries* (London, 1966), pp. 104-12; see *ODNB* for Bray and his plans.

[12] W. R. Aitken, *History of the Public Library Movement in Scotland to 1955* (Glasgow, 1971), pp. 6-12.

[13] G. W. Shirley, *Dumfriesshire Libraries* (Dumfries, 1932), p. 2. Kirkwood's plan for libraries in 'ye South of Scotland' is cited, without details, in NLS MS. 20800, fols. 53-57.

Library was reconstituted as a subscription, though non-proprietary, library for local citizens, not solely for local ministers. Books could be borrowed for five shillings a year, and a catalogue of 1784 shows that it was still thriving. Although most borrowers were students of divinity, many subscribers came from well-known county families, including James Ewart (1736), Robert Riddell of Glen Riddel, James Laurie (1749), William Irvine, Esq. (1751), Thomas Dickson, MD (1752), Gilbert Gordon, collector of Excise (1752), Andrew Ewart, clerk to the Custom House, and Captain Riddell (1771). John Ewart, for instance, borrowed over a hundred volumes between 1768 and 1780, mostly history, including William Robertson's *History of Scotland* and Sir John Dalrymple's *Memoirs of Great Britain and Ireland*, as well as Lucian, René Descartes, Ossian, and William Whitlock. The books are now in New College, Edinburgh.[14]

This development may have been influenced by a similar arrangement at the Leightonian Library in Dunblane. Though opened in 1688 as a diocesan library under the terms of the will of Archbishop Robert Leighton, its trustees decided to convert it into a general subscription library in October 1734, just anticipating the Dumfries Presbytery. Anyone could borrow provided that they 'shall be first matriculated to the said Library and pay at least half a crown each person'. Although the Leightonian Library was inevitably predominantly a theological collection, contemporary publications on other subjects were actively sought during the eighteenth century, including writings by Adam Smith, Count Volney, George Anson, Captain James Cook, Adam Ferguson, William Robertson, and Edward Gibbon. Although lighter literature was largely eschewed, the most popular book for borrowing was John Moore's novel, *Zeluco*, while Robert Burns's *Poems Chiefly in the Scottish Dialect* was soon reduced to single leaves. The library enjoyed a new lease of life when mineral wells were discovered nearby in 1813, and temporary membership was granted to visitors for 2s.6d. a fortnight. The full subscription was 10s.6d. by 1831, but only five shillings by 1843 as interest dwindled. The library was dilapidated by the 1890s, but the books still survive and have been restored. Although William Aitken dismissed the library at Dunblane and the parish library of Saltoun as 'scarcely public libraries', the former at least clearly played a part in the rise of the private subscription library.[15]

---

[14] Kaufman, *Libraries and their Users*, pp. 141-2. The loans register is in the Ewart Library, Dumfries. The author is grateful to the late John Howard, sometime librarian of New College, Edinburgh, for further information on Kirkwood derived from that Library's collections; cf. J. V. Howard, 'John Hutton, M.D., and the Dumfries Presbytery Library, 1714-1826', *Records of the Scottish Church Historical Society* 32 (2002), 41-69.

[15] G. Willis, 'The Leighton Library, Dunblane: its History and Contents', *Bibliotheck* 10 (1981), 139-57; cf. Aitken, *Public Library Movement*, p. 2; Robert Chambers, *Picture of Scotland*, 4th edn. (Edinburgh, 1840), p. 441. The Leightonian Library remains open to the public; the book collection is now administered by Stirling University Library.

The Beginnings of Circulating Libraries: Allan Ramsay

The lending of books by booksellers for a fee can be traced back to the time of the Restoration, both in Britain and abroad, though there are no references to this practice in Scotland before the 1720s; at least, there is no evidence. The earliest recorded instance of a French bookseller lending books comes from a Scottish traveller. John Lauder, later Sir John, the future Lord Fountainhall and distinguished judge, borrowed a book in Poitiers in 1665. He was then a young law student, travelling through France and, although buying a large number of books on the way, he recorded that he 'payed 18 souse for the lean [loan] of Romances from Mr Courtois, as Celie and the sundry parts of Almahide, penned by Scuderie'.[16] Newspapers, or newsletters, are known to have been lent out by the late seventeenth century. Burgh council members in Montrose were borrowing them by 1694, while this practice attracted complaints from subscribers to a newsroom in the Dumfries townhouse in 1696.[17]

Although Scottish and English booksellers may have lent books on an *ad hoc* basis, organized lending from a separate stock came much later. Allan Ramsay, though now best known as a poet, is the first person in Great Britain known to have started a formal circulating library as opposed to lending books from his stock-in-trade. Ramsay started his library in Edinburgh in 1725 and charged an annual subscription, although a nightly fee was available. An invoice sent to his patron, Sir John Clerk of Penicuik, reads: 'To Annual Reading for 1726 10 [shillings]'.[18] Similar invoices are preserved for succeeding years. Ramsay's library is well-known from the story related by Robert Wodrow in 1728. Wodrow, an ecclesiastical historian and former university librarian of Glasgow, was somewhat deficient in the humour department. He launched a diatribe against the state of society in Edinburgh by condemning the salacious nature of Ramsay's book stock:

> profannes is come to a great hight, all the villanous profane and obscene books and playes printed at London by Curle and others, are gote doun from London by Allan Ramsey, and lent out, for an easy price, to young boyes, servant weemen of the better sort, and gentlemen, and vice and obscenity dreadfully propagated.

---

[16] *Journals of Sir John Lauder*, edited by Donald Crawford, Scottish History Society, vol. 36 (Edinburgh, 1900), pp. 157-8. Lauder is presumably referring to Madeleine de Scudery's *Clélie* (1654-61) and *Almahide* (1661-63).

[17] Bob Harris, 'Communicating', in *A History of Everyday Life in Scotland*, edited by Elizabeth Foyster and Christopher A. Whatley (Edinburgh, 2010), pp. 175, 187.

[18] *The Works of Allan Ramsay*, edited by Alexander M. Kinghorn and Alexander Law (Edinburgh, 1970-72), vol. 4, p. 183.

> Ramsay has a book in his shope wherein all the names of those that borrou his playes and books, for twopence a night, or some such rate, are sett doun; and by these, wickednes of all kinds are dreadfully propagat among the youth of all sorts. My informer, my Lord Grange, tells me he compleaned to the Magistrates of this, and they scrupled at meddling in it, till he moved that his book of borrouers should be inspected, which was done, and they wer allarumed at it, and sent some of their number to his shope to look throu some of his books; but he had nottice an hour before, and had withdrauen a great many of the worst, and nothing was done to purpose. This, with the Playes and Interludes, come doun from England this winter ... dreadfully spreads all abominations, and profaness, and leudness; and a villanous, obscene thing, is no sooner printed at London, than it's spread and communicat at Edinburgh.[19]

Ramsay had become a bookseller in the Luckenbooths, later Parliament Close, by 1722 and had originally been a peruke-maker. He was a founder-member of the Easy Club, established in 1712 for 'Mutual Improvement in Conversation'. One of its fundamental purposes was to read *The Spectator* at each meeting, and the Club did appear to possess a library, if modest.[20] People who ran libraries did not always belong to the book trade, and Ramsay demonstrates the connection between libraries and fashion – libraries often aimed at attracting the fashionable members of society.[21] Clearly Ramsay was perceived by Wodrow and others as a provider of cheap entertainment rather than more serious fodder. By 1734 Ramsay was complaining to Clerk of Penicuik that the bookselling business was so low that he might have to take a cheaper house, and he was famously thwarted by the authorities when he attempted to run a theatre (to which Lord Grange was also opposed).[22] He is said to have incurred further Presbyterian opprobrium by adding translations of French plays to his library in 1736. He retired in 1740 and his library passed to John Yair and by 1758 to Yair's widow, Margaret.[23]

In England, the Bath bookseller, James Leake, was lending books by 1728, though no-one knows when his library actually commenced; he had joined his

---

[19] Robert Wodrow, *Analecta*, Maitland Club, vol. 60 (Edinburgh, 1843), vol. 3, pp. 515-6. James Erskine, Lord Grange, was a prominent judge (*ODNB*).

[20] *Works of Allan Ramsay*, vol. 5 (1972), pp. 8 & 56.

[21] K. A. Manley, 'Booksellers, Peruke-Makers, and Rabbit-Merchants: the Growth of Circulating Libraries in the Eighteenth Century', in: Robin Myers, Michael Harris, & Giles Mandelbrote (eds.), *Libraries and the Book Trade* (New Castle, Del.: Oak Knoll, 2000), pp. 29-50 (here p. 32).

[22] *Works of Allan Ramsay* (Edinburgh, 1970), vol. 4, p. 194.

[23] *Caledonian Mercury*, 30 September 1746, 12 August 1758.

father-in-law's long-established bookselling business in 1722.[24] He was the first person in England known to have organized a circulating library (though the phrase was not used before the 1740s) and pioneered the fashionable libraries which flourished in English spas and coastal towns. These libraries became the social centres of holiday resorts such as Margate and Brighton, along with gaming and evening assemblies. This stratum of 'sociable' library development never spread to Scotland. The well-known circulating library of the poet Allan Ramsay and his successors, for instance, which existed from 1725 to about 1851, became primarily a literary rather than a social centre. Although Scottish spas and seaside towns existed, they never developed in the same way as at Bath or other English resorts, or at least not in the period covered here.

The Variety of 'Community' Libraries

'Community' libraries can take many forms, and in Scotland the desire for reading-material of all kinds was met in many different ways, whether through permanent institutions, such as the proprietary library, or more transient collections. An anonymous Englishman, for instance, who toured the country in 1815, encountered a library on a packet-boat plying the Forth and Clyde canal from Edinburgh to Glasgow, though it is unlikely to have contained the weighty tomes of land-based libraries:

> This passage boat is uncommonly elegant; and a proof of the universal diffusion of literature among the Scots is afforded by the well-thumbed state of the books, which form a neat little library for the use of the passengers. Burns' works formed a part. It is astonishing the reputation they [his works] have attained ...[25]

In 1820, an enterprising Inverness vintner, William Geddes, announced a steamer service to Fort Augustus along Loch Ness, with books and music provided. A passenger on a cruise around the Western Isles on the *S.S. United Kingdom* in 1827 also commented that its library 'contains a number of elegantly bound books'.[26]

The community library was nothing new in Scotland; Innerpeffray and the Leightonian Library in Dunblane are well known, though the latter was chiefly used by the clergy. The Innerpeffray Library, near Crieff, was founded

---

[24] [Thomas Goulding], *An Essay Against Too Much Reading* (London, 1728), pt. 2, p. 5 ff. The *ODNB* is in error to state that Leake was lending by 1731. Cf. Manley, 'Booksellers, Peruke-Makers, and Rabbit-Merchants', pp. 33-35.

[25] 'An English Commercial Traveller', *Letters from Scotland* (London, 1817), p. 115.

[26] *Inverness Courier*, 24 June 1820; *Caledonian Mercury*, 9 July 1827.

around 1680 for young students, but its register of loans reveals regular use by local farmers and tradesmen, despite its rural location (it is situated three miles down a country lane from Crieff, itself a small town not on any major routes). Between 1747 and 1800 1,483 loans were made of 370 works to 287 borrowers; no subscription was charged. Religion was the largest single class, but history became increasingly popular.[27] Although historians such as R. A. Houston have questioned the usefulness of Innerpeffray Library, since only a small proportion of the local populace are known to have borrowed from it, what is more significant is that such a resource of information and knowledge was freely available to all who ventured there; and many did.[28] Not all visitors may have borrowed books, but availability was as significant a factor in its usefulness. It remained a lending library until 1968 and is still preserved intact.[29]

Many libraries were set up by local benefactors, as in Jedburgh in 1714 and Lochmaben in 1726, both based in schools. The library bequeathed by Rev. John Gray (1646-1717) to the burgh of Haddington was freely available to residents from 1729 and was mainly theological, but between 1732 and 1796 2,837 loans were made to about 400 readers, the most popular books being, in order, the *Universal History*, Charles Rollin's *Ancient History*, the novels of Henry Fielding, and John Callander's *Collection of Voyages*. By the end of the eighteenth century the library was being used as if it were a private subscription library, with history still the most popular borrowing category. It benefited from an active management committee, and the borrowers included many women and teenagers.[30]

In Logie, Fife, the local laird, Walter Bowman (1699-1782), an antiquary who mainly lived in England, entailed his heirs to make available for the use of the parish his library of old and valuable works bought on the continent. Women and children were excluded, and readers had to wash their hands first (for which purpose 'a bason of water and a towel' were provided), but these precautions ensured the books' survival until 1949 when they were sold off.[31] In general, reliance on benefactors continued well into the nineteenth century.

---

[27] Paul Kaufman, 'Innerpeffray: Reading for all the People', in his *Libraries and their Users* (London, 1969), pp. 153-62.

[28] R. A. Houston, *Scottish Literacy and the Scottish Identity* (Cambridge, 1985), pp. 173-8.

[29] Cf. www.innerpeffraylibrary.co.uk, including an online catalogue.

[30] Kaufman, 'Community Libraries', pp. 265-8; Aitken, *Public Library Movement*, pp. 5-6; V. S. Dunstan, 'Glimpses into a Town's Reading Habits in Enlightenment Scotland: Analysing the Borrowings of Gray Library, Haddington, 1732-1816', *Journal of Scottish Historical Studies* 26 (2006), 42-59.

[31] Alexander Anderson, *Old Libraries of Fife* (Kirkcaldy, 1953), p. 2; A. H. Millar, *Fife: Pictorial and Historical* (Cupar, Fife, 1895), vol. 1, p. 179; cf. *ODNB*.

For instance, the horticulturist, Archibald Gorrie (1778-1857) of Annat Gardens, who introduced the pansy, set up a village library in Rait, Perthshire, in about 1812, consisting of around 300 volumes of, largely, biography, history, and religion.[32]

Another unusual individual benefaction was the collection of books presented in the 1770s to the Boar's Head (later the Gardenstone Arms), in Laurencekirk, Kincardineshire, by Francis, Lord Gardenstone, an eccentric judge, best known for keeping a pig in his bedroom.[33] Gardenstone did effect many improvements for his tenants in the model village begun by him in 1768, of which he was inordinately proud ('as if he had founded Thebes', as James Boswell caustically remarked). Dr Samuel Johnson visited the inn in August 1773 after Boswell told him that 'Lord Gardenston had furnished it with a collection of books, that travellers might have entertainment for the mind, as well as the body. He praised the design, but wished there had been more books, and those better chosen'.[34] George Colman the younger took his breakfast in the room where, he wrote, the books were housed in 'a glazed book-case ... mounted upon a bureau, after the fashion of sundry snug little back parlours, in England'.[35]

The library was subsequently, in 1782, moved to a specially-built annexe, where the room was described as 'a model of elegance and good taste'.[36] The Elgin bookseller and librarian, Isaac Forsyth, passed through Laurencekirk in 1791 and considered it:

> the neatest village, perhaps, in Scotland, supported by the benevolent and liberal Lord Gardenstone. He has built a good inn and an excellent library, well stocked with books, some fossils, corals, stuffed birds, paintings, and statues, and particularly with the famous [visitors'] album. The genteeler part of the neighbourhood have the use of the books freely.[37]

John Ramsay of Ochtertyre also thought well of the library: 'Many a [traveller] has been agreeably amused on a bad day or long night with the library, which is well chosen for desultory reading'. He was also struck by the

---

[32] J. C. Loudun, *Manual of Cottage Gardening* (London, 1830), p. 63.

[33] J. R. Barker, 'Lord Gardenstone's Library at Laurencekirk', *Bibliotheck* 6 (1971), 41-51; for Gardenstone, see: *ODNB* and James Paterson, *Kay's Edinburgh Portraits* (London, 1885), vol. 1, pp. 34-36.

[34] *Boswell's Life of Johnson*, edited by George Birkbeck Hill, revised by L. F. Powell, 2nd edn. (Oxford, 1964), vol. 5, pp. 75-76.

[35] George Colman, *Random Recollections* (London, 1830), vol. 2, pp. 78-79.

[36] *Aberdeen Magazine* (1790), 560.

[37] Isaac Forsyth MacAndrew, *Memoir of Isaac Forsyth* (London, 1889), p. 39.

portraits on display of the villagers, which Gardenstone had commissioned.[38] Gardenstone was commended in the *Statistical Account* of 1794: 'The public-spirited proprietor of this village has also built and fitted up an elegant inn with a library of books adjoining to it, chiefly for the amusement of travellers who might stop there'.[39]

However, the library was not maintained after his death, and the *New Statistical Account* recorded in 1838 that the books had much diminished.[40] In 1869 102 volumes were placed under the care of the Brechin Diocesan Library and subsequently found their way to the University of Dundee Library, where 157 separate works can still be identified.[41] Some did survive *in situ* until the end of the nineteenth century, including Aristophanes, Isaac Newton's *Principia*, Isaac Watts's *Logic*, Jethro Tull's *Horse-hoeing Husbandry*, John Dryden's *Virgil*, *Gil Blas*, Herman Boerhaave's *Aphorisms* on diseases, Niccolò Machiavelli (in Italian), and Samuel Clarke's *Sermons*. Other identifiable works include William Shakespeare, Francis Bacon, Sir Walter Raleigh, Virgil, John Rushworth, David Hume, and John Locke.

The annexe itself was demolished in 1962. Clearly the library was an eclectic collection, and although not a subscription library, it was still influential. Like the Leadhills miners' library, it proved a valuable example of how a library could be provided for community use. It was far more than just an 'inn' library and originated as Gardenstone's own private library; in addition it was said to be 'his Lordship's practice to insert his Critical Observations on the margins of the respective books, and to interline with his pen some of the most remarkable passages',[42] though in one book he wrote: 'every traveller is welcome to damn me as a bad critic, if he thinks proper'.[43]

Libraries in inns were, on the whole, unlikely to be academic book collections, but do demonstrate a perhaps unexpected side to the idea of 'community' libraries and could reveal unexpected riches. The geologist John MacCulloch, writing in 1824 in what became a controversial book about the Highlands, included a story involving Bonnie Prince Charlie. He boasted of

---

[38] John Ramsay, *Scotland and Scotsmen in the 18th Century*, edited by Alexander Allardyce (Edinburgh, 1888), vol. 1, p. 377.

[39] *OSA*, vol. 5 (1793), p. 178.

[40] *NSA*, vol. 11 (1845), p. 150.

[41] George Birkbeck Hill, *The Footsteps of Dr. Johnson* (London, 1890), pp. 109-10; Thomas Kelly, *Early Public Libraries* (London, 1966), p. 104; *Catalogue of the Brechin Diocesan Library: Appendix No. 2* (Brechin?, ca. 1880), 160-267. The 157 surviving works can be traced in Dundee University Library's online catalogue by a provenance search.

[42] *Boswell's Life of Johnson* (Oxford, 1964), vol. 5, p. 490; Lord Gardenstone, *Miscellanies in Prose and Verse*, 2nd edn. (Edinburgh, 1792), preface.

[43] Barker, 'Lord Gardenstone's Library', p. 49.

the story's accuracy because, while staying at an inn, he had chanced upon a book by John Home (presumably *The History of the Rebellion in the Year 1745*, published in 1802) which detailed the whole affair, 'a very unusual piece of good luck'. MacCulloch continued:

> My landlord's library at Kinloch Rannoch had one prime merit, at least in the eyes of the Roxburgh club: for it was very black. Nothing is much more amusing at times, than the libraries of these highland inns: and I need scarcely say how creditable to the people it is, to find these unexpected books in these unexpected places. To be sure, they are often 'neither new nor rare'; still you 'wonder how the devil they got there'. I have met with Adam Smith's *Wealth of Nations* in a house of dyvots and thatch; if that is a phenomenon, what will you say of [John] Lemprière's *Dictionary*, and of Montaigne; Montaigne, himself, in his own egotistical amusing native dress. On the same shelves, I have seen Pope's *Odyssey*, Virgil, not Dr [Joseph] Trapp's I assure you, but the genuine Mantuan in his own cloak; a *Treatise of Mensuration*, [Hugo] Grotius *de Veritate*, [Matthew] Quin's *Book-keeping by double entry*, [John] Clarke's Ovid, [William] Guthrie's *Grammar*, the *Spectator*; and far more, and more strange mixtures. As to the good books, such as [James] Hervey and [Thomas] Boston, and countless more, and countless worse and more unintelligible, always excepting John, the great John Bunyan, there is always store of them.[44]

But not all private libraries intended for public use were successful. In Lanark in 1762, Dr William Smellie, a man-midwife (and friend of Tobias Smollett) whose lectures in London on obstetrics had made him well-known, bequeathed £200 for a school, along with his library, to remain in the schoolroom. In a codicil of 1763, the year of his death, he directed that no books should be lent, but in order to make the perusal of his books more comfortable, he considerately left 'my large reading desk, with the table flap that hangs to it, and stands in the lobie, with the leather chair, and smoking little chair, in the study – as also the high steps there, to take down the books, which must be contained in locked tirlised [i.e. fitted with grills] doors'. The schoolmaster would be librarian, and answerable to the ministers of the presbytery. If any money was left after building the school, classics and other useful books were to be bought, and a catalogue printed.

However, although the building work was completed by 1775, no rules for the library were formalised until 1803. In 1814 the library's trustees agreed that the books could be lent, but in 1816 they decided that the library was not a success and should be broken up. This was carried out in 1819 when the

---

[44] John MacCulloch, *The Highlands and Western Isles of Scotland* (London, 1824), vol. 1, pp. 454-6.

books purchased after the original bequest were divided amongst those who had belonged to the library. The books of the original bequest were left in the schoolroom, where they 'have, consequently, become useless lumber, and, for want of proper attention, must soon be destroyed by moths'.[45] And so the noble intentions of the donor were rendered useless, and the books remained behind locked doors. Not until 1931 were the books rescued and transferred to the local public library in Lanark, the Lindsay Institute.[46]

An unusual subscription library was established in Govan by Mrs Agnes Thom, widow of Rev. William Thom (1710-90), former minister there, in 1818. She bequeathed her own books and £100 for a library to be run by the parochial schoolmaster. Membership originally cost five shillings *per annum*, and sixpence per quarter by 1842; it possessed no less than 1,100 volumes by 1849. This library was unusual in that it was set up by an individual (as was Stirling's Library in Glasgow, but that was on a much larger and ambitious scale), and, unlike those provided by other benefactors, for example William Smellie, it succeeded as a public library but without its members having any control. The library's offerings ranged from Josephus and Plutarch to Robert Burns and *French Lovers* (by Robert Lesuire?), by way of Euclid, Malachy Postlethwayte, James Hervey, Edward Gibbon, Virgil, Alexander Cruden, Daniel Defoe, and Lord Byron; there was even a Koran. How successful this library was, is difficult to assess. The accounts show that very little was spent on it, and in 1837, when a complaint was made that the library was languishing, the schoolmaster argued that he had never agreed to promote it. But the library still existed in 1896 when it was proposed to hand it over to the parish.

Similarly curious in its inception was the library of the Ormiston Friendly Association for the Protection of Property, in Haddingtonshire. This benefit society, established in 1784 by, amongst others, the Earl of Hopetoun, had from 1817 spent some of its subscription money on books. A hundred volumes had been acquired by 1835. This may have been a lowly library, but evidently the residents of this small village felt the urge to acquire literature as a communal collection.[47]

Another aspect of communal book-lending which should not be overlooked was the practice of private individuals lending their own books not just to their friends but amongst a wider community. By its very nature this kind of activity is rarely documented, and yet borrowers' registers and other evidence survive to suggest that in some areas informal lending from private libraries fulfilled

---

[45] W. Davidson, *History of Lanark* (Lanark, 1828), pp. 65-69.

[46] Antonia J. Bunch, *Hospital and Medical Libraries in Scotland* (Glasgow, 1975), pp. 65-72; cf. also *ODNB* for Smellie.

[47] *NSA*, vol. 2 (1845), p. 150.

a useful purpose amongst a wide circle, and was a practice which in some cases was close to being institutionalized by rules and regulations. In 1765, for instance, (Sir) James Grant, M.P., of Castle Grant, Morayshire, permitted local gentry to borrow one book at a time from his library. Only his clerk, James Grant, was permitted to enter the library, and no more than six books could be lent out altogether.[48] Mark Towsey has drawn attention to the late-eighteenth and early-nineteenth century borrowers' registers of the Brodie family of Brodie Castle, near Nairn, and the Urquharts of Craigston Castle, Aberdeenshire, who lent books not just to local gentry but also to professional men and ministers, and, too, to a number of women.[49] Many other people also lent out books, naturally, and the quasi-formal practice of lending can be viewed as the provision of a substitute for a local subscription library. And what their friends and acquaintances borrowed tended to be the same kind of superior non-fiction as private subscription libraries were founded to provide, as will be considered later.

Informal lending can be found in a commercial context as well. The Glasgow booksellers (but not circulating librarians), James Brash and William Reid, seem to have lent books for free to favoured customers. One such was Mary Archbald, a farmer's wife on the far-distant (from Glasgow) island of Little Cumbrae. She, for instance, received Walter Scott's *The Lay of the Last Minstrel* from them in 1805, which her son transcribed. When she emigrated to upstate New York in 1807, she knitted fur gloves for the pair in appreciation.[50] Brash and Reid also, in 1804, permitted the young poet, John Struthers, to borrow books after closing on Saturdays until Monday morning. The books were covered in paper to keep them clean, but Struthers, a strict Sabbatarian, had to wait until early on Monday to read them.[51] Other booksellers may have operated in a similar philanthropic manner, but evidence is wanting.

The Earliest Subscription Libraries: Leadhills and Other Miners' Libraries

The Leadhills miners' library was an influential forerunner of Scottish subscription libraries. Founded as 'The Society for Purchasing Books at

---

[48] NRS GD248/25/2/20; cf. online catalogue.

[49] Mark Towsey, *Reading the Scottish Enlightenment* (Leiden, 2010), pp. 48-54.

[50] Alison M. Scott, '"This Cultivated Mind": Reading and Identity in a Nineteenth-Century Reader', in *Reading Acts: U.S. Readers' Interactions with Literature, 1800-1950*, edited by Barbara Ryan and Amy M. Thomas (Knoxville, 2002), pp. 29-52 (here p. 51); Towsey, *Reading the Scottish Enlightenment*, p. 97.

[51] *Poetical Works of John Struthers, with Autobiography* (London, 1850), vol. 1, p. lxxxviii.

Leadhills' on 23 November 1741 with 23 members, the rules were officially ratified on 15 April 1743 as a society 'for our mutual Improvement'.[52] Usually described as the earliest working-class Scottish subscription library, Leadhills was not proprietary and charged in its earliest years at least 2s.6d. entry fee, later raised to a maximum of five shillings, plus 2s.6d. as the annual subscription, amended in 1761 to 'at least 2s.6d.'. (As in later libraries, the entry fee was payable on first joining and constituted purchase of a share). But the designation 'working-class' is misleading; the Leadhills miners were an élite compared to other miners. They only worked for six hours per day (at a period when it was normal to work at least eight) but began at between 5 a.m. and 6 a.m.; pickmen could earn up to £20 per year while labourers could be paid up to £14 per year, well above the national average. Unskilled workers might earn about £12 per year.

The level of literacy amongst the 'miners' at this period is demonstrated by the subscription list to James Durham's *Commentary upon the Book of the Revelation* (Glasgow, 1739), which includes no fewer than eighteen miners from Leadhills (some became library members) and a further twenty from neighbouring Wanlockhead. This contrasts with the popular book by the Presbyterian, Isaac Ambrose, *Prima, Media and Ultima* (Glasgow, 1737), whose subscription list only includes eight names from Leadhills and two from Wanlockhead out of a total of 648 subscribers.[53] There is no doubt that the miners were literate and keen for knowledge; but they were mostly not working-class. The original library members were clerks employed by the Scotch Mining Company and miners (half of whom were English) who leased plots of land from the Company by making 'bargains' with the manager.[54] They then employed others for the pick and shovel work: in other words, the library's members were capitalist adventurers rather than manual workers, though the membership list does include a handful of identifiable 'pickmen'. The library's official book stamp also showed a pick and shovel. No less than 50 men had become members of the society by 1747, 100 by 1766, 150 by 1782, 200 by 1792, and 250 by 1806 (these figures are cumulative). Member no. 840 was enrolled in 1902.

Library historians have long debated whether the library at Leadhills was a product of company paternalism or of genuine self-help by the workers,

---

[52] Paul Kaufman, 'Leadhills: Library of Diggers', in his *Libraries and their Users*, pp. 163-70; cf. J. C. Crawford, 'The Ideology of Mutual Improvement in Scottish Working Class Libraries', *Library History* 12 (1996), 49-61; J. C. Crawford, 'The Leadhills Library and a Wider World', *Library Review* 46 (1997), 539-53.

[53] For more examples of book purchases by the working classes at this period, see: J. C. Crawford, 'Reading and Book Use in 18th-century Scotland', *Bibliotheck* 19 (1994), 23-43 (here pp. 24-26).

[54] W. S. Harvey, 'Miners' Bargains at Leadhills during the 18th Century', *Glasgow Spelaeological Society Journal* 2 (1970), 1-21.

or perhaps the personal foundation of the manager, James Stirling. Dr John Crawford, for instance, has suggested that the prime influence might be traced to Episcopalian Jacobitism, while Peter Jackaman favoured corporate philanthropy fuelled by nonconformity, citing the influence of the Quaker-dominated London Lead Company (which ran the mines at Wanlockhead until 1755).[55] Some miners – and possibly Stirling himself – may even have encountered the circulating library begun in Edinburgh by Allan Ramsay (himself a native of Leadhills, whose father had been an overseer there) and considered the notion of borrowing books. It is conjectural that an influence on its foundation may have been the Dumfries Presbytery Library, recently revived on a subscription basis and situated not many miles away.

Encouragement for the Leadhills Library's formation must be attributable, if only in part, to James Stirling (1692-1770) of Garden, Stirlingshire, the Oxford-educated mathematician and Fellow of the Royal Society employed from 1734 as the reforming manager of the mine. He was also a Jacobite, for which he had been expelled from Balliol College in 1715. As a young man, he is said to have discovered the secrets of Venetian glass-manufacture and had to flee that city for his life.[56] Before Stirling's time, the Leadhills miners had been noted for indiscipline and trouble-making, and his achievement was to bring order and introduce social improvements such as better housing, a school, doctor, and a reduction in the number of vendors of alcohol.[57] There is no evidence that he initiated the library, but it would have been an understandable development. He himself possessed a private library, and the need for the workers to have their own collection could have arisen from his example or from the need for a more accessible library.[58]

Stirling and other managers of the mines were expressly barred from taking any part in the management of the library, but he became an honorary member, as did Archibald Stirling of Garden (James's nephew, son-in-law, and successor), the Earl of Hopetoun, and a number of people who may have made donations, such as John Kingan, Church of Scotland minister at Crawford (the parish in which the mines lay), and Robert Wells, a merchant in Charleston, South Carolina. (The last-named was probably related to James Wells, who had signed the original articles of 1743. Robert had emigrated to America in 1752 and became a printer and bookseller. He subsequently served on the committee of the Charleston Library Society; he printed that library's rules in

---

[55] Crawford, 'Leadhills', p. 540. For arguments on both sides, see: P. Jackaman, 'The Company, the Common Man, and the Library', *Library Review* 29 (1980), 27-32.

[56] John. O. Mitchell, *Old Glasgow Essays* (Glasgow, 1905), pp. 85-106.

[57] Ramsay, *Scotland and Scotsmen*, vol. 2, p. 311.

[58] A manuscript catalogue (1771) of Stirling's own library is amongst the Stirling of Garden family papers held privately in Aberdour.

1762 and their catalogues of 1770 and 1772.)[59] The library was never intended to become private property but was for the community, and no ownership shares could be bought in the enterprise so that 'the Good, we hereby intend, may not be subverted by the fraudulent Design or Combination of one or more Members of the Society', as the original rules stated. However, the right of membership could be transferred on the death of a member to his heir, or, indeed, assigned elsewhere during his lifetime on leaving the area permanently, if the society approved. But the books could not be sold off for the benefit of individuals.

The rules allowed for a preses, clerk, treasurer, librarian, officer (whose job was to carry out the orders of the committee and summon members to meetings, etc.), and three inspectors, whose duty was to report on any damage committed on the books; the latter were given the right to enter members' houses to examine books on the spot. The clerk was responsible for handing over parcels of books to the librarian, who had to provide security for them and attend the meetings at which books were exchanged. The latter was also responsible for the library's book-press and for keeping a catalogue. Both he and the clerk had use of the books for free. No overseer or grieve at the mines could be an office-holder for fear he might use his influence prejudicially. Each member had to purchase a copy of the rules so that they could not claim ignorance.

The Society met quarterly to conduct general business, such as appointing officers and the committee, and to ballot on new members (who had to wait at least six weeks for the ballot to take place). There was a fine of sixpence for non-attendance, unless an acceptable excuse was submitted in writing within a fortnight. An annual dinner was held at a public house (when the expense could 'on no Pretence' exceed sixpence each for liquor): 'The Preses shall have a Power of preserving Decency and Order, and of imposing Fines for any irregular Behaviour; and such Members as cannot attend, must give timeous Notice to the Preses'.

The committee met on the first Wednesday of each month to order new books. Books were allotted to members by rote at a meeting held on the second 'lawful' day of each month, at which a strict ritual was observed:

> 1. The Books, which have been in the Hands of the Members, during the preceding Month, shall be delivered to the Librarian, and being marked as received by him or Assistant, and inspected by the Inspectors, shall be committed to their places in the Library.

---

[59] James Raven, *London Booksellers and American Customers: Transatlantic Literary Community and the Charleston Library Society, 1748-1811* (Columbia, S.C., 2002), pp. 41, 53, 81, and *passim*.

2. The Members being all seated, shall then receive Books for the ensuing Month; the Privilege of the first Choice, as also every succeeding Choice, devolving upon every member in his turn, according as he stands in the Librarian's List, so that he who chuses first this Night shall chuse last the next.

3. Any Member who cannot attend in Person, may be allowed to employ a Proxy, to whom he must give a written List of the Books he wants, signed with his own Hand; but if any Books in the said List by another Member chusing before, the Proxy may chuse any other Book in the Library of the like Size, in Place of that he missed.

4. No Member shall receive, at one Time, more than four small Duodecimo Volumes, or three larger, or two Octavos, or one Quarto or Folio, but with such Quarto or Folio he may have one small Volume. But it may be allowed any of the Members to exchange Books amongst themselves, during the Course of the Month, providing always that the Member receiving them in the Library shall be accountable for any Damages they may sustain.

5. Members reading a Book of more Volumes than one, shall not be deprived of the next succeeding Volume, by Members chusing before them.[60]

The ritual of choosing books in rotation is found in other clubs, most notably in England, as, for instance, in the Dalton-in-Furness Book Club in Lancashire, which was in existence in the 1760s and still meets today in similar fashion.[61] It was also employed at the meetings held every fourth Saturday by members of the Monkland Friendly Society, of which Robert Burns was librarian, as he explained:

At every meeting, all the books, under certain fines and forfeitures, by way of penalty, were to be produced; and the members had the choice of the volumes in rotation. He whose name stood, for that night, first on the list, had his choice of what volume he pleased in the whole collection; the second had his choice after the first; the third after the second, and so on to the last. At next meeting, he who had been first on the list at the preceding meeting, was last at this; he who had been second, was first; and so on ...[62]

---

[60] From the printed rules (1761), pp. 13-14, in the Hornel Library, Broughton House, Kirkcudbright.

[61] E. H. Boddy, 'The Dalton Book Club: a Brief History', *Library History* 9 (1992), 97-105, with account of a visit to the society made by the present author.

[62] *OSA*, vol. 3 (1792), p. 599.

The Leadhills and Wanlockhead libraries and their procedures were probably well-known at Dumfries, where Burns worked. At Leadhills, though, the system of rote was eventually abandoned as it became increasingly unfeasible, with too many members and changing attitudes.

All books had to have the society's bookplate pasted inside and could be kept for one month (folios and quartos for two months), with a fine of a penny for late return. Lost books had to be replaced or payment made at double their value, and books could not be lent, or even shown, to non-members. Wisely, books were lent out to members who did not live in the village in 'a Bag sufficient to keep out Rain', but to reduce the risk, people could only belong to the library if they resided in Leadhills or Wanlockhead (or unless mines were subsequently discovered within six miles).

A diary of 1745, anonymous, but attributed to Matthew Wilson, a senior clerk at the mine and a member of the library, reveals much of the life of the community and indicates his own reading; he was also on the library's committee. He is found reading the poem, *Leonidas* by Richard Glover, and 'In the Interval of Business and diversion this week I read part of [Paul de] Rapin's *Hist. of England*'. In July, 'Some of my spare hours this Week were spent in reading [Johann] Cramer's *Elements of the Art of Assaying Metals*'. He also read Sir Edward Coke's *Dilections* [sic][63], Abbé Vertot's *Revolutions of Portugal*, and Peter Rae's *History of the Late Rebellion*. On Saturday 30 November he spent all his spare time reading and calculated he could read Samuel Puffendorf and Rapin at the rate of sixteen pages an hour, and *Don Quixote* at twenty-eight pages. A week later he has speeded up Rapin to thirty pages an hour.[64]

The diarist attended quarterly library meetings, held at 7 p.m., and frequently dined with Stirling, hearing tales of his adventures in Italy. Wilson spent much of his time poring over the mine's accounts and ordering provisions. He was frequently sent by Stirling to Edinburgh, where he observed Bonnie Prince Charlie riding through the city. The capture of the capital caused a cessation to most business around the country. When the Highlanders were rumoured to be approaching Leadhills, many people hid their valuables in the mines, but in the event only three turned up and swiftly galloped away. Clearly Wilson was no manual worker, and his diary shows how much other miners – viz. the adventurers – were earning. One miner, William Otto, also a member of the library, was earning over £54 yearly, partly because he was paid to employ boys for a six-day week and philanthropically gave them Saturday afternoons off; but he pocketed the pay for those half-days himself.

---

[63] Presumably the diarist means 'deliberations' or 'declarations' and refers to Sir Edward Coke's law reports.

[64] J. Williams, 'A Leadhills Diary for 1745', *Dumfriesshire & Galloway Natural History & Antiquarian Society Transactions*, 3rd ser. 54 (1979), 105-31.

The books acquired for the library were the high-quality non-fiction which people came to expect in any subscription, as opposed to common circulating, library by the end of the century. A manuscript catalogue of 1767 lists 191 titles in 497 volumes and reveals a very serious collection indeed, in which almost 30% is made up of history and almost 24% of religion. The stock includes Herodotus, George Stanhope on Thomas à Kempis, Samuel Puffendorf, Paul de Rapin, Hugo Grotius, William Whiston's Josephus, Ralph Cudworth's *Intellectual System*, Philip Doddridge, William Shakespeare, Joseph Butler's and John Tillotson's sermons, Jonathan Swift, William Sherlock on death, Edward Chamberlayne's *State of Britain*, *Life of Marlborough* by W. H. Dilworth, *Life of Peter the Great* by John Banks, Thomas Burnet's *Theory of the Earth*, *The Spectator*, Pieter van Muschenbroek's *Philosophy*, *Ancient Universal History* in twenty-one volumes, Charles Drelincourt on death, Johann Cramer on metals, James Hervey's *Meditations*, Plutarch, Bishop John Pearson on the creed, Voltaire, George Anson, John Milton, John Hill's *Essays on Natural History*, *Whole Duty of Man* (attributed to Richard Allestree), John Campbell's *Lives of the Admirals*, Isaac Watts, Tobias Smollett's *History of England*, and so much more. This was no library for entertainment, and the only sops to lighter reading are Allan Ramsay's *Poems*, *Don Quixote*, and Smollett's *Roderick Random*.[65]

In 1760, when the library was estimated to be worth £60, concern was felt that members might try to capitalize on their property. A rule was therefore added that the Earl of Hopetoun, the landowner who leased the mineral rights to the Company, could sue the members if their numbers fell below seven and advertize for new members within six miles of the village. The earl was specifically prevented from disposing of any of the library's property 'excepting that if at any time Leadhills being gone to Decay and the Members of the Society by that means Extinct', he could transfer the books to another mining village within his barony, provided it was for the public benefit, 'since it was the original Intention of the Founders thereof to render the Benefit of it Publick and perpetual'. Previously there had been a rule that if there were seven or fewer members, and a new subscriber should be refused membership, then he could sue the 'refusers'. Successive earls continued support, and in 1791 the third earl permitted the library to build a new house, paid for out of the sale of their previous building, with new slates granted by the earl from one of his quarries.

In August 1803 Dorothy Wordsworth, accompanied by her brother, William, and Samuel Taylor Coleridge, stayed in Leadhills and discovered with some surprise, and with some condescension, the library:

---

[65] Catalogue in the possession of the Marquis of Linlithgow, to whom the author is most grateful for permission to examine this item.

> We talked with one of the miners, who informed us that the building which we had supposed to be a school was a library belonging to the village. He said they had got a book into it a few weeks ago, which had cost thirty pounds, and that they had all sorts of books. 'What! Have you Shakespeare?' 'Yes, we have that', and we found, on further inquiry, that they had a large library, of long standing, that Lord Hopetoun had subscribed liberally to it, and that gentlemen who came with him were in the habit of making larger or smaller donations. Each man who had the benefit of it paid a small sum monthly – I think about fourpence.[66]

During the nineteenth century the library remained in use, but the mines declined and were barely worked 'owing to the suspension or spiritless working of the mines, during a long, baffling House of Lords lawsuit' between the then earl and the Company, according to Dr John Brown, who visited in 1865; but, he noted, they 'have a capital library'.[67] The Leadhills Library had acquired 3,855 volumes by 1905, but existed largely as a reading room throughout a large part of the twentieth century. The library still survives.

A library run along almost identical lines was founded in neighbouring Wanlockhead on 1 November 1756 with the title 'Society for Purchasing Books in Wanlockhead'.[68] Library provision was part of a programme of social reforms, including new housing, enacted after the sacking and prosecution of disruptive miners in 1755 following disturbances led by a shocking combination of women and men dressed as women.[69] As at Leadhills, it is unclear whether the newly-purged miners were the driving force behind the library's establishment, or the mining company. The land was owned by the Duke of Buccleuch but was mined from 1755 by Crawford & Co., who built a church in that year; there was no church in Leadhills. The library's rules were copied from Leadhills. The entry fee was three shillings plus four shillings per year, the latter being reduced by half in 1783, at which level it remained until 1921. The fee was paid quarterly, when the miners were paid. Members met once a month to select books, and, as at Leadhills, the mine managers were not to interfere in the library's administration. Books were probably arranged on the shelves according to size and date of acquisition, and there was no direct access for the members. Although it grew slowly, with only 116 volumes in 1783, there were 3,805 volumes by 1904.

---

[66] William Knight (ed.), *Journals of Dorothy Wordsworth* (London, 1910), vol. 1, pp. 178-9.

[67] Quoted in: J. Moir Porteous, *God's Treasure-house in Scotland* (London, 1876), pp. 91-94.

[68] John C. Crawford and Stuart James, *The Society for Purchasing Books in Wanlockhead, 1756-1979* (Glasgow, 1981).

[69] 'J.', 'Short Account of the Miners of Leadhills and Wanlockhead', *Christian Observer* 23 (1823) 26-29; reprinted in Jean Goldie, *Family Recollections* (Edinburgh, 1841), p. 43.

Despite constant financial problems, the library maintained its own building; its membership reached a peak of 147 in 1850 but fell to sixty-eight by 1876. The character of the library also shifted during the early nineteenth century, as happened too at Leadhills, caused by the Disruption of 1843. At the Leadhills Library many works of controversial divinity are said to have been introduced at this period by adherents to the Free Church.[70] Although the Duke of Buccleuch encouraged the aims of the Wanlockhead library, he looked askance at Leadhills because so many miners were Evangelicals; he only permitted the latter a chapel in Wanlockhead in 1859. It is notable that religion was the largest class in the Wanlockhead library, reaching over one third of total stock for most of the nineteenth century. History was originally the second largest section but was overtaken by fiction by the 1820s. Although mutual improvement might have been the original impetus behind both the Leadhills and Wanlockhead libraries, the miners' tastes and attitudes all too obviously changed as the new century progressed. The Wanlockhead mines closed in 1934, but 2,500 books still survive *in situ* in the care of the Wanlockhead Museum Trust (founded in 1974).

The amount of religious literature at Wanlockhead is significant because it is unusual. Most Scottish subscription libraries concentrated on history, biography, travels, and popular science. But religious differences were never far away, particularly in small villages. The Fenwick Library, Ayrshire, for instance, was founded in 1808, apparently by weavers and shoemakers (its earliest records are lost), in a village noted for its support for the Covenanting tradition. Its 1827 catalogue proclaims the role of libraries in the diffusion of knowledge and emphasizes that books, 'under the blessing of God, have often provided the means of directing the bewildered traveller to the way that leadeth to eternal life'. Out of 283 volumes, no fewer than 118 (or 41%) are on religion, followed by history (17%); the library possessed but one novel.[71] Fenwick and Wanlockhead stand out for revealing attitudes amongst their respective villagers.

Libraries existed at other lead mines. At Ben Cruachan, Argyllshire, in about 1784, the miners 'taxed themselves in a moiety of their wages for the purchase of books and the gradual establishment of a library for their amusement in this sequestered situation'.[72] At some time before 1786 lead miners working for the Earl of Breadalbane in Perthshire (but employed by the same company which

---

[70] 'A Trip to the Gold Regions of Scotland', *Gentleman's Magazine* 132 (1853), 596.

[71] J. C. Crawford, 'Recovering the Lost Scottish Community Library: the Example of Fenwick', *Library History* 23 (2007), 201-12.

[72] Thomas A. Thornton, *Sporting Tour through the Northern Parts of England* (London, 1804), p. 241.

managed the mines at Leadhills) were also collecting books, as reported by *The Times*:

> It is remarkable that a new species of literary characters have lately been discovered near Tyndrum, on the North side of Loch Lomond, in Scotland. ... The miners having a good deal of spare time, and little temptation to spend their money, formed some time since a little stock to purchase books. At first they got pieces of amusement, and then bought works of science, particularly treatises on mineralogy and other branches of natural philosophy. We are assured these subterraneous readers have now a well-assorted library of 7 or 800 volumes. Philosophy seems to have humanized and exalted their minds, as they are exceedingly attached to their noble Patron; remarkably affectionate to their wives and families; and uncommonly courteous to such strangers as visit their sequestered place of abode.[73]

In 1792 antimony miners in Jamestown, Dumfriesshire, were given books by the mine owners, the Westerhall Mining Company, including (in the original orthography of the minute books) [John] Tillitson's *Sermons*, [William] Guthrie's *Grahamar*, [Peter] Rae's *Wisdom of God*, [William] Robertson's *History of Scotland*, [Thomas Nettleton's] *A Treatise on Virtue*, Seneca's *Morals*, [Adam] Ferguson's *Lectures*, [Antoine] Lavoiser on chemistry, and [Axel] Cromstead on mineralogy. Other well-wishers donated worthy tomes, including a book on the American Constitution and James Hervey's *Meditations*. On 1 August 1793 the miners formed themselves into a society to purchase further books which 'will tend greatly to our Improvement', raising five shillings each towards their first purchases, which included George Ridpath's *Border History*, Samuel Richardson's *Sir Charles Grandison*, Tobias Smollett's *Peregrine Pickle*, Robert Burns's *Poems*, John Erskine on laws, James Thomson's *Seasons*, John Mason on self-knowledge, works of Knox [presumably John Knox], *The Letters of Junius*, Samuel Johnson's *Rambler*, *History of the Devil* by Daniel Defoe, and, perhaps with pangs of longing, Hardwicke Lewis's *Excursion to Margate*.

The library's procedures were based on those at Leadhills, whose rules were solicited in 1794, and monthly meetings were held for the exchange of books. The usual officers were chosen, including preses, clerk, and 'Liberarien', and fines were detailed. The library had transferable shares, and as early as August 1794 one share duly passed to a former member's nephew. With the dissolution of the mining company, the library was moved around nearby villages until a purpose-built building was eventually provided in 1860, following a bequest of money and 5,400 books from Thomas Telford in 1834. It survives as the

---

[73] *Daily Universal Register* [i.e. *The Times*], 4 January 1786.

Westerkirk Library.[74] Its rules, revised in 1843, show the library's indebtedness to Leadhills, including a similar plan for distributing books by rote:

> The day of the full moon, or the first lawful day following, at six o'clock in the morning, (November to February inclusive); at seven o'clock in the evening, (March to October inclusive), is appointed as the monthly meeting for the exchange of Books which have been taken out the preceding month; each Book shall be delivered to the Librarian, after being regularly marked as returned in the Calendar, and properly examined by the Inspectors. The members shall have their choice of Books for the ensuing month by rotation, as they stand in the Clerk's list, new members or entrants being allowed the first choice on their entrance. Any member reading a work consisting of more volumes than one, shall not be deprived of his right to the succeeding volumes by another member having a prior choice.

A fine of a penny was charged for non-return of a book at a monthly meeting, and twopence per month thereafter. Members could exchange books amongst themselves, but not lend to non-members, or face a fine of a shilling (in 1778 the latter offence cost a fine of 2s.6d. in the Ayr Library). The cost of new books would be defrayed from Telford's bequest. Any members could suggest books, but if funds were insufficient, preference was given to books proposed by the committee of management; final selection was by a ballot. The shares were transferable, but could only be transferred once. Occasional readers could pay sixpence per quarter, or three shillings a year if they lived in a neighbouring parish.[75]

A library for colliery workers at Newton, near Edinburgh, existed by around 1800 but had dissolved by 1830, though books remained in 1845. The local minister ascribed its decline to the influx at the beginning of the century of hundreds of miners, 'chiefly of the most reckless characters', who had no interest in reading. A subscription library was also established for workers at Bannockburn Colliery in 1828, which soon had forty members and 175 volumes,[76] and similar libraries appeared (probably shortly after 1825) at Bertram Shotts Ironworks, Lanarkshire, and Crawfordston Colliery, Tarbolton, Ayrshire.[77]

---

[74] A. McCracken, 'The Glendinning Antimony Mine (Louisa Mine)', *Dumfriesshire & Galloway Natural History & Antiquarian Society Transactions*, 3rd ser. 42 (1965), 140-8, appendix; *Westerkirk Parish Library Restoration Project 1992-1997* (Westerkirk, 1997).

[75] From the rules given in the library's catalogue, attributed to 1843; cf. *Life of Thomas Telford* (London, 1838), vol. 1, p. 662.

[76] *Stirling Journal*, 28 August 1828.

[77] *NSA*, vol. 6 (1845), p. 759 for Bertram Shotts; *NSA*, vol. 5 (1845), p. 603 for Tarbolton.

Kelso and the Borders: the First Proprietary Subscription Libraries

Kelso Library (1750) is the first known Scottish proprietary subscription library, preceding the Liverpool Library (1758), often (though inaccurately) regarded as the first in England and a model for the Warrington (1760), Leeds and Halifax (both 1768) libraries. Kelso was followed by Hawick and Ayr (both 1762), then Duns (1768), Selkirk (1772), Kirkcudbright (1777), and Greenock (1783). The Gentleman's Society of Dumfries allegedly started in mid-century, but its exact date is unrecorded. According to some sources, this Society was founded in about 1745 or 1750. This dating comes from a history of libraries in the county, of which the oldest version, which appeared in 1907, gives the source as 'Oliver and Boyd for 1845'. This refers to the *Edinburgh Almanack* for 1845, though the reference appears in the 'western supplement'. Sadly, every almanack from about 1840 to 1860 used exactly the same phrase: 'established a century ago'. So there is no trustworthy evidence as to when that library was really founded, not even the decade. Indisputably it existed by 1767 when the library subscribed to Thomas Short's *Comparative History of the Increase and Decrease of Mankind in England*. The Jedburgh Company Library existed by the late 1770s and may have been founded in the 1760s.

A subscription library did exist in Berwick-upon-Tweed by 1753; whether Berwick counts as part of English or Scottish library history is an interesting speculation. The Berwick Public Library subscribed to John Werge's *Collection of Original Poems* (1753) and also to John Jebb's *Excerpta Quaedam e Newtoni Principiis Philosophiae Naturalis*, an edited version, in the original Latin of Newton's *Principles of Natural Philosophy*, published in 1765. In 1769 the Berwick Library was considered a model for a proposed subscription library in Alnwick, Northumberland, though that was not to materialize, and similarly in 1785 for the proposed subscription library in Perth. Clearly the Berwick Public Library had a long life and was considered influential in its own time; its existence has never previously been identified. Kaufman was not aware of it, and whether it existed before the nearby Kelso Library is unknown. Kelso and Berwick libraries might well be part of a chain encompassing the already mentioned Pocklington Library in Yorkshire, and therefore a more direct development of English library history.

The prototype for subscription libraries was the Library Company of Philadelphia, founded in 1731 by Benjamin Franklin and friends, and whose intentions of providing a library for the public good can be traced back to Thomas Bray's parochial libraries and John Locke's ideas of mutual improvement. This library, which can fairly claim to be the first private subscription library, was initiated by fifty men who pledged forty shillings each towards the first parcel of books and ten shillings a year thereafter. The forty shillings represented a share, and new members paid more as the library increased. Ten years later original shares were reckoned to be worth £6.10s. Non subscribers could borrow books by leaving a deposit. In 1743 the library received a charter from the State's Proprietors and so became a legal entity in its own right. This became the pattern for North American proprietary libraries, which spread rapidly. By 1750 another eleven private subscription libraries had been founded there, mostly in Connecticut, but also including the Redwood Library (1747) in Newport, Rhode Island, and the Charleston Library Society (1748) in South Carolina; the latter pair still survive. A further nine appear during the 1750s.[78] The Library Company of Philadelphia purchased its books from London, and one of its earliest benefactors was a Scottish plantation owner in Antigua, Walter Sydserfe. But whether it was consciously used as a model for similar libraries in Scotland and England cannot be presumed.

Kelso, famous at this period for its racecourse, may not have been the most prepossessing town in Scotland to be (arguably) the birthplace of the Scottish subscription library movement, though many of the library's members lived outside the town itself. Visiting the town in October 1758, the Englishman (Sir) William Burrell, future lawyer and Member of Parliament, described what he observed:

> The town of Kelso is meanly built; most of the houses are covered with turf or thatch. The inhabitants, by their neighbourhood to England, have so far condescended to imitate them in cleanliness as to cover the inside walls of their rooms with paper, which gives them an air of neatness, and I must do them the justice to add the bedding and linnen is extremely good. But in all other respects they preserve the filthy customs of their countrymen, from which they will not be persuaded to secede. The streets are filled with human excrement from one end to the other, which renders walking unsafe and disagreeable.[79]

The Kelso Library was founded by twenty local citizens who signed a contract for ten years. The annual fee was ten shillings (increased to one guinea in 1804), while the founders paid £10 for their share of the library. That was a considerable amount, and this library was for the better-off. The ten-year contract was adopted at Hawick, Duns and Perth, and signified that the library could not be dissolved during that period. The second ten-year period at Hawick began at Martinmas 1773 with a payment of eight shillings sterling.

---

[78] A summary list of the earliest such libraries is given in: James Raven, 'Social Libraries and Library Societies in Eighteenth-century North America', in: Thomas Augst and Kenneth Carpenter, *Institutions of Reading: the Social Life of Libraries in the United States* (Amherst, Mass., 2007), pp. 24-52 (here pp. 31-32).

[79] *Sir William Burrell's Northern Tour 1758,* edited by John G. Dunbar (East Linton, 1997), p. 122.

Duns Library's shares cost £2 plus six shillings a year, but new members were obliged to pay all annual subscriptions since the commencement of the library in 1768, even if they had joined several years after the ten-year term had commenced. This was soon changed as 'it will be a great Bar or if not a total stop to future Subscribers to be charged with the original Subscription and the annual payments that may be due at the time'. When the second ten-year contract expired in 1788, it was agreed that the library would continue indefinitely, unless dissolution was approved by a majority of two-thirds.[80]

The Duns Library's laws also specified that there could be no more than fifty members. Limiting membership is found elsewhere and suggests one way of ensuring exclusivity; but in small Borders towns, it is unlikely that that number could be reasonably exceeded anyway. The Edinburgh Subscription Library (1794) originally restricted membership to seventy-five, but this was soon increased to 400. Limits could easily be moved upwards, and one reason for fixing a limit was so that entry money and annual subscriptions could be reviewed if the library proved popular.

The Kelso Library's minute books for its first forty years of existence were lost early in the nineteenth century[81], and all that is known of its administration for this period comes from several surviving catalogues and from the diary of one of its most assiduous founder-members, Rev. George Ridpath (ca. 1716-72), minister of nearby Stichill and author of a posthumously-published *History of the Borders*.[82] Though the diary only begins in 1755, it does reveal the date of the library's foundation. The founders signed a contract for ten years, reviewed after five, and Ridpath's diary covers its renewal in 1760. Since he also refers to the anniversary dinners, held originally on the same date each year, it can be deduced that the Library was founded on 5 November 1750, though the minute books of a century later reveal that the library officially opened for business on 3 February 1751. The anniversary meeting was later moved to July as a more convenient time of the year.

Ridpath's diary records his borrowings, with comments. Books were then issued for a month. He devoured Voltaire's *History of Europe*, Emanuel Bowen's *Complete System of Geography* (which he found 'full of blunders'), *Philosophical*

---

[80] Borders AO, DL/3/1, Duns Library minute book, 7 November 1770, 12 November 1788.

[81] The minute books for the period 1793-1848 disappeared from Kelso Public Library during the 1960s or 1970s, but were extant when Paul Kaufman was preparing his article, 'Library News from Kelso', *Library Review* 17 (1960), 486-9. Extracts from the minutes were sent to Kaufman by Frank Beckwith of the Leeds Library, and copies are now amongst the Beckwith papers in the Brotherton Library, University of Leeds. The minute books after 1849 are in the National Records of Scotland, having passed to the Crown as *ultimus haeres*. The author is most grateful to Dr. Tristram Clarke of the NRS for his assistance in tracing them.

[82] *Diary of George Ridpath, 1755-61*, edited by Sir James B. Paul, Scottish History Society, 3rd ser. 2 (Edinburgh, 1922).

Transactions, *Scots Magazine*, Thomas Stanley's *Lives of the Ancient Philosophers* ('which entertained me much'), Joseph Warton's Virgil, (Paul de?) Rapin, Sir John Dalrymple on feudal property, Juan d'Ulloa's *Voyage to South America* ('very entertaining ... one of the best works of that class'), Montesquieu, Laurence Sterne's *Tristram Shandy* ('too learned for the ladies and even the bulk of male readers'), Apuleius's *Golden Ass* ('remarkable for a luxuriancy of fancy and expression, and a very useful moral allegory appears ...'), and so much more. On 8 April 1760, he 'Slept on [Samuel] Butler's *Remains*'. Presumably his voracious reading helped him to write his sermons, which were said to last for up to two hours.

Details of administration are also revealed. Members could not handle the books; they had to present written requisitions to the librarian. Stock selection meetings were held every quarter, usually on the same days as meetings of the local presbytery since there were members in common, and up to six books could be borrowed at a time. In the 1750s books were acquired from the Edinburgh booksellers, Kincaid and Donaldson, and Ridpath would compare prices with those advertised in the *London Magazine*: 'I find they have dealt with us fairly enough', he noted on 10 November 1755, 'being much oftener, and a good deal more, under, than over, the prices there'.

Stock selection was not taken lightly. On 3 November 1756 he 'attended a library meeting, where we gave commissions for a good many books. Agreed also to return the *General Dictionary*, which I did not much oppose as I saw it would be in vain, and as it is certain that the other parts of the work are greatly inferior to [Pierre] Bayle's'. (He was presumably referring to Thomas Dyche's *Dictionary*.) On 2 February 1757 the meeting was held at night 'where we sate till 12'. Increasing debt forced the library's committee to hold back on ordering books in 1757 and 1758, and a new crisis arrived when the custodian of the books informed them that he could keep them in his house no longer. In fact the librarian, John Waldie, was the proprietor of the Cross Keys Inn and obviously found the presence of so many books an inconvenience to his business.

After three years of stagnation, Ridpath was at last able to make up a list of suggestions, and on 7 November 1759 they gave 'a pretty large commission for new books and also gave orders for new presses for holding our books, which are to be put up so soon as these are ready, in a room in the town house which Ramsay has procured us the use of and at the expense of the Duke of Roxburghe made a very decent, convenient place. Our finances now are in tolerable good condition'. The library certainly benefited from the town's wealthy residents, though Ridpath was wary of expecting too much. As preses of the library, he wrote on the following day to 'Mr Baillie of Mellerstain, acknowledging the favours of Lady Murray [who had recently died] to our Library, and desiring the continuance of them on his part. This was thought proper last night by the meeting, tho' I did not much approve of it, as having too much the air of begging'.

Fitting-up the new room and moving the books became a preoccupation for Ridpath, and he began compiling a shelf-list of the books which he then used as the basis for a (non-extant) alphabetical catalogue, completed during February 1760. (Ridpath was subsequently asked to prepare a catalogue to be printed, which was completed in 1761, but no copies have survived.) The new librarian was to be R. Telfer, a local bookbinder. The ten-year contract for the continuance of the library was approved on 5 November 1760, when all the members agreed to pay ten shillings a year for ten years. A motion that books should be lent out for half-a-crown per quarter to non-shareholders, which would have produced plenty of money, was rejected, presumably because most members felt this might have damaged the long-term value of the shares.

The Kelso Library was always called the Kelso Library, though it was locally often known as the 'Old Library'. Sir Walter Scott, who lived in Kelso as a school-boy in 1784, confused the issue when he wrote that

> a respectable subscription library, a circulating library of ancient standing, and some private book-shelves, were open to my random perusal, and I waded into the stream like a blind man into a ford, without the power of searching my way, unless by groping for it. My appetite for books was as ample and indiscriminating as it was indefatigable, and I have since had too much reason to repent that few ever read so much, and to so little purpose.[83]

It is not immediately clear whether the subscription and circulating library he mentions are one and the same library (which almost certainly is what he meant); but elsewhere he refers to 'a good though old-fashioned library', and it is clear he means the Kelso Library alone.[84] He added:

> The vague and wild use which I made of this advantage I cannot describe better than by referring my reader to the desultory studies of Waverley in a similar situation, the passages concerning whose course of reading were imitated from recollections of my own.[85]

When Scott settled at Abbotsford, he does not appear to have joined any of the nearby subscription libraries, though many of his friends belonged to the Selkirk Library, while he himself was said, possibly apocryphally, to have been

---

[83] J. G. Lockhart, *Life of Sir Walter Scott* (Edinburgh, 1902), vol. 1, p. 29; quoted in Kaufman, 'Community libraries', p. 294.

[84] The *ODNB* does indeed claim that Scott belonged to both a subscription and a circulating library in Kelso, but there is no evidence for the latter at this period.

[85] Preface to the 1829 edition of the *Waverley* novels.

a frequent visitor to the Galashiels Library.[86] He certainly supported the idea of subscription libraries, for instance by donating thirty volumes to the Fort William Subscription Library in 1820.[87] The presence of three Edinburgh circulating library catalogues – those of William Wilson, Robert Kinnear, and Joannah Tansh – dating from 1810 to 1826 at Abbotsford suggest, though, that he was a library borrower.[88]

A printed catalogue of the Kelso Library of around 1793 shows seventy-one subscribers, including eleven ministers, three women, and four baronets. Members included the Duke of Roxburghe; George Baillie of Jerviswood and Mellerstain (brother of the Earl of Haddington); Dr Andrew Coventry, first professor of agriculture at Edinburgh University; Admiral William Dickson; and Sir John Buchanan Riddell, MP. How often such people used the library is unknown, and this applies to many other of the older subscription libraries; the Earl of Selkirk, for instance, was a member of the Kirkcudbright Library, but it would appear unlikely that he often borrowed or attended meetings.

The Kelso Library contained 1,292 titles in 1793, a substantial size, including fiction, but mostly 'good' non-fiction. The stock included *Journals of the House of Commons, State Trials*, James Anderson's *Diplomata et Numismata Scotiae*, Anthony à Wood's *Athenæ Oxonienses*, works by John Locke and Niccolò Machiavelli, John Millar on distinctions of rank in society, William Marsden's *History of Sumatra*, the Russian code of laws, the *Decameron*, James Boswell's travels in Corsica and the Highlands, Boethius, two copies of Edmund Burke on the French Revolution, a copy of the French constitution of 1791, Frederick II's works (in thirteen volumes), a guide to the lakes of Cumberland, William Gibson on diseases of horses, Bryan Higgins on cement, Kitt [sic] on fruit trees (the author is really Thomas Hitt), agricultural reports of England, John Phillips's *Cyder* (a poem), John Milton, the *Annual Register* (in thirty-two volumes), *Monthly Review* (eighty-one volumes), *Analytical Review* (twenty-seven volumes), Sir John Sinclair's *Statistical Account* (sixteen volumes), the ubiquitous J. G. Zimmerman on solitude, the plays of Sir John Vanbrugh, and a large selection of novels such as Tobias Smollett's *The Atom*, Thomas Bridges's *Adventures of a Banknote*, Isabelle de Montolieu's *Caroline of Lichtfield*, Ann Radcliffe's *Udolpho*, as well as *The Lounger*, and much more. There were numerous lives and travels, and also some books on religion, but the latter were not such heavy tomes as in many other libraries.

By way of comparison, the Hawick Public Library also produced a catalogue at about the same time, which reveals forty-one proprietors, including eight

---

[86] Robert Hall, *History of Galashiels* (Galashiels, 1898); Kaufman, 'Community Libraries', p. 294.

[87] *Caledonian Mercury*, 6 November 1820.

[88] These catalogues are amongst a selection of books acquired by the National Library of Scotland in 1934; the remainder of the collection is still at Abbotsford.

ministers, one baronet (Sir George Elliot of Minto), a brewer, tanner, and several surgeons. Its smaller stock included similar non-fiction to the Kelso Library, with many classics in translation and the works of Edward Stillingfleet, Robert Boyle, Luis de Camoëns, Enrico Davila, Ossian, Thomas Pennant, and others. Its members also acquired a number of journals such as the *Critical Review*, *Transactions* of the Society of Arts, the *English Review*, the *Analytical Review*, and more.

The Ayr Library, too, was of similar size and stock. There were seventy-three members in 1792, ten of whom had been founder-members thirty years earlier. Their stock was solidly non-fiction, including John Locke, Laurence Sterne, Adam Smith, Edward Gibbon, and much more in similar vein, while the members were drawn from the gentry and professional classes. Yet another example of the period was Greenock Library, which had seventy-five members in 1793. The town's population (15,000) was over ten thousand more than Kelso, and it was a very different kind of place. Not only was Greenock a busy port, but its shipyards had attracted many Gaelic-speaking Highlanders looking for work; these were not the people who would typically join such a library. Greenock Library did achieve a membership of 170 by 1809, while membership of the Kelso Library had barely increased, if at all.

The inclusion of three women members in the Kelso Library's list of membership for 1793 shows that ladies were never excluded from these libraries. In the Ayr Library the Countess of Dumfries and Stair became a member in 1797; only one woman had been a member in 1776, increasing to five by 1785 (including Lady Cunningham and Lady Crawford) and twelve by 1811. Whether they played any role in the administration is unknown, since it was the custom of the period that women need not attend meetings in person but could vote by proxy. Undoubtedly many ladies would have used their husband's membership of a library to read books themselves. But the ratio of women to men was usually low. When the Wigtown Library was established in 1795, there were forty-four original subscribers, of whom five were women, a reasonably high proportion. Just as interesting is the make-up of the male members, who include no less than eight reverend gentlemen, six writers (i.e. lawyers), three surgeons, several bankers and merchants, the sheriff and his depute, as well as several landed gentry, including the Earl of Galloway, and their factors. This library was clearly comparable to Kelso in its composition.

Returning to the Kelso Library, the books were kept for many years in the Council House. Because its decrepit condition exposed the books to some risk, the library acquired its own building for £36 in 1795 in Chalkheugh, an attractive location overlooking the Tweed; ten new shares were created at £8 each to raise money. Repairs to the building and the embankment beneath it were necessary in 1811. A house was also bought for the librarian, though pulled down in the 1830s because of its state and because it produced no profit. The 1802 catalogue of the Kelso Library shows that its membership had only increased by one, and indeed it had probably reached its optimum size, considering the existence of two other libraries in the town. The stock had risen by less than 200 titles, and only the librarian was permitted to handle the books. It was resolved in 1805 that none of the original shares (there were then eighty) should be sold for less than £10, though during the course of the century new shares did become available at a lower price. The next catalogue dates from 1814 after a series of frenetic notices in the local newspaper, threatening fines and exclusion if books were not returned for checking. Now that the library was well-established, up to six books could be borrowed at a time; folios and quartos could be borrowed for two months, and octavos or smaller for one month. Magazines and reviews could not be lent until bound. This catalogue lists seventy-seven members, now including eleven women, but only about 200 more titles had been bought.

The two other proprietary libraries in the town (despite its relatively small population of 4,000 by 1801), were clearly intended for the lower classes who may not have been welcomed in the Kelso Library itself: the New Library (1778) and the Modern Library (1800). In 1811 the manager of the latter was a linen-draper. Both libraries merged in 1858 when together they held 4,000 volumes. The first known commercial circulating library appears in Kelso in 1816, run by Archibald Rutherford but is unlikely to have offered much competition to the three subscription libraries. In the Oliver and Boyd logbooks, an account of booksellers' credit worthiness, Rutherford is described as: 'Doubtful; Too much of a Florist [i.e. he devoted a lot of time to his garden] & get the name of taking a dropp'.[89]

As for other libraries in the vicinity at this period, the Jedburgh Library began in about 1793 as primarily a theological library, but ran into trouble when the orthodox members objected to certain works of religious controversy, particularly by Dr Edward Young, the 'Bard of the Night'.[90] The library still lasted for fifty years, concentrating on religious works, and it was said that the Bard of Avon knocked vainly on its doors for admission. Another subscription library in Jedburgh, known as Waugh's Library – although no-one of that name is known – was established in about 1785 and lasted sixty years; that was said to accept with open arms the books rejected by the previously mentioned library. There also existed the Jedburgh Company Library, which preceded both. This was said to have declined after 1835 when its directors failed to introduce fresh blood but stayed in office for year after year 'and vetoed all works proposed at general meetings, unless those appearing in their own

---

[89] The logbooks are in the NLS; I am grateful to Dr Bill Bell for providing copies.

[90] Alexander Jeffrey, *History & Antiquities of Roxburghshire* (Edinburgh, [1857]), vol. 2, p. 115.

vocabulary'.[91] By 1834 Jedburgh also boasted a book club for the 'higher class'. The Hawick Trades Library, founded in 1802, was clearly for tradesmen and still existed in 1850. The Coldstream Library eventually merged with the local Mechanics' Institute and still survived in the 1930s. The St Mary's Library, Melrose, was founded in 1798 and possessed 2,500 volumes in the 1860s; it then charged 2s.6d. entry and ten shillings a year.

Subscription Libraries and Shares

In subscription libraries, the price of shares reveals the type of people at whom the library was aimed, as at Kelso and Duns, where the founder-members were local gentry, clergy, nobility, and farmers. The Duns Library was initially permitted to store its books in the town house, an indication of its perceived importance for the community. Alexander Hay, a local landowner who gave the required permission, wrote to the library's clerk in 1768:

> It must give me great pleasure to think that Dunse is in a way of becoming a Seat of Literature, Arts and Sciences, tho' I must owe I should have still more was there a possibility of its becoming a Settlement of Industry, Trade and manufactures.[92]

This letter also hints at the intellectual pretensions which founder-members of libraries at Duns and elsewhere must have felt.

The Selkirk Library cost two guineas entry and 7s.6d. a year, a considerable sum. Similarly, the Dundee Library, established 1792, was for the better-off, while the Dundee Public Library, founded by a handful of young men in 1796, was for the working classes, had no transferable shares, and charged only five shillings entry. Fees could be waived for those who could not afford the quarterly charge of one shilling. It was started as a reaction against other libraries seen as too expensive or which, like common circulating libraries, were 'mostly composed of trash of novels, better fitted to debauch the morals than enlighten the mind'.[93] Amongst its first purchases were William Godwin's *Political Justice*, Voltaire's *Age of Louis XIV*, Antoine Lavoisier on chemistry, Comte de Buffon's *Natural History*, and Samuel Johnson's *Lives of the English Poets*.

Because of its low subscription, income was limited, and this did create problems, as in 1800 when no further new books could be ordered until the

---

[91] Ibid, pp. 114-5.

[92] Borders AO, DL/3/1, Duns Library minute book, 25 December 1768; also quoted in: Crawford, 'Reading and Book Use', p. 36.

[93] *Scots Chronicle*, 27 January 1797.

fees had been raised. Members of libraries were usually obliged to buy a copy of any printed catalogue, and at the Dundee Public Library in 1800, some objected; but the committee argued that they could not print it any more cheaply, and those who refused to buy would not be permitted further books. By 1805 the library had debts of £100, chiefly because of unpaid-for catalogues. (In the same year the Kilmarnock Public Library had to negotiate credit from its book supplier because it was owed over £25 in unpaid subscriptions.) In 1807 two managers were accused of planning to sell off the best books; they were removed from the committee. Yet despite all these problems the Dundee Public Library managed to survive; in 1809 a library belonging to the local medical men was even deposited with them. Ironically, the Dundee Public Library became so flourishing that in 1815 it took over its more expensive rival, the Dundee Library. Duplicates were sold, and money was even lent to the Scottish Episcopal Chapel to earn interest. The whole collection eventually passed to the Municipal Library.

The price of shares would naturally tend to increase, though in some libraries new shareholders were denied a share in books bought prior to their own membership. Duns Library's regulations stipulated that each subscriber would have an equal voice in its management but they should

> have interest, share, and concern in the books of the Library, only in proportion to the time he has been a member, and to the sums he has paid in.

Despite the masculine wording of the rules, three women were members of the Duns Library by 1789; its membership included not only eight gentlemen of the cloth, but also a dissenting minister, bleacher, butcher, schoolmaster, several writers, and two soldiers.

In Ayr Library members paid an annual six shillings. The original members paid no entry money, but new members paid one shilling a year for each year of the library's existence (unless a share had been transferred to them), replaced in 1803 by a consolidated payment of five guineas.[94] At Greenock Library (1783), subscribers also paid six shillings per year plus ten shillings for a share, and an additional two shillings for every year of the library's existence.[95] In the Kilmarnock Library (1797) proprietors paid at least one guinea plus one shilling for each year of the library's existence, as well as five shillings *per annum*. Annual subscribers, without shares, were admitted to the Hawick Library at ten shillings a year from at least 1773 (and probably earlier) but had to sign an undertaking not to exercise any claim as a shareholder; and they had

---

[94] Allan Leach, *Libraries in Ayr, 1762-1975* (Ayr, 1975): reprinted from *Ayrshire Collections*, 2nd ser. 11 (1975), 69-84 (here p. 71).

[95] James T. Hamilton, *Greenock Libraries* (Greenock, [1969]), p. 39.

to give a month's notice before joining. Three-quarters of the governing body of Stirling's Library (which was not a proprietary library) approved annual subscribers in 1792, but that could not be implemented because total consent was necessary.[96] The Greenock Library permitted annual subscribers at one guinea *per annum* from 1812, and the Stewarton Library at six shillings *per annum* from 1825.

By the mid-nineteenth century many older subscription libraries found increasing difficulty in attracting new shareholders, and annual subscribers became common. At the Montrose Library, schoolteachers and university students were admitted free from its foundation in 1785, while at the nearby Arbroath Library from 1810 poor schoolmasters of the parish were allowed to join at half-a-guinea a year, but had no share. The reasoning was that the teachers of the subscribers' children should be well-informed. (Their librarian at this time was a schoolteacher.) This privilege was later extended to clergy, though, unusually, no ministers had been members at the library's commencement.

Rules about share-dealing in Scottish libraries were far more complex and comprehensive than were found in any English subscription libraries, reflecting a differing attitude (and legal situation) towards matters of inheritance. Shares could usually be transferred. In the Duns Library, a proprietor could 'transfer his share at his pleasure', and if not transferred by death, then it would descend to the heir. Share transfers involved signing a lengthy, solemn document, duly witnessed. However, when in 1771 David Graham, teacher at the English School, produced a share transfer from Adam Dickson, previously minister in Duns, Graham refused to pay arrears owing by Dickson. Graham's right to borrow books was withdrawn, but he was permitted to transfer the share, though he failed to do so. The share passed to the new minister of the Associated Congregation who paid £1.14s. for Dickson's arrears; the same share subsequently passed down to successive ministers before being forfeited during the 1840s. Arrears in payments continued to be a considerable problem.

Many libraries carefully regulated the transference of shares after death. In the Cupar Library, founded 1797, share transfers had to be approved by the committee, and rules were complex:

> the widow of a subscriber, if he has no child, or if his heir be a minor, shall succeed to the right of her husband, while the heir is under age, and she remains unmarried.[97]

Shares could be sold: the *Dumfries Weekly Journal* of 19 September 1797, for instance, carried an advertisement for 'a share of the Theatre and Gentlemens

---

[96] Thomas Mason, *Public and Private Libraries of Glasgow* (Glasgow, 1985), p. 63.

[97] Cupar Library catalogue (1813).

Library'; another share was advertized on 28 June 1808. In the Greenock Library shares could be transferred 'by sale, gift or will' to any person who agreed to abide by their regulations. In 1824 an Edinburgh stockbroker was selling shares in Scottish foundries, oil companies, breweries, and in the Edinburgh Subscription Library.[98]

The rules of the Paisley Library Society (1802) prevented shares being seized by creditors. New members from anywhere in Renfrewshire paid three guineas and two shillings for each year the library had existed. Gifts of books were accepted in lieu of the subscription. Non-subscribers were admitted at £1 a year or six shillings per quarter. On death, rights were forfeited if the heirs did not pay any arrears within two years, or five years if the deceased member or heir was abroad. A member's widow had rights of free entry, but on a second marriage had to pay for admission. Children could enjoy rights free of entry payment but had to pay half a guinea on reaching their majority. Shares could be temporarily transferred if a member was abroad, but if they were out of Renfrewshire for longer than a year they were considered to be absent; anywhere outside Renfrewshire was considered abroad, of course.[99]

At the Fenwick Library, shares were transferable, but creditors of any member would have no claim on the library. In the case of a member dying and leaving several heirs portioners, the share would descend to the eldest. If an heir did not wish to receive the share, he could receive one guinea after six months in exchange, minus any fines. At the Kirkcudbright Subscription Library, shares could pass to the eldest son or daughter if there was no will, and if they were prepared to pay fifteen shillings entry money. In the Peterhead Reading Society its committee could adopt a deceased member's heir-at-law as a member of the library, or they could buy the share back.

The Renton Subscription Library, near Dumbarton, was founded in 1797 following an earlier suggestion by William Stirling, a local industrialist whose firm donated twenty guineas to start the library. The factory library for his workers has previously been mentioned. One of the smaller, cheaper libraries, Renton Library initially did not allow shares to be transferred but bought them back with interest, as when, in 1802, John Campbell and several other members gave notice that they were quitting the town. In 1805 David Davids left and was given £1.5s.6d. as a subscriber plus four and a half years' interest. In 1811 a member resigned without giving a reason, and payment was denied.[100] In the Cabrach Library, Banffshire, unmarried women were permitted to pay only half the entry money for a share, but on marriage their husband had to pay the

---

[98] *Caledonian Mercury*, 11 November 1824.

[99] *Regulations of the Paisley Library Society* (1802).

[100] From the Renton Subscription Library minute book in Dumbarton Public Library.

other half.[101] In the Inshewan Reading Society, shares could be temporarily transferred to a subscriber's 'son or his brother or his son-in-law, providing he is of a good moral character', during any absence of the original member, and they would also inherit on death.

The Paisley Library's founders were conscious of their obligations to posterity and their role as an instrument in the education of their fellow townsfolk, as expressed by Thomas Crichton, a local teacher:

> There was a time, in this country, when Knowledge was closely locked up from the bulk of the people, in the dead languages, accessible only to the learned recluse, shut up in his library, within the walls of a college. It is happy for us, however, that these gloomy days of Gothic Ignorance have taken their flight, and that, in this happy Island, many have access to vast treasures of useful literature in their own language.[102]

As a celebration of the library's opening, Crichton continued his theme with a somewhat grandiloquent poem of 4,000 lines, beginning:

> Hail! friends of Science! friends of human kind!
>   Yours is the noblest task t'improve the mind;
> To form, mature, to execute a plan
>   Design'd to rouse the latent powers of man;
> To teach the Youth, within his studious bower,
>   To spend, improv'd, his idle vacant hour.
> 'Tis yours, to chase the mental fogs away;
>   Conduct from Error's night to truth's bright day;
> Reclaim from Vice's dark, entangling snare,
>   Lead smoothly on to Virtue's temple fair;
> Prepare for action, on Life's bustling stage,
>   By all the wisdom of the letter'd page.
> To place before the mind a world all new;
>   Designs like these, ye friends of Man, pursue.[103]

The idea of permanence was important in subscription libraries. People were subscribing to a share in knowledge, to be passed on to future generations. Many subscription libraries lasted into the twentieth century. Yet not every library accepted that the value of its collection would increase. At the Kirkcudbright Subscription Library (1777), membership was declining by 1807, even though the population was increasing, and people were 'better

---

[101] Taylor, *Cabrach Feerings*, p. 109.

[102] [Thomas Crichton], *The Library: a Poem* (Paisley, 1804), preface.

[103] [Thomas Crichton], *The Library*; this verse is reprinted in: Tom Leonard (ed.), *Radical Renfrew* (Edinburgh, 1990), p. 53.

enabled, and more disposed to acquire Literary Information'. But the Library needed to sell new shares to provide more capital and income. It was decided to reduce the subscription on the grounds that people wanted the latest information and that older books were becoming out-of-date. They appear thus to have anticipated the self-renewing as opposed to the ever-increasing library.

The committee of the Dunfermline Subscription Library decided in 1823 that their library was not as successful as others because their shares were the wrong price. Other libraries were flourishing because they had a lower entry charge but a higher annual fee (Dunfermline charged £4 entry and 7s.6d. a year). The price of books had doubled since the library began in 1789, and they no longer bought quartos. Their annual income was only around £35, out of which came the librarian's salary of £6; room rent, heating and lighting, £5.14s.; insurance, ten shillings; police assessment on the rent, five shillings; and binding costs in the previous year of £3.8s.10d. The entry money was reduced by one pound.

Unusually, the Perth Library's rules of 1785 were drafted to ensure that the library remained permanent by vesting the property in trustees on behalf of the burgh rather than the subscribers; it thus became a more general community library, though still only available to subscribers. The trustees had to be subscribers who were also peers, members of parliament, provosts, ministers, or other public officials. The minutes emphasize that the library must never be confused with a common circulating library, and therefore they refused to consider permitting annual members who did not hold a share. The insistence on entry money plus an annual subscription was to ensure that the character of the library was maintained. It is worth noting that the library's main promoter was an Episcopalian clergyman, Adam Peebles, reinforcing that up to this period Scottish subscription libraries were closely associated with local establishment leaders. When the Glasgow Public Library became incorporated in 1811, it claimed that this was to ensure that its books were held in trust for the public.[104] However, the Ayr Library's main motive in seeking incorporation was to protect its property from members who inherited shares but ignored the rules, claiming that they could not be bound by them.

Eventually, and particularly after 1800 as more competing libraries emerged, non-proprietary members, who did not own shares, tended to be welcomed rather than deterred by subscription libraries. In the Stirling Subscription Library, strangers were permitted at one shilling per month plus a security of one guinea.[105] In the Lilliesleaf Library it was agreed in 1825 that 'half year servants should be allowed to read from the Library, provided they

---

[104] *Picture of Glasgow* (Glasgow, 1812), pp. 177-8.

[105] *The History of Stirling*, 2nd edn. (Stirling, 1817), pp. 187-90.

pay three shillings half yearly or 1ˢ6ᵈ quarterly'. At Selkirk French prisoners-of-war could use the library if they were officers, and their borrowings between 1811 and 1814 were recorded, mostly novels such as Tobias Smollett's *Peregrine Pickle*, *Delia* [by Miss Pilkington?], Oliver Goldsmith's *The Vicar of Wakefield*, Gottfried Bürger's *Leonore*, Alain Le Sage's *The Devil on Two Sticks*, Ann Radcliffe's *The Mystery of Udolpho*, and the works of Henry Fielding. At Arbroath Library, in 1799, army officers and strangers could use the library for 1s.6d. per month, plus a deposit of two guineas; a similar arrangement was observed in the Cupar Library. It is worth noting that regimental libraries did exist, usually for officers only, but information is scanty. For instance, when the Marquis of Huntly dined with his regiment, the 42nd Royal Highlanders, at Musselburgh Barracks in 1810, he donated 'a handsome sum of money' to the regimental library; by 1840 the Regiment had collected 1,500 volumes.[106] And when the 93rd Regiment (Highlanders) were quartered in Ireland in 1820, their officers were said to possess a 'small well chosen library'.[107]

Non-members who borrowed could pose a problem. Complaints were made in the Duns Library in 1788 and again in 1793 that sons of members were borrowing books, even though they lived in separate families to the subscriber whose ticket they were using; the ticket-holders were fined five shillings. In 1817 the problem re-surfaced when apprentices were found to be borrowing books in the names of their masters, but without their knowledge.[108] However, in 1825 a non-subscriber in the Paisley Library was not borrowing books but was seen too frequently there. An ingenious remedy was found to prevent this abuse of the privilege of membership:

> A gentleman whose attendance at the library, where he was not a subscriber, had grown more frequent than his company was acceptable, the regular visitors had many debates, whether to give him a polite notice to quit, or suffer him to remain; an old crusty gentleman going in one day soon settled the business; perceiving, not only the disagreeable visitor, but a large mastiff belonging to him, taking up the whole of the fire-place, he very coolly opened the door, and, giving the mastiff a tremendous kick, which made him raise a hideous yell, he exclaimed in a broad accent, 'Come, dom it, you are no subscriber at any rate'. The gentleman followed his dog, and never more annoyed them by his presence.[109]

---

[106] *Caledonian Mercury*, 15 August 1810, 28 September 1840.

[107] *Freeman's Journal*, 28 November 1820.

[108] Borders AO, DL/3/1, Duns Library minute book, 17 December 1778, 30 November 1793, 1 April 1817, 3 November 1818.

[109] *Paisley Advertiser*, 19 February 1825.

A significant level of co-operation is also found between libraries: in or about 1806, for instance, catalogues were exchanged amongst the subscription libraries of Arbroath, Greenock, Kelso, Ayr, Kilmarnock, Dundee, Perth, Paisley, Coldstream, Duns, Darlington, Sunderland, and North Shields, and with the Newcastle Literary and Philosophical Society, and all members were permitted reciprocal use. The credit for the original proposal was claimed by John Clennell (1772-1822), agricultural writer and later co-founder of the Hackney Literary and Philosophical Society in Middlesex; he also suggested an appropriate form of joint membership ticket, just as James Millar of Elgin was to do in a scheme discussed below.[110]

A slightly different attitude towards book collection was adopted at the Peterhead Reading Society, founded in 1808 as an antidote to the local circulating library. Here the phrase 'reading society' was adopted rather than library because the original intention was to allow books to be sold off, and the money raised to be either redistributed to the members themselves or spent on more books 'to form the foundation of a Library which might in time and by gradual accumulation become an ornament & benefit to the Town'. Interestingly, several founder-members agreed to subscribe for up to three years if no books were sold, and in the end it was resolved to form a permanent library, though with the proviso that unworthy books could be sold and the money used for further books.

A reminiscence by one of the founder-members, Alexander Murray, a merchant, reveals typical problems:

> Although Mr Clark [the local bookseller] had a library of old books for circulating, they were all trash such as we did not think worth reading, so we each subscribed a guinea yearly to purchase new books on history, the arts and sciences, etc., but excluded novels. Each member recommended books to the value of his subscription, and a committee had the choosing of them. At first our library was of no great extent, but afterwards we had to get Mr Clark to give it a shelf in his shop on condition of our purchasing our books through him, but finding that our books were read by all and destroyed in that public place, we had book presses made and the library removed to the end of the news room and coffee room, to be under the care of Mary Findlater, then [viz. 1814] the curator of the news room. As the presses were raised seven or eight feet, Mary, when a book was wanted, could only give you the key and show you the high steps. This did not suit every reader, especially if old

---

[110] James M'Bain, *History of the Arbroath Public Library from 1797 to 1894* (Arbroath, 1894), p. 13; cf. *Rules of the Subscription Library, North Shields* (1806), p. 29, and John Clennell on literary associations in *The Tradesman* (1815), p. 284.

> or lame, and many of the readers sold their right, and I sold mine for two guineas after having been a subscriber for ten years. The Society then made every share into two at half a guinea, and have now a small house for their books, and Sandy Scott for librarian, who attends a while every other day.[111]

Despite its problems, this library continued until 1932, though all its old books were donated to the Municipal Library in 1893.

Many libraries did decline after initial enthusiasm had worn off, and it is worth remarking that libraries often owed a debt to individuals who had promoted the idea of book learning, as had William Stirling in the Renton Library. The story was similar at the Kirkcudbright Library, as Robert Heron observed in 1793:

> It has already introduced a good deal of knowledge into this country, which it must otherwise have wanted. The late Mr William Laurie of Barnsoul, who was distinguished among the gentlemen of this country, by his learning, his virtues, and his amiable manners, was principally active in forming this Library, and in regulating its concerns.[112]

Rev. Dr Robert Douglas was instrumental in the establishment of both the Selkirk Library (1772) and the Galashiels Library (1797). The Edinburgh Subscription Library, founded in 1794 by James Hall and James Peddie, both doctors of divinity and dissident Presbyterians, became one of the largest proprietary libraries, with shares costing initially twelve guineas; founding members included solicitors, brewers, builders, an upholsterer, apothecary, and merchants. The books were kept until 1807 in the Rose Street Chapel Session House. The librarian had to produce a security and not lend books on the Sabbath nor before 10 a.m. nor after 4 p.m. Fines for late returns of books were shared between library and librarian.[113] It had over 400 members from the 1820s until 1880, when it contained 40,000 volumes, and lasted until 1900, when it was resolved that the books should be sold off to pay their debts, and that the members could join the Philosophical Institution by way of compensation.

The latter library's rival, the Edinburgh Select Subscription Library, was established in 1800 by ten young men, mostly small tradesmen who objected to the expense of the older library. Their library was called 'Select' because their

---

[111] Alexander Murray, *Peterhead a Century Ago*, edited by Andrew Murray (Peterhead, 1910), pp. 53-54.

[112] Robert Heron, *Observations Made in a Journey through the Western Counties of Scotland* (Perth, 1793), vol. 2, p. 194.

[113] *Catalogue of the Edinburgh Subscription Library, 1794-1833* (Edinburgh, 1833), p. 153.

intention was 'to procure for their mutual use a collection of books, rather select than numerous, and chiefly such as are above the purchase of individuals'.[114] The new library initially only charged five shillings entry, though rapidly increased to one guinea as it became so popular; there were fifty-one members by 1803. But membership declined when in 1810 a new house was bought for £195, mostly borrowed. There was a feeling that the money would have been better spent on their principal function, buying books, and there was talk of selling off the library. By 1814 there were 119 members but an income of only £88. Several more moves were to take place until, during the 1820s and 1830s, the membership began to increase rapidly. Despite its original limited intentions and 'select' nature, it achieved 593 members by 1841 with an income of £400, and possessed 30,000 volumes at its final dissolution in 1882.

Glasgow Public Library, founded in 1804, had 550 members by 1818 and took over the privately-established Stirling's Library (1791) in 1871.[115] The latter had been bequeathed to the city by Walter Stirling in 1791. But this was no free library (though the donor may have intended it to have been)[116] nor a proprietary library, and its users paid five guineas entry money for a life subscription. The first subscribers only paid three guineas but raised £1,000 during the first year. The library continued to grow, for instance receiving 500 volumes as a bequest from a subscriber in 1826.[117] The building eventually became for many years the main lending library branch of the City Libraries service. Outside the cities, subscription libraries were often small and frequently lacked a permanent home; yet the Montrose Library, for example, still amassed 20,000 volumes by 1884.

The Growth of Circulating Libraries: the Capital City

Subscription libraries could only ever cater for a relatively small proportion of the population, but circulating libraries, which charged variable fees depending on the number of books customers wished to borrow at a time, or even just by the night, could be more flexible. And yet, after Allan Ramsay, further libraries did not appear for a whole generation. The real impetus for library growth was not to come until the 'revolutionary' years of the 1790s, when more and more people from all classes sought knowledge and information.

---

[114] *Sketch of the Origin and Progress of the Library* (1834).

[115] Kelly, *Early Public Libraries*, pp. 102-3.

[116] Mason, *Public and Private Libraries*, p. 35.

[117] *Glasgow Herald*, 29 May 1826.

In Edinburgh in 1756 William Gray and Walter Peter were running a library in the New Exchange, from 1758 run by Gray alone. Like Ramsay, Gray charged ten shillings yearly, 5s.6d. per half year, three shillings per quarter, or one penny per night.[118] By 1772 his stock consisted of 1,711 titles, of which over one third consisted of novels and 'entertainment', the latter meaning popular lives and biographies; divinity made up one-fifth of the whole stock. The business was bought by Alexander Mackay in 1794. Further libraries in Edinburgh were run by John Wood with 1,400 volumes by 1764, Alexander McAslan by 1765, Alexander Brown by 1774, James McLeish by 1778 (whose library still existed in the 1840s under the management of Quentin Dalrymple), and others. An advertisement by McAslan from 1768 states that 'Religious, instructive and entertaining BOOKS [are] lent out to read', showing that at this period circulating librarians were sometimes anxious to emphasize the importance of religion before entertainment; he charged the same fees as Gray, above.[119] William Coke, bookseller in Leith for fifty-five years, ran a library by 1764. Coke was described as indefatigable, like a squirrel in a cage, always endeavouring to reach the top. He was said to walk from Leith to Edinburgh and back several times a day if necessary just to purchase a sixpenny-pamphlet for a customer, and it was calculated that he must have walked the equivalent distance of twice the circumference of the world.[120]

Yair's library, formerly Ramsay's, remained the dominant circulating library in the capital and was bought in 1779 by James Sibbald, who had previously worked as a farmer, through the bookseller Charles Elliot, Sibbald's cousin. Sibbald claimed 20,000 volumes, and his aims were high; he was not a man to undersell himself:[121]

> Libraries of this kind are seldom intended for any thing more than merely books of amusement, such as poetry, novels, &c. Valuable books in the arts and sciences, and even of history are often excluded on account of the expense and risk; and pamphlets, however interesting they may be for the day, share the same fate, from the consideration of their temporary nature. Some of the principal branches of literature are thus, in a great measure, inaccessible to any but the great and opulent; and these, from want of opportunity to examine such new publications as they incline to purchase, are frequently deceived by a promising title page, or the partial verdict of a review.

---

[118] *A Present for Children*, 2nd edn. (Edinburgh, 1761) for advert.

[119] Daniel Defoe, *Robinson Crusoe* (Edinburgh, 1768), advert. at rear.

[120] Charles Timperley, *A Dictionary of Printers and Printing* (London, 1839), p. 870.

[121] *Caledonian Mercury*, 1 January and 2 December 1780.

> To obviate these inconveniences, is the intention of this extensive Library. The selection has been made with the utmost attention, and at a great expence, and the acting partner having been in London for near a twelvemonth past, has had an opportunity of collecting a great number of such curious, scarce, and valuable books, as are never to be met with in a circulating library; and likewise of forming his plan upon that of the British, and other libraries of the greatest reputation.
>
> The lovers of History and Biography, of Geography and Natural History, of the Arts and Sciences, and of Divinity and Ecclesiastical History, will severally, in this collection, find an opportunity of gratifying their favourite inclination at a very moderate expence. For the accommodation of gentlemen in the Medical Line, a proper selection has been made of the best authors on Anatomy, Physic, Surgery, &c.
>
> And for the amusement of our gay readers, who chuse to mix the agreeable with the useful, it has been assiduously studied to collect the greatest part of the books of Poetry and Romance, that have been published in the English language; and to enrich this department with the addition of some of the most celebrated in the French and Italian. The music consists chiefly of favourite operas, and the best and newest songs, adapted to the voice and harpsichord, or violin; and, as libraries entirely musical, although not known here, meet with great encouragement in London, at an high subscription, it is not doubted that this branch, *as only an addition*, will, to many ladies and gentlemen, prove a very agreeable gratification.
>
> No expense nor trouble will be spared to add, from time to time, with the utmost expedition, every new publication that can serve either to enliven the mind, improve the understanding, or promote the cause of virtue.[122]

Sibbald's model was the 'British Library', one of the largest circulating libraries in London, claiming 100,000 volumes and run by the well-known bookseller and publisher, John Bell (1745-1831), not to be confused with the Edinburgh bookseller and publisher of that name. Under Sibbald, Ramsay's old library became a noted literary centre (and Ramsay's name was frequently employed in advertisements). He regarded non-fiction as an important part of his business, though that did not attract the young Walter Scott to Sibbald's library, as he describes in his autobiography of 1808:

---

[122] *Edinburgh Advertiser*, 17 December 1779.

> I fastened also, like a tiger, upon every collection of old songs or romances which chance threw in my way, or which my scrutiny was able to discover on the dusty shelves of James Sibbald's circulating library in the Parliament Square. This collection, now dismantled and dispersed [not so; the library had moved to another address] contained at that time many rare and curious works, seldom found in such a collection. Mr Sibbald himself, a man of rough manners but of some taste and judgment, cultivated music and poetry, and in his shop I had a distant view of some literary characters, besides the privilege of ransacking the stores of old French and Italian books, which were in little demand among the bulk of his subscribers. Here I saw the unfortunate Andrew Macdonald, author of *Vimonda*, and here too, I saw at a distance the boast of Scotland, Robert Burns.[123]

There exists a famous painting by William B. Johnstone of Sibbald's circulating library, showing young Walter sitting next to a bookcase while Robert Burns holds court in a room full of Scottish literary giants, such as Adam Ferguson, Alexander Nasmyth, James 'Abyssinian' Bruce, and Lord Monboddo, who just happened to have called in at the same time. Scott is portrayed sitting amongst the shelves, reading a book, though no-one knows for certain whether readers could approach the shelves themselves. Circulating library rules never permitted that; instead, subscribers were instructed to send in a list of ten to twenty numbers, representing titles in the catalogue which was the only means of 'access' to the library; the librarian searched for the books. Since the painting was executed seventy years after its setting (1786), it is, sadly, hardly a contemporary historical document.[124]

Twenty years later Scott recalled Sibbald's library further:

> I was plunged into this great ocean of reading without compass or pilot; and, unless when some one had the charity to play at chess with me, I was allowed to do nothing save read from morning to night. I was, in kindness and pity, which was perhaps erroneous, permitted to select my subjects of study at my own pleasure, upon the same principle that the humours of children are indulged to keep them out of mischief. As my taste and appetite were gratified in nothing else, I indemnified myself by becoming a glutton of books. Accordingly, I believe I read almost all the romances, old plays, and epic poetry in that formidable collection, and no doubt

---

[123] Lockhart, *Life of Scott*, vol. 1, p. 48; quoted in Kaufman, 'Community Libraries', pp. 293-4.

[124] Illustrated in Kaufman, *Libraries and their Users*, opposite p. 134, and Richard Sher, *The Enlightenment and the Book* (Chicago, 2006), p. 113 (both black & white).

was unconsciously amassing materials for the task in which it has been my lot to be so much employed.[125]

Writing again of the period 1784/85, Scott's friend, John Irving, recalled:

Every Saturday, and more frequently during the vacation, we used to retire, with three or four books from the circulating library, to Salisbury Crags, Arthur's Seat, or Blackford Hill, and read them together. ... The books we most delighted in were romances of knight-errantry; the *Castle of Otranto* [by Horace Walpole], [Edmund] Spenser, [Gabriello] Ariosto, and [Matteo] Boïardo were great favourites.[126]

The 1780 catalogue of Sibbald's library claimed a stock of 20,000 volumes (which translated into 4,338 titles), lent for 10s.6d. per year, or 3s.6d. per quarter, or a penny per shilling value of each book for a 'reasonable' time. Subscribers could pay an extra guinea a year for 'WHOLE New Political Pamphlets, Reviews, Magazines, Parliamentary Registers, Trials, &c.' from London.[127] Sibbald also lent prints and music, though it is said that this side of the business went into a decline when he was discovered colouring the prints himself. He leased his library, known as the Edinburgh Circulating Library, to Alexander Lawrie and James Symington in about 1790 for £200 per year, later reduced to a hundred guineas yearly. This caused embarrassment in 1793 when John Murray, the London bookseller, objected to being asked to send bills to Lawrie and Symington for books ordered by Sibbald: 'I never heard their names mentioned in the business till your last, and I shall forbear send more numbers since you seem not to desire to have them'. Murray considered that transferring an account to others was 'improper & cannot be complied with', adding: 'If they are good men they cannot hesitate to settle this article with you. If they are not you are not kind to desire of me what you would not do yourself'.[128] Sibbald took over personally again in about 1799 until his death in 1803.

Sibbald's catalogue of around 1800 shows that the collection then numbered 5,223 titles, made up of: History, biography, voyages, and travels 1,223; Arts, science, trade, agriculture 587; Medicine 320; Divinity 273; Poetry, plays, *belles-lettres* 1,169; Novels and romances 1,009; Pamphlets 97; French and Italian 352; Appendix 187. Leaving aside the last two categories, and counting

---

[125] Preface to the 1829 edition of the *Waverley* novels.

[126] Lockhart, *Life of Scott*, vol. 1, p. 132; quoted in Kaufman, 'Community Libraries', p. 294.

[127] *Caledonian Mercury*, 1 January 1780.

[128] NLS, MS. 41906, John Murray's letterbooks, 22 June & 15 July 1793. For an account of Murray's business, see William Zachs, *The First John Murray and the Late Eighteenth-Century London Book Trade* (Oxford, 1998).

plays, etc., with fiction, then non-fiction comprised approximately half of the stock. Considering that the reputation of circulating libraries became so tarnished by their perceived association with cheap romantic fiction, it is important to remember that the largest libraries provided access to enormous collections of serious non-fiction. But, equally, the ratio of fiction to non-fiction was not necessarily paralleled by the ratio of fiction to non-fiction books lent; unfortunately, issue statistics just do not exist.

Returning to Ramsay's time, no other circulating library is known in Edinburgh before 1756 when William Gray and Walter Peter appear as partners. From 1794 this library was run by Alexander Mackay in the High Street, and in 1805 he took over the former library of Ramsay and Sibbald. This combined library continued until 1851, when many books were sold off. By 1831 the library was run by William Wilson (who had begun as a circulating librarian by acquiring the library of Lawrie and Symington, formerly Walter Berry's) and was recalled by James Bertram, future editor of the *North Briton*, as 'of historic interest, as having been founded by Allan Ramsay. Many of the books that had been handled by the poet and his successors were yet in the library when, by the kindness of the proprietor, I was placed on the "free list"'.[129]

Sibbald's competitors were in a minor league, but increased rapidly, though not until the 1790s was there a significant increase in library provision in Edinburgh. Alexander Brown began a new library in North Bridge Street in 1782. His catalogue of around 1786 reveals a stock of 1,719 titles, including over 600 novels and over 600 poems, plays, and essays. He charged ten shillings per year for borrowing one book at a time, changeable once a day, and higher subscriptions for more (e.g. £1 for four books, etc.). Books could be kept out for a month, unless new, when the borrowing period was a maximum of six days.[130]

Specialized libraries emerged, including music circulating libraries, which will be considered later. A lending library for newspapers at twopence per hour was advertised by John Forbes, bookseller in South Hanover Street, Edinburgh, in 1797. He kept a reading room but offered to supply Scottish, English, or Irish newspapers to ladies and gentlemen who wished to read at home if they sent their servants,

> at the Trifling Expence of twopence for one Hour's reading. It must be obvious to every candid Person that an hour is sufficient for the perusal of any Paper, and that it must go through three or

---

[129] James G. Bertram, *Some Memories of Books, Authors, and Events* (London, 1893), p. 88.

[130] Catalogue in NRS, CS96/1573.

four hands before it clears itself; therefore an early return will be considered as a particular favour.[131]

This kind of specialized service was not confined to the largest cities. Subscription newsrooms and coffee rooms were found more frequently from the 1790s, and were often run by booksellers or on a proprietorial plan similar to private subscription libraries; but their organization was different to the services offered at some circulating libraries, and they constitute a separate topic to the present work. Some circulating libraries did have newsrooms attached; the biggest in Scotland was probably James Taylor Smith & Co.'s General Newspaper Saloon and British and Foreign Public Library in Edinburgh, which in 1825 offered at least 138 British and sixty-six foreign newspapers.[132]

In 1800 there were at least seven circulating libraries in Edinburgh, and ten in 1820. (There were probably more; much of this information derives from trades directories, but stationers or other tradesmen who ran libraries were often entered only under their main occupation.) One of the most successful was run by John Sutherland, whose library lasted for about fifty years and whose success was owed to the works of Sir Walter Scott, both in terms of loans and sales. Like many circulating libraries of the early nineteenth century, Scott was a saviour. James Bertram remembered being told in the 1830s by an Edinburgh bookseller that the libraries, rather than the booksellers, made most money from Scott: 'Willie Wilson, John Sutherland, Elder [&] Ogilvie, and Mrs Tansh must have cleared thousands of pounds among them during the past two-and-twenty years by the lending of these books'.[133]

Bertram recorded that it was John Sutherland who first hit on the idea of splitting each volume of the latest *Waverley* novel into two to help keep his customers satisfied. While unhappily apprenticed to Sutherland, William Chambers read Scott's novels to a baker during the winter of 1815/16, the reward being his breakfast, while Bertram noted that Sutherland himself arranged for *Rob Roy* and *Heart of Midlothian* to be read to workmen in neighbouring shops. Bertram, too, recalled

> seeing, in a Scottish provincial town, the novel of *Guy Mannering* bound in portions of a hundred pages, each of which even at that time (1832) was lent to read at the price of twopence per night. As it ran to ten parts, the reading cost one shilling and eightpence; and the feat of perusal in one case was achieved, not in ten nights, but in a gallop of ten hours![134]

---

[131] Advertisement in Falkirk Archives Office, GD171/4248/1-2.

[132] *Caledonian Mercury*, 5 May 1825.

[133] Bertram, *Some Memories*, pp. 100-1.

[134] Ibid., pp. 101-4.

William Wilson, the successor to Ramsay and Sibbald, was said to have doubled his profits by splitting other triple-decker novels into six parts, as he had done with the *Waverley* books.[135]

William Chambers, later the periodical publisher, began a circulating library in Leith Walk in about 1820 'which, owing to the frequent issues of the *Waverley Novels*, was tolerably successful'.[136] His brother, Robert, also ran a library in Edinburgh, in the late 1820s. Although the latter's business just falls outside the period covered by the present work, it is worth noting because of the survival of its loans register for the years 1828/29.[137] It is in fact the earliest – and possibly the sole – record of borrowings from a Scottish commercial circulating library; such records are equally rare in England. Robert Chambers catered for a wide cross-section of Edinburgh society, but his library was aimed at the better-off. Subscribers included Lady Molesworth, General Drummond of Culdees Castle, Crieff, Lord Robert Kerr, and Lady Belhaven. Each customer is allotted a page in the register, and loans are recorded and crossed out on return. Occasionally an industrious reader will have a new page later on in the volume. Analysing the social status of the readership is revealing, though it should be borne in mind that the figures may be slightly higher than the reality, because it is not always possible to discover whether a person entered twice really is the same person or another customer, perhaps a relative, of the same name. The register shows 192 men as subscribers, including one lord, one knight, five doctors, three esquires, two professors, four reverends, one colonel, one major, eight captains, two lieutenants, one staff sergeant, and one Solicitor-General. There were also 119 women, of whom seventy-four were described as Mrs, thirty-six as Miss, seven as Lady, and two as Hon. Mrs.

In the absence of similar sources, it is difficult to draw conclusions from Chambers's register, but the total number of over 300 subscribers suggests a thriving business (though many customers only subscribed for short periods and were presumably visitors to the capital). His library was situated centrally in the New Town, in Hanover Street, and so was bound to attract fashionable attention. But there were many other libraries in the area. The largest libraries in Edinburgh were probably Mackay's (successor to Ramsay) in the High Street and John Sutherland's in Calton Street, but other libraries contained several thousand volumes each.

Chambers's register does suggest that fiction was the main interest. For instance, Miss Wright of 37 Queen Street, who became a subscriber on 18 June 1828, borrowed *A Marraige [sic] [in] High Life*, by Caroline, Lady Scott,

---

[135] James Thin, *Reminiscences of Booksellers and Bookselling* (Edinburgh, 1905), pp. 28-29.

[136] William Chambers, *Memoir of Robert Chambers*, 8th edn. (Edinburgh, 1874), p. 156.

[137] NLS, Dep. 341/413.

James Fennimore Cooper's *Red Rover*, *Great St Bernard* by George Croly, and *Zellah* (error for *Zelia*?), as well as Reginald Heber's *Journal* and Joanna Baillie's *Plays*, while J. Dyer of Stockbridge, who subscribed £1 on 20 May, borrowed *Blackwood's Magazine*, *The Sporting Magazine*, Friedrich Schiller, and Walter Scott's *Rob Roy* and *Guy Mannering*, etc. Lady Don of Heriot Place paid 2s.6d. for a month and borrowed songs, the *Public Journals* for 1823, Scott's *Woodstock*, *Poetical Album* (edited by Alaric Watts) and more, while Miss Skene of 74 Great King Street, requested Mary Russell Mitford's *Our Village*, Mrs C. D. Burnett's *At Home*, *Locomotion* (by William Kitchiner?), Charles Maturin's *Fatal Revenge*, *Romantic Tales* (by Matthew Lewis?), Vice-Admiral Lord Collingwood's *Memoirs*, *Widow's Lodgings* by John Ballantyne, Edward Bulwer Lytton's *Disowned*, *Vathek* by William Beckford, etc. These random examples tend to confirm the view that fiction had become the staple diet of most circulating library customers, especially the ladies, but meaningful comparisons with other circulating libraries are frustratingly impossible without similar records. Chambers's surviving library catalogue for 1829 does, though, confirm that his library contained mainly fiction and the popular forms of non-fiction. His collection only boasted 942 titles, which hardly amounts to a large library; he gave up lending books in 1832.

The Spread of Circulating Libraries: Glasgow, the Provinces, and Overseas

Outside Edinburgh, the next town to benefit from a circulating library business was Perth, where Robert Morison commenced in 1752, lending books from eight shillings per year down to one shilling per month, or one penny per night. He was already postmaster, bookbinder, bookseller, stationer, and 'glasier' (as his father had been before him). The last-named was a curious but understandable occupation. Glaziers and bookbinders both used curved-edge tools and so belonged to the same guild, the Incorporated Society of Wrights.[138] Morison's descendants continued to run circulating libraries into the nineteenth century. David Morison, a stationer, began to lend periodicals in 1810. Amongst much more he offered the *Literary Panorama*, Rudolf Ackermann's *Polite Repository* (though presumably the *Repository of Arts* is meant), *European Magazine*, *La Belle Assemblée*, and *Gentleman's Magazine* at sixpence for three days after publication, fourpence during the second week after publication, threepence during the third week, and so on. Other magazines, such as the *Edinburgh Review*, *Quarterly Review*, and *Farmer's Magazine*, were lent for ninepence after the first fortnight.[139] He started a

---

[138] D. Crawford Smith, *The Historians of Perth* (Perth, 1906), p. 77 and following.

[139] *Perth Courier*, 22 February 1810.

circulating library for books in 1819, and his 1824 classified catalogue of the Perth Library was far superior to similar catalogues of the period.[140] Though he was no trained architect, he successfully designed a new building in the style of a Roman temple to house the Perth Library and the Perth Literary and Antiquarian Society.[141]

The first recorded circulating library in Glasgow was established in 1753 by John Smith the elder (1724-1814), and was run at various addresses in succession. The bookshop probably commenced in 1751; it was common for a bookseller to have established himself before embarking on a potentially risky undertaking such as a lending library. Indeed, the first John Smith had already led a risky life, having been wounded in Flanders in 1747. Unusually for a bookseller, John Smith came from a landed background, being the youngest son of the second laird of Craigend, Stirlingshire, and brother to Archibald, who subsequently purchased Jordanhill, Glasgow. John was succeeded by his son and grandson in turn, John Smith the younger (1753-1833) and John Smith 'the youngest' (1784-1849). The library boasted 3,000 volumes by 1773 and 20,000 by 1816 but was discontinued in 1828 and offered for sale, though after 1835 a 'Select reading club' was started, whose books were sold off annually until 1892.[142] The company still flourishes as a campus book retailer.

Also in Glasgow, David Home opened a library in 1759, James Knox by 1767, and Archibald Coubrough claimed 4,000 volumes in 1778. As in Edinburgh, there was no real expansion of libraries until the 1790s, coinciding with a demand for knowledge which was one of the few benefits of the French Revolution. Two new libraries were operating in the 1780s, while another five or six started in the 1790s, including John McFadyen's musical circulating library. An interesting and slightly unusual variation on the usual model of a circulating library was Alexander Molleson's 'Traveller's Library' at 19 Glassford Street, founded in 1808. His advertisement read:

> Application being occasionally made for the loan of Books by Travellers and others, who find it inconvenient to buy, or are undetermined till they have read the Books, and would give a reasonable compensation for the use of them, this Institution has been contrived for their accommodation.[143]

Proprietary subscription libraries did not as a rule flourish in towns where there were substantial circulating libraries, Edinburgh and Glasgow excepted.

---

[140] J. C. Crawford, 'The Bibliography of Printed Catalogues Issued by Publicly Available Libraries in Scotland 1765-1930: an Analysis of the Database', *Bibliotheck* 23 (1998), 27-48 (here pp. 36-37).

[141] Smith, *Historians of Perth*, pp. 100-1.

[142] John Smith & Son Ltd., *A Short Note on a Long History* (Glasgow, 1925).

[143] *Glasgow Herald*, 4 July 1808.

Although Aberdeen possessed a private subscription library, the Aberdeen Reading Society, founded in 1805, it appears to have been something of a minnow amongst libraries; no catalogues survive. The Caledonian Literary Society, also established in 1805, was apparently intended as a substitute for a subscription library and had collected 1,000 volumes by 1809. The society's aim was to promote mutual improvement and 'amusement' by means of a library, but it may not have lasted for many years.

There was, though, a massive circulating library in Aberdeen, which originated with a library established by Alexander Angus in 1764. He had been a bookseller since about 1744. His catalogue of 1765, which was arranged alphabetically by first letter of author or title and is the oldest complete surviving Scottish circulating library catalogue, lists 1,157 titles of mainly novels. No fewer than twenty-eight titles begin with the words *Adventures of ...*, and ninety-nine with *History of ...* Editions of Cicero and Voltaire nudge against works with titles such as *Cases of Polygamy, Concubinage, Adultery, and Divorce*, or *Jilts, or Female Fortune Hunters*, and *New Boghouse Miscellany*. He charged ten shillings yearly, as had Allan Ramsay, for two books at a time, or a penny per night. Within a dozen years the basic subscription was increased to 10s.6d. a year (with a monthly rate available for 1s.6d.). Subscribers had to pay sixpence for the catalogue, which became common practice for most libraries (and also implied acceptance of the rules printed inside). A second library appeared in the city in 1765, which lasted for about thirty years, while Angus was succeeded by John Burnett in 1795.

Alexander Brown began a library in Aberdeen in 1789 and offered about 6,000 volumes by 1795. His first catalogue, of 1789, records 3,536 titles and reveals that, like Sibbald in Edinburgh, his stock was almost equally divided between fiction and non-fiction. He founded a separate music library of some 2,000 items in 1798, which cost an extra £1.5s. per year. In 1804 Burnett and Brown merged their libraries to form the United Public Library. The new library, boasting 50,000 volumes, was for a time kept in the Athenaeum, which operated as a newsroom and 'Literary lounge', in Castle Street. Subscribers to the latter were allowed an extra book from the United Library. This privilege continued when the latter moved to Broad Street in 1810 following complaints from readers exhausted from climbing to the second floor of the Athenaeum, where the books had been kept.[144] The library was open from 8 a.m. to 9 p.m., charging one guinea yearly for one book at a time (or two for subscribers in the country), including all new books, or fifteen shillings a year for books in the catalogue only (i.e. excluding the latest books). Subscribers could pay more for further books, and non-subscribers could borrow a book for twopence per night and a deposit to the value of that book. This library remained a major literary

---

[144] W. R. McDonald, 'Circulating Libraries in the North-east of Scotland in the 18th Century', *Biblioteck* 5 (1968), 119-37; *Aberdeen Journal*, 30 May 1810.

resource for Aberdeen into the early twentieth century, merging in 1915 with the circulating library of David Wyllie & Son (a subscriber who died in 1912 claimed to have belonged to the latter library, which had originally been run by Alexander Watson by 1821, for seventy-five years).[145]

George Moir of Aberdeen was a hosier by trade but established a circulating library in 1800. His library excluded novels and politics and explicitly sought support from his Christian brethren. His library consisted of improving literature, lent at 3s.6d. *per annum* or twopence per week per book. He would lend free to young people who could not afford even that.[146] This represents another aspect of circulating library provision: that not every library was run purely for making a profit from lending sensational literature, and that some people were prepared to counter the perceived evils of the average circulating library. Indeed, the preface to Moir's catalogue quotes the criticism of Professor James Beattie on reading a romance: 'The time spent in reading it was lost; and there was more danger from the indelicacy of particular passages, than hope of its doing good by the satire – the moral sentiments – or the distributive justice, dispensed in winding up the catastrophe'.[147]

Outwith the cities, the earliest identified 'country' library was James Meuros's Ayrshire Circulating Library, which was operating in Kilmarnock by about 1760,[148] with a branch in Ayr from 1766.[149] Although Meuros, an unwitting defendant in the legal case over perpetual copyright in 1774, continued as a bookseller in Kilmarnock until the early 1820s, no further references to his lending activities have been found; the longevity, or otherwise, of many individual circulating libraries is often impossible to determine. Another bookseller who operated in more than one locality was William White, who ran a library in Irvine by 1780 with 1,269 titles in 3,000 volumes, and a branch in Beith. One book at a time could be borrowed by residents, or four by country dwellers, but borrowers were asked to send a list of up to twenty requests at a time.[150]

Libraries can be identified in Dundee (by 1765), Dalkeith (1768, still in existence in the 1840s and presumably later),[151] Paisley (1769, when there

---

[145] 'A Century of Bookselling 1814-1914: David Wyllie ...', *Aberdeen Book-Lover* (November 1914).

[146] A copy of Moir's catalogue (1800) is in Aberdeen University Library.

[147] Quoted in: 'Character of Mr. James Beattie', *Scots Magazine* 58 (1796), 586.

[148] Fragmentary catalogue in the British Library.

[149] *Edinburgh Advertiser*, 14/17 January 1766.

[150] *A Sale and Circulating Catalogue of Books to be Lent to Read. To be had of William White* ([Irvine?], [ca. 1780]) (Ardrossan Public Library).

[151] *NSA*, vol. 1 (1845), p. 529.

were two), and Banff (1770). George Caldwell's Paisley Circulating Library was unusual in that it started as a private collection. Caldwell was a silk-weaver with a passion for collecting and reading. At the age of 25 he was persuaded to turn his private library into a commercial venture, and so he lent books from the front of his shop while continuing to work at his loom at the rear. Eventually, lending and selling books became more profitable than weaving, combined with printing chapbooks and prints.[152] As a rule, circulating libraries charged an annual subscription, but borrowing rates by the night persisted. According to the 1789 catalogue of Caldwell's library, subscribers paid nine shillings a year, or 1s.6d. per month, but non-subscribers paid a penny per night for books of three shillings value or less, or twopence for more expensive works. His stock of 442 titles included novels, popular histories, and sermons. Non-fiction was an essential element in circulating libraries. In the 1790s James Imlach's library in Banff was typically described as 'a choice circulating library, which, besides the usual *light summer reading* of the times, contains a select collection of the works of the eminent writers, both ancient and modern'.[153] Being a seaport, Banff could receive books and the latest periodicals from London for Imlach's shop easily and rapidly.

The real growth period started in the 1780s. Alexander Davidson was running a library in Inverness (at the sign of Pope's Head) by 1782, when he produced a catalogue (for which subscribers had to pay threepence) of some 550 titles, which would have amounted to over one thousand volumes. He produced an appendix only a year later, showing that the library had more than doubled in size to 1,165 titles.[154] Although there were many novels, there was plenty of good non-fiction as well. His catalogues are unclassified, but the proportion of fiction to non-fiction would appear to be approximately fifty-fifty, as with Sibbald and Brown above. Books were lent on the following terms: one penny per night, 1s.6d. per month, three shillings per quarter, five shillings per half year, or ten shillings per year. Davidson's rules from 1782 are worth printing in full as being not untypical of a circulating library of the period.

CONDITIONS.

I. Subscribers are to pay at the time of subscribing.

II. The payment of One Penny for each night a book is kept, to be made when the book is returned.

---

[152] Robert Brown, *Paisley Poets, with brief Memoirs of Them* (Paisley, 1889), vol. 1, p. 369; cf. J. C. Crawford, '"The High State of Culture to which this Part of the Country has Attained": Libraries, Reading and Society in Paisley, 1760-1830', forthcoming.

[153] *OSA*, vol. 20 (1798), p. 369.

[154] The catalogue and appendix of Davidson's library is in Inverness Public Library, and the author is grateful to its librarian for assistance.

III. Whoever loses a book, or spoils it in the reading, more than can be reasonably allowed in common wear, or writes upon it, must pay the price at which it is valued in the catalogue; and if the book should consist of more volumes than one, then the other volumes are to be taken, together with the one lost or spoiled, and paid for accordingly.

IV. One book must be returned, and paid for, before another can be demanded. Readers in the country who are subscribers, will be allowed two books, or two volumes of a book at a time.

V. No Subscriber to keep a new book above eight days; as keeping a book too long prevents its circulating among other readers.

VI. Readers in the country are to send for and return the books at their own expence.

VII. Every reader, is to give in their name, place of abode, and the value of the book they take out, if required.

VIII. Subscribers to prevent being disappointed in the books they want, are desired to send in six or eight different numbers taken from the catalogue.

IX. Subscribers to pay three-pence for their catalogue.

Isaac Forsyth (1768-1859), an apprentice of Alexander Angus of Aberdeen and friend of Alexander Brown of the same city, began his Elgin Circulating Library in 1789 in The Tower, an impressive building in the High Street next to his home; he had begun business as a bookseller and stationer in the previous year.[155] Forsyth may well have been influenced by the success of Angus's library, though it is noteworthy that throughout his career Forsyth acquired his stock not from Aberdeen but, by using direct ships, from Edinburgh and London. He regularly ventured himself to the English metropolis to buy new books. He charged 10s.6d. yearly, and less *pro rata*, or one penny per night for one book for non-subscribers. In his first catalogue of 1789, containing 1,092 volumes, he sought public support for

> a Collection which has been procured with a great Deal of Trouble, and at a very considerable Expence, where he hopes that the Man of Letters will see something not unworthy of his Attention, while those who are pleased with the lighter Species of Reading may find, in a beautiful Variety, Instruction judiciously blended with Amusement.[156]

---

[155] Jane Thomas, '"Forming the Literary Tastes of the Middle and Higher Classes": Elgin's Circulating Libraries and their Proprietors, 1789-1870', in: John Hinks and Catherine Armstrong (eds.), *Worlds of Print* (New Castle, Del., 2006), pp. 91-111.

[156] From the preface to Forsyth's *Catalogue of the Elgin Circulating Library* ([Elgin], 1789).

Forsyth had collected 4,000 volumes by 1812 and circulated books throughout north-east Scotland, reflecting his town's importance as a commercial and transportation centre. His system was explained in 1810 when he offered to deliver weekly parcels for an extra annual fee. For a parcel to be sent to Inverness or Portsoy cost five shillings, Nairn, Keith, Cullen or Forres four shillings (the last twice a week), and Fochabers three shillings. He also promised to dispatch books by the weekly packet from Burghead to Sutherland and the Ross-shires, while boxes or parcels could be conveyed at five shillings per year to Dornoch or Tain. Many city circulating libraries offered to send books to both town and country (in 1823 Alexander Mackay advertised that he would send books from Edinburgh 'to the most distant parts of Scotland'),[157] but Forsyth's enterprise is the only Scottish example to be advertised with costings.[158] To protect the books, 'stout leather bags, with locks, are furnished at prime cost'.[159]

Forsyth's bookselling and lending amounted to a successful business, but he also became known as a banker, in which he lost a great deal of money, as he did when he ventured into the manufacture of straw hats. Many other circulating librarians also dealt in 'fashionable' trades (after all, Allan Ramsay had been a peruke-maker), but diversification (Forsyth also became a farmer and was secretary of the Morayshire Farmers' Club) was not always profitable. Forsyth continued his library personally until the age of seventy-six, but by that time the library was ailing, and he had long lost the vitality of his youth.

A short-lived circulating library was operated by William Farquhar in Peterhead by January 1794; but he moved to Edinburgh later in the same year and does not seem to have continued his library. Farquhar, a would-be poet, was no Allan Ramsay. He did, though, set out a poetical 'mission statement' for his Peterhead library, though in a rather different style to Sibbald's effusions:

> Here's Willie Farquhar's hinmost shift,
> At a'thing else he had no thrift:
> Come in then, lads, an' gi'e 'm a lift,
>   His buiks are bonny,
> An' ye may plainly see his drift,
>   Is to mak' money.
>
> Gin ilka chiel in Peterhead
> Wad come to's shop for buiks to read,
> He sud get warks wad fill his head
>   Wi' thrifty notions;

---

[157] *Caledonian Mercury*, 3 November 1823.

[158] *Inverness Journal*, 4 May 1810.

[159] *Aberdeen Journal*, 15 November 1826.

> Or, gin he thought it was as guid,
>   Wi' sleepy potions.
>
> For Authors are like ither men,
> They dinna a' tak' up the pen,
> Wi' an intent their win' to spen',
>   To mak' ye vogie,
> For sometimes sleepin' recommen',
>   As weil's a cogie.
>
> But there are unco few o' mine,
> That are o' this wile dozen'd kin;
> Na, they are buiks that fill the min',
>   Nae wi' fool buff,
> But wi' Benevolence divine,
>   An' sic guid stuff.[160]

On a more elevated plane must be the circulating library of the sober and eminently respectable Alexander Elder, who, in the words of Robert Chambers, a youthful customer, became 'a dealer in intellectual wares' in Peebles during the 1790s. The library may not have been widely appreciated, as was commented on in 1802: 'A bookseller in the county town has set up a circulating library; but meets with small encouragement. From the thin dispersed state of population, the number of readers cannot be many, and those who do read do not read much'.[161] Chambers himself, who later ran a circulating library in Edinburgh but became far more famous and successful as a publisher, recalled using Elder's shop in around 1810:

> It seems a curious reminiscence of my first bookseller's shop, that, on entering it, one always got a peep of a cow, which quietly chewed her cud close behind the book-shelves, such being one of Sandy's means of providing for his family. Sandy was great in Shorter Catechisms, and what he called *spells*, and school Bibles and Testaments, and in James Lumsden's (of Glasgow) halfpenny coloured pictures of the 'World Turned Upside Down', the 'Battle of Trafalgar', &c., and in penny chap-books of an extraordinary coarseness of language.[162]

---

[160] Quoted in: James T. Findlay, *A History of Peterhead* (Aberdeen, 1933), pp. 277-8.

[161] Charles Findlater, *General View of the Agriculture of the County of Peebles* (Edinburgh, 1802), p. 256.

[162] Chambers, *Memoir*, p. 54. William St. Clair refers to the same story by Chambers in his *The Reading Nation in the Romantic Period* (Cambridge, 2004), p. 242, but claims, strangely, that Elder was a local farmer who set up his shop and library 'in the shed where he kept his cows'. There is no evidence to suggest that Elder was anything other than a bookseller who kept a normal bookshop. And a cow.

Chambers provides a fascinating glimpse of a literary tradesman who was to become richer than most of his neighbours and considered Elder to be 'enterprising and enlightened beyond the common range of booksellers in small country towns, and had added a circulating library to his ordinary business'.

Elder provided Chambers and his brother, William, with quills for pens 'which he would hand us over the counter with a civil glance over the top of his spectacles, as if saying: "Now, laddie, see and mak' a guid use o't"'. But, perhaps more importantly, the father of the two Chambers had encouraged them to use the library, so that by the age of nine or ten they

> had read a considerable number of the classics of English literature, or heard our father read them; were familiar with the comicalities of Gulliver, Don Quixote, and Peregrine Pickle; had dipped into the poetry of Pope and Goldsmith, and indulged our romantic tendencies in books of travel and adventure.[163]

Chambers considered Elder's stock to be a cut above the average wares of a country bookseller, especially as his customers were probably not very demanding. When Elder acquired the various volumes of the *Encyclopedia Britannica*, fourth edition, only the Chambers's father was sufficiently interested to purchase it; sadly it was sold within a year to satisfy the latter's creditors. Chambers senior, a cotton merchant, was obliged to leave Peebles after advancing credit to French prisoners-of-war who returned to France after making promises to re-pay their debts, but, strangely, were never heard from again. Robert Chambers never abandoned his regard for the novels of Fielding, Sterne, and Smollett, as fostered by Elder's library, even though those novelists had become unfashionable by the mid-nineteenth century.

William Chambers, too, had appreciative memories of Elder's library:

> With Elder's field of literature laid open to us, Robert and I read at a great rate, going right through the catalogue of books without much regard to methodised study. In fact, we had to take what we could get and be thankful. Permitted to have only one volume at a time, we made up for short allowance by reading as quickly as possible, and, to save time, often read together from the same book; one having the privilege of turning over the leaves. Desultory as was this course of reading, it undoubtedly widened the sphere of our ideas; and it would be ungrateful not to acknowledge that some of my own success, and not a few of the higher pleasures experienced in life, are due to that library in the little old burgh.[164]

---

[163] Chambers, *Memoir*, pp. 54-55.

[164] Ibid., pp. 58-59.

William Chambers in 1859 donated a building for a museum and library, including 10,000 volumes, in Peebles (the Chambers Institute, which still exists under that name), though he doubted whether the youth of that period would appreciate it as much as he had appreciated Elder's library.[165]

The library in Peebles was relatively prosperous, but the lot of a provincial library owner was not always a happy one. The memoirs of George Miller (1771-1835) of Dunbar are a mine of information about the travails of the provincial book trade.[166] As Alexander Somerville wrote of Miller, he 'certainly lived before the age was ripe for him, and died, I fear, before he was fully appreciated'.[167] Miller and his brother, James, succeeded to their father's bookshop and stationery business in 1789, to which they added a circulating library in the same year. They began with 507 volumes, which had doubled a year later. But James objected to his brother's secret marriage, and their partnership was dissolved. George, whose matrimonial adventure had obliged him to leave the Secession Church and join the Wesleyan Methodists instead, set up a rival business with a freshly-acquired stock of 1,000 volumes. Another brother, John, subsequently started the first circulating library in Dunfermline. George found his new circulating library an 'unprofitable and troublesome business', though

> of essential use in bringing customers to the shop and enabling me to seek out and establish a business for myself – a disadvantage which my brother, who had fallen so smoothly into the old-established business of my father, never knew what it was to labour under.[168]

By 1806 George Miller's Dunbar and County Circulating Library had 2,500 volumes, which he considered 'a pretty good collection surely for a country town, but was very much excessive [in costs] in the getting'. Interestingly he reveals that he then catered for thirty-five yearly, twenty-nine half-yearly, and eight quarterly subscribers, 'a very handsome number'.[169] In fact he is the only Scottish circulating library proprietor before Robert Chambers in 1829 whose membership figures are recorded. In 1811 he added a reading room and a shop known as the India Tea Warehouse. But he complained of attempts to oust him, as well as his disappointment in his sons (one had left the town, another was mad). The success of Miller's library depended on its popularity amongst soldiers at the local barracks, opened in 1803, when Miller had anticipated

---

[165] Ibid., pp. 321-2.

[166] W. J. Couper, *The Millers of Haddington, Dunbar and Dunfermline* (London, 1914).

[167] Alexander Somerville, *The Autobiography of a Working Man* (London, 1951), p. 47.

[168] Couper, *The Millers*, p. 59.

[169] NLS, MS. 5409, fol. 87r, George Miller's autobiography, 1806.

a 'golden harvest'. The end of the Napoleonic wars removed that source of income. The library was transferred in 1814 to Haddington, where George had operated a printing-press for a number of years and published short-lived magazines. One unsuccessful venture was the *Cheap Magazine* which preceded by many years the similar publications of Charles Knight and the Chambers brothers; but Miller's efforts were not repaid in such small towns as Dunbar and Haddington, and Miller failed to make a profit.

By 1816 Miller's debts had spiralled, unbelievably, to over £9,500. He claimed assets of over £10,500, consisting mostly of unsold publications issued in numbers and unbound books. Rival booksellers claimed that Miller, who was well-respected, was capable of securing 16s. in the pound for his assets, but a series of sales only realized £584.[170] A third son, another James, continued the library for a short time, but it was dissolved in 1819. George Miller blamed the library's final failure on the popularity of the famous itinerating libraries of Samuel Brown, which began in 1817:

> It is evident that East Lothian should have been the last place to which these gentry should have turned their attention. But it unfortunately so happens that there are many well-meaning people in the world who are very unwilling to help forward any laudable measure except they themselves take the lead, and others who are ready to object to any selection or collection of books in which they have not been consulted.[171]

George Miller had, it seems, been in conflict with a supporter of Brown who objected to Miller printing handbills advertizing strolling players, a pursuit which did not find favour with devout churchmen. Over the following years Miller had several times to sell off part of his bookstock to fend off bankruptcy, but his library venture was never revived.[172]

Inevitably the majority of circulating libraries were found in the Lowlands, and the majority of these were small affairs which often only lasted a short time. Janet Hamilton (1795-1870), for instance, a popular poetess in her time, devoured the contents of her village library when young. She lived in Langloan, Coatbridge, and subsequently started a circulating library of her own (probably after 1825), which, according to her biographer:

> true to poetic experience, turned out a losing concern. She had no lack of readers, but they failed to return the volumes they took

---

[170] NLS, MS. 5409, George Miller's autobiography, 7 September & 12 October 1816, ff.

[171] Couper, *The Millers*, pp. 131-2.

[172] G. Hogg, 'Latter Struggles in the Life of a Provincial Bookseller and Printer: George Miller of Dunbar, Scotland', in: *Periodicals and Publishers: the Newspaper and Journal Trade, 1750-1914*, edited by John Hinks, Catherine Armstrong, and Matthew Day (London, 2009), pp. 139-59.

out, so that her library was literally exhausted, for she lost all her books.[173]

A diversion might be taken at this point to consider the spread of Scots abroad. Many booksellers emigrated to the colonies during the eighteenth century, including several who were to start up circulating libraries. In North America organized circulating libraries began to appear in the 1760s. Amongst their founders was John Mein, a former bookseller in Edinburgh, who opened Boston's first circulating library in 1765 with 700 titles in 1,200 volumes. His opening advertisement sets a familiar tone:

> Something of this kind has been long wanted to amuse the *Man of Leisure*: to afford an elegant and agreeable relaxation to the minds of *Men of business*, and to insinuate knowledge and instruction, under the veil of entertainment to the FAIR SEX – here likewise the *Divine* and the *Christian* may find in the works of the *Pious* and the *Learned*, that exalted satisfaction, which flows from the serious study of the *Christian Religion* ...

About one quarter of the stock was fiction, and there were also thirty-seven French titles. But Mein's library only lasted for five or six years. He was in business with Robert Sandeman of the Sandemanians, but, as a loyalist, Mein became increasingly unpopular and in 1771 departed to England (rather than Scotland).[174]

William Aikman, from Bo'ness, opened a library in Annapolis in 1773 but, being a loyalist too, soon found it prudent to leave the continent. He removed to Kingston, Jamaica, where he commenced the first circulating library on that island in or just after 1775. But the inhabitants did not appreciate this novelty, and he sold off his stock in 1781.[175] Robert Aitken, a member of the Antiburgher sect who had run a library in Paisley, moved to Philadelphia in 1771 and started a successful library; he was followed there by Robert Bell in 1774. Samuel Loudon established a library in New York in 1774, and though he suspended it for ten years during the revolution, he was not a loyalist and returned to continue the library afterwards.[176] In Canada, William Lyon Mackenzie briefly ran a library before entering Canadian politics. He had previously run a library with his mother in Alyth, Perthshire, and the failure of

---

[173] Janet Hamilton, *Poems, Sketches and Essays*, revised edn. (Glasgow, 1885), pp. 16-17.

[174] David Kaser, *A Book for a Sixpence: the Circulating Library in America* (Pittsburgh, Pa., 1980), pp. 29-31.

[175] Ibid., pp. 36-37; Roderick Cave, *Printing and the Book Trade in the West Indies* (London, 1987), pp. 229-31.

[176] Cf. *ODNB* for Aitken, Loudon, and Mein; Kaser, *Book for a Sixpence*, pp. 37-39.

that venture in 1817 was said to have coloured his feelings towards those who enjoyed wealth at the expense of small tradesmen like himself, who did not.[177]

Scots, too, were prominent in proprietary subscription libraries abroad. Near to home, many members of the Belfast Reading Society (1788), precursor of the Belfast Library, bore surnames of Scottish origin, while, much further away, at least six founder-members of the Charleston Library Society (1748) were of Scottish descent.[178] In what is now Ontario, the Niagara Library was founded in 1800 in the town of Newark, now known as Niagara-on-the-Lake. Its founders were Scottish Presbyterians, and its earliest purchases included sermons of Hugh Blair and James Fordyce, and works by John Bunyan, Philip Doddridge, William Wilberforce, and Ossian, as well as Robert Burns, the *Edinburgh Magazine*, *Edinburgh Review*, and *Scots Magazine*.[179] And furthest away, in New South Wales, the committee of the Bathurst Book Society, founded in 1837, was almost entirely composed of Scottish Presbyterians, some of whom had attempted a similar venture in the 1820s.[180]

The Business of Circulating Libraries

Libraries such as Sibbald's in Edinburgh and Smith's in Glasgow charged a relatively high price. A yearly fee of ten shillings was not going to attract the workers, and they were aiming deliberately at the higher classes of society. By 1805 John Smith of Glasgow charged one guinea. Most libraries adopted similar subscriptions, and one guinea a year was normal before 1820. In about 1815 Robert Kinnear of Edinburgh charged two guineas yearly for country subscribers, who could borrow eighteen volumes at a time, though by 1824 William Hunter, also of Edinburgh, charged three guineas for ten books in town or eighteen in the country; he also offered a nightly rate of threepence for a quarto, twopence for an octavo, or one and a half pence for a duodecimo, but double for new publications. In London subscriptions of up to five guineas were 'normal' by then.

Price-fixing was common in England, especially in London and Bath, where identical rates were often jointly announced by several library owners.

---

[177] *ODNB*; *Dictionary of Canadian Biography* (Toronto, 1976), vol. 9, p. 497.

[178] Raven, *London Booksellers and American Customers*, p. 38; cf. John Killen, *A History of the Linen Hall Library 1788-1988* (Belfast, 1990), chapter 1.

[179] Janet Carnochan, *Niagara Library* (Niagara-on-the-Lake, 1900); see also, for instance, A. L. Bordsen, 'Scottish Attitudes Reflected in the Library History of North Carolina', *Libraries & Culture* 27 (1992), 121-42.

[180] K. A. Manley, 'Early Australian Book Clubs: Bathurst, Parramatta, Perth', *Library History* 10 (1994), 76-87 (here pp. 77-79).

Subscription rate rises appear to have been co-ordinated in Scottish towns as well, for example Aberdeen. In Dundee the owners of the only two rival circulating libraries in 1805, Robert Miller and William Chalmers, jointly increased their subscriptions to fifteen shillings a year and *pro rata* to two shillings per month or one and a half pence per night, citing the great rise in the price of books as their reason.[181] But the example of Sibbald and his peers spawned many, cheaper rivals, who may have lent books for a small fee per night only rather than for an annual subscription. James Smith, who ran the Inverness Circulating Library, advertised in 1820 that he was adopting an arrangement for accommodating his customers based on the practice followed in the south of Scotland, so he claimed. In order to prevent the most popular works being kept out for too long, he proposed to charge non-subscribers sixpence per night, while subscribers must pay threepence per night which would be increased to sixpence if they kept these books out beyond one night.[182]

The phenomenon of 'Minerva' libraries was started by the London publisher, William Lane, in the late eighteenth century and continued by his successor, A. K. Newman & Co. Lane published cheap romantic fiction specifically tailored for young females who flocked to circulating libraries for the latest novels. He extended his business by offering whole 'Minerva' libraries for sale, complete with instructions. Anyone – not necessarily a bookseller – could buy a box of perhaps 200 novels and set up an instant circulating library themselves which, he advertised, was 'an undertaking advantageous as well as genteel'.[183] In the *Caledonian Mercury* for 20 August 1812, for instance, A. K. Newman offered three 'circulating libraries for the winter': one contained 727 volumes for 1s.6d. per volume, the second was 1,000 volumes for two shillings per volume, while the third consisted of 637 volumes at 3s.6d. per volume (the price varied according to size, and all were half-bound in calf).

A typical advertisement for just such a small library is found in 1806 for John Baxter's Minerva Circulating Library, situated in Horse Wynd in Dundee:

> [Baxter] Most respectfully informs the Ladies and Gentlemen of Dundee, that he has just received a Parcel of NEW BOOKS, which he intends giving out to Read *per Night*. His Stock for that purpose is not yet extensive, but as he intends to add to it monthly, every New Publication of esteemed merit, and as he will be particularly

---

[181] *Dundee, Perth, & Cupar Advertiser*, 22 February 1805.

[182] *Inverness Journal*, 7 January 1820.

[183] *World*, 25 March 1788.

> careful in making a proper selection, he hopes to gain a share of public favour.[184]

His advertisement shows that he did include some non-fiction, but the fact that he advertised it as the 'Minerva' Library shows the kind of customers his library was aimed at.

Many circulating libraries were not run by booksellers at all, but often by stationers or even other tradesmen who were simply diversifying their business, especially in small towns. In Eyemouth, for instance, a Mr Patterson ran a shop by 1806 which contained a stationery business, library, and post office, all of which was perfectly typical. Untypically, he was also master of the kirk school. Thomas Carlyle, who entered Annan Academy as a schoolboy in 1806, used a circulating library of novels and romances run by a local cooper, John Maconachie.[185] John Montgomery, who ran a library in Oldmeldrum, Aberdeenshire, before 1810, when he was bankrupt, was a merchant and druggist and owned a herb still.[186] John Hill & Co. of Dumfries began a library in 1803 and advertized that they sold violins, silk purses, combs, and umbrellas; they obviously aspired to attract the female customer.[187] In nearby Dalbeattie, James Murray was a general merchant and draper who also kept a circulating library by 1825. He was, though, described by the traveller for Oliver & Boyd, the publisher, as 'Doubtful. ... May be trusted £10 [i.e. credit]'. Small businessmen were not always safe risks to their suppliers (the same source referred to William Robertson, who ran a circulating library in Lanark, as 'Middling good; Very untidy in his business').

When A. Macmillan & Co. began a circulating library in Castle Douglas in 1817, they reassured their existing customers that they would continue to sell hardware and groceries as well as books.[188] John Smith of Beith and William Straton of Dundee were both grocers who ran libraries. The book trade has never been the sole preserve of the bookseller: William Brownlie of Paisley, for example, appears in a trades directory as bookseller and cow feeder (though apparently did not run a library).[189] Robert Galloway, who ran a library in Glasgow, had originally been a shoemaker, while his brother, George, traded in Edinburgh as both shoemaker and bookseller.[190] Robert Dick of Stranraer was

---

[184] *Dundee, Perth, & Cupar Advertiser*, 6 June 1806.

[185] Edwin W. Marrs, Jr., *The Letters of Thomas Carlyle to his Brother Alexander* (Cambridge, Mass., 1968), p. 7.

[186] *Aberdeen Journal*, 19 December 1810.

[187] *Dumfries Weekly Journal*, 13 December 1803.

[188] *Dumfries & Galloway Courier*, 28 January 1817.

[189] *Paisley Directory* (1812).

[190] Alexander Campbell, *An Introduction to the History of Poetry in Scotland* (Edinburgh, 1798), p. 309.

both librarian and shoemaker, while Matthew Paul of Anderston was a tailor and librarian. Some librarians may well have practised completely different professions. In 1806, apparently in Edinburgh, a 'woman, who lately kept a house of ill fame, being brought before a magistrate, was questioned as to her line of life. 'Please your Worship', said she, 'I keep a *circulating library*, the neatest volumes you ever saw".[191]

Robert Nicoll (1814-37), the poet, opened a circulating library in Dundee in 1834 (he was apparently no relation to his namesake, Robert Nicoll, who ran a library in the same city in the 1780s), and therefore is too late to be included in the Listing. However, his experiences of reading as a boy and the economics of starting a library himself are of relevance to the present study, since they relate to a time only a few years later than the present focus period. Nicoll was brought up as a farm hand on his father's farm in Perthshire and took every opportunity of reading, whether in the fields or wherever he might be. In 1826, at the age of twelve, he saved up 1s.6d. to pay for a quarter's reading at David Peat's circulating library in Perth and borrowed the *Waverley* novels to read in the woods.[192] He became a grocer's apprentice in Perth's High Street, and continued to read voraciously. He wrote that 'a gentleman lent me his right to the Perth Library, and thus I procured many works I could not get before, – Milton's prose works, Locke's works, and, what I prized more than all, a few of [Jeremy] Bentham's, with many other works in various departments of literature and science which I had not the good fortune to read before'.[193] Nicoll himself could never afford to collect a library of his own, and his biographer wrote: 'Many men have a pride in amassing books, which they never read. Robert Nicoll's pride lay in reading without amassing'.[194] By now he was a confirmed Radical.

In 1832 a circulating library was opened on the opposite side of the road by Peter R. Drummond, who recorded: 'He heard the announcement of my poor books as the hungry lion hears the timid footsteps of his prey, and prepared to devour them'.[195] Nicoll became keen to embark on a literary or journalistic career but was still only eighteen and lacking money. Then, in 1834, he had the chance of taking a shop in Dundee. He had been befriended by a wealthy, if eccentric, draper who lent Drummond £40 on Nicoll's behalf. Drummond laid out the money on books and stationery, purchased in Glasgow, buying as much again on credit in Nicoll's name. With a letter of introduction, 500

---

[191] *Caledonian Mercury*, 6 October 1806.

[192] P. R. Drummond, *The Life of Robert Nicoll, Poet* (Paisley, 1884), p. 37.

[193] Ibid., p. 112.

[194] Ibid., p. 127.

[195] Ibid., p. 89.

volumes of 'Minerva Library' books were ordered from A. K. Newman & Co. of London, while Drummond supplied a further 1,000 from his own library, valued at two shillings per volume, and re-paid over a long period. So, in a modest fashion, began Nicoll's library.[196] It was only to last two years, but his story does reveal how one young individual could set himself up in business on a modest scale, but with friends and a little financial aid.

Workers' Libraries

During the 1790s, the example of proprietary subscription libraries and the expansion of local circulating libraries led to a greater awareness of what libraries could offer to all classes. Many small subscription libraries founded from the 1790s onwards were clearly intended as working class equivalents of the Kelso and Duns libraries and those similar libraries founded shortly afterwards. It is, though, worth noting that the Belfast Reading Society (1788), founded by artisans (many of Scottish Presbyterian stock) as a permanent subscription library, with transferable shares, preceded similar libraries in Scotland.

The new smaller libraries charged low fees and often did not offer shares. The first *Statistical Account of Scotland*, compiled under Sir John Sinclair during the early 1790s, provides the best evidence of how many of these subscription libraries developed during this period. These accounts were written by local established ministers, and so it will not be surprising that they in general approved of public libraries for encouraging reading, or at least the 'right' kind of reading. Dr Samuel Charters, minister of the parish of Wilton, near Hawick, and a proprietor of the Hawick Library, for instance, wrote to Sir John Sinclair: 'Lending books to the parishioners I have found useful, and think that parish libraries, consisting not only of religious books, but of such as the *Statistical History*, might be a public good'.[197] Charters had already written elsewhere:

> A little money may be usefully laid out on well-chosen books for lending to the poor. The poor have leisure hours; they can read, and some of them love reading; but they cannot purchase books, and may fall on improper ones ...
>
> Parish libraries would be an useful institution. Reading forms the mind. The influence of books at the Reformation was mighty, and is at all times great. In the dawn of knowledge, it was an object with

---

[196] Ibid., pp. 128-9.

[197] *OSA*, vol. 15 (1795), p. 641.

[Bishop] Leighton and others, to furnish the clergy with books. By private and circulating libraries, the middle ranks are now furnished. By a parish library, knowledge would descend. Under a minister's direction, poisonous books would be excluded, and good ones chosen, suited to the young, the thoughtless, the busy, the sick, the mourner, the melancholy, the aged. An appetite for controversy will subside when better food is provided.[198]

Robert Burns, writing in 1792, also commended libraries for the workers to Sinclair:

To store the minds of the lower classes with useful knowledge, is certainly of very great consequence, both to them as individuals, and to society at large. Giving them a turn for reading and reflection, is giving them a source of innocent and laudable amusement; and besides, raises them to a more dignified degree in the scale of rationality.[199]

Rev. Dr John Smith wrote of the Campbeltown (Argyllshire) Public Library (ca. 1790): 'This institution promises much utility, by diffusing general knowledge and a taste for reading'.[200] Joining this library cost only six shillings a year and was amongst the first to charge such a low fee, with no shares, to attract the ordinary reader, rather than the professional man or the landed gentry, as in Kelso. Similarly at Cambusnethan whose minister wrote: 'The inhabitants ... have given a good specimen of their character and taste, in the institution of two libraries, supported by an annual subscription, and containing a judicious selection of books, entertaining, historical, moral, and religious'.[201] These libraries were usually small, possessing only a few hundred volumes, but often appeared to have lasted many years. The Cabrach Library (1815) still existed in 1915, when it had only recently relaxed its original rule that no novels or plays should be purchased.[202]

Libraries for workers was a cause which appealed to John Millar, Professor of Civil Law at Glasgow University and a supporter of workers' education. A social philosopher, he was a major figure in the Scottish Enlightenment. In 1796 Millar's carriage broke down at Langloan while he was travelling between Glasgow and Edinburgh. During this delay, Millar had a chance encounter

---

[198] S. Charters, 'On Alms', in: *The Scotch Preacher* (Edinburgh, 1789), vol. 4, pp. 122-3.

[199] *OSA*, vol. 3 (1792), p. 598.

[200] *OSA*, vol. 10 (1794), p. 561.

[201] *OSA*, vol. 12 (1794), p. 574.

[202] James Taylor, *Cabrach Feerings* (Banff, 1920), pp. 106-11.

with a labourer who, because of an injury, was resting inside his cottage, reading Henry Brooke's *Fool of Quality*.[203] The man explained that the book

> belonged to a Reading Society, which, about three years ago, he and eighteen others, all mechanics or labourers like himself, had formed. That, for the two first years, they contributed sixpence per month, to be laid out in the purchase of books. That they had now above a hundred volumes upon different subjects of instruction and amusement, and which having considered as a sufficient stock to begin their library, they had lately reduced their contribution to one shilling each per annum, exacting however ten shillings from every new subscriber. They meet twice a year to name a Librarian from among themselves, and to vote what new books their funds are to be laid out upon. He told me there was a Society upon a similar plan in the neighbouring village of Monkland; and that, in the village of Airdrie, two miles off, there was a very numerous one, with a large and general collection of books.[204]

This was the same library which Janet Hamilton, already mentioned, was to belong to. She recalled that Brooke's *Fool of Quality* was the only novel owned by the Society, the preference being for religion. Further enquiries by Millar revealed about forty similar libraries in the Glasgow area (with nine in its immediate vicinity, including two in Gorbals and one at Gillespie's cotton mill in Woodside, and ten in Paisley) as well as in Falkirk, Kilmarnock, Catrine (Ayrshire), Campbeltown (Argyllshire), and the Rothesay cotton mills on the Isle of Bute.[205] Voyages and travels were the prevailing taste, and the general effect on the workmen

> had been strikingly beneficial. That in place of spending their money in alehouses, they uniformly, after finishing the necessary labour of the day, employ themselves in reading to their families ... and that the whole of their regular and orderly conducts forms a marked contrast to that of the generality of other tradesmen.

Millar knew too of Leadhills, whose valuable library 'most people who visit Scotland, I believe, have heard of'. Millar published details of these small libraries anonymously in the *Scots Chronicle*, a newspaper edited by his former pupil, John Maitland, Earl of Lauderdale. His intention was to encourage similar libraries, where the workmen themselves ran the society and selected what books they wanted, without owning expensive shares. He examined

---

[203] Cf. Crawford, 'Ideology of Mutual Improvement', pp. 55-60, which discusses the presumed authorship of the following quotations.

[204] *Scots Chronicle*, 25 October 1796.

[205] Ibid., 30 December 1796, 20 January & 10 February 1797.

the catalogues of several such libraries and found that history was popular, though he wished to see more natural history and education.[206] Millar's final letter, published in a London magazine, recorded a total of fifty-one 'workers' libraries', many founded by weavers, who enjoyed the facility of being able to read and work simultaneously; weavers were closely associated in Scotland with radicalism.[207] The same magazine had already published favourable comments on the original letters in the *Scots Chronicle*, ensuring that the idea of small subscription libraries run by and for working men was publicized south of the border.[208] These Scottish libraries may even have been a influence on the founding of the Kendal Economical Library in 1797, the first known subscription library in England specifically founded for artisans.

The library at Airdrie (1792) has been mentioned and was one of the earliest workers' libraries near Glasgow. The original members comprised weavers, wrights, two innkeepers, a shoemaker, a distiller, an excise officer, a surgeon, and several farmers. The first president was the local minister, and other ministers also joined. The first librarian, James Downie, was also the schoolmaster, and his only payment was exemption from paying any subscription; he was still librarian at his death in 1823. Books were only issued before 9 a.m. and after 4 p.m., presumably so as not to conflict with the librarian's duties as a schoolmaster, and because workers would have difficulty in visiting at other times. Although the entry money of ten shillings was relatively high, the annual subscription of two shillings was very low, and this clearly acted as no deterrent to the local population. Members were initially summoned to meetings by the town officer, who received a penny from each subscriber for the privilege. Meetings were held in the local taverns in turn.[209]

As in so many other libraries, the earliest works bought included the familiar Charles Rollin, David Hume, Comte de Buffon, Alexander Pope's Homer, Ossian, Oliver Goldsmith's *New and Accurate System of Natural History*, James Beattie's *Evidences of the Christian Religion*, John Erskine, Isaac Watts's *The Improvement of the Mind*, and books on agriculture. But, as in so many other libraries, within a few years more and more members went into arrears with their subscriptions, and many were removed in 1800, including Rev. Andrew Fairbairn, an independent minister, who had never paid any entry money or subscription, though he had donated Johann G. Eckhardt's *Roman History* in five volumes. The library grew modestly, though in 1824 hardly more than £6 could be afforded for further books. Although it disappeared during the 1830s,

---

[206] Ibid., 10 February 1797.

[207] *Monthly Magazine* 4 (October 1797), 275-7.

[208] Cf. 'Benevolus', in *Monthly Magazine* 4 (July 1797), 30.

[209] J. Gardner, 'An Airdrie Library in the Eighteenth Century', *Airdrie Advertiser*, 30 July 1921.

it cannot be dismissed as a failure; for over forty years it provided a unique resource for the literate workers of the town.

The Tillicoultry Reading Society in Clackmannanshire was another workers' library whose existence was revealed in response to Millar's request for further information. This society had been established in January 1793 by two or three youths who suffered under the disadvantage of living far from any circulating library. As one of its members, Walter Monteath, reported:

> We have already a very respectable collection of books, including the most approved histories, civil and religious. We have not expended one penny on plays or novels. Our Society at present consists of twenty-three members; and one and all of us are of that order of men who earn their bread *by the sweat of their brows*.[210]

According to their rules, only moral people could join, and any improper behaviour was punished. Transferable shares were part of the membership, and could be passed to an heir unless their character prevented it, in which case the next in line would inherit. Women could belong but were not admitted to their public meetings. This may seem draconian in the modern age, but in those days it was considered perfectly normal to prevent any embarrassment by being in close proximity with men. (When George Miller of Haddington fell into debt and held a series of book sales, he invited the ladies to attend as there would be many items of particular interest to them. As an incentive, a police officer would be present 'to preserve order'.)[211]

By 1800 approximately a hundred subscription libraries can be identified in Scotland, of which at least half could be described as working-class. Only two comparable working-class libraries existed in England, in Birmingham and Kendal. After 1800 small, cheap subscription libraries for workers, including so-called trades libraries, spread all over Scotland, and dividing book clubs began to appear. Mere statistics are difficult to interpret, but the idea of permanent storehouses of knowledge had found favour in Scotland, while commercial circulating libraries existed in virtually all towns for recreational reading. Although many subscription libraries may only have enjoyed a relatively small membership, their importance in encouraging mutual improvement – an idea which was to be taken further by mechanics' institutes (also Scottish-inspired) – cannot be denied, and in particular the dissemination of knowledge to all classes of society.

The Dalkeith Subscription Library, founded in 1798, only charged one shilling for its shares and one penny a week. Despite its low charges, its members clearly had intellectual pretensions and held a robust idea of which

---

[210] *Scots Chronicle*, 21/24 February 1797.

[211] NLS, MS. 5409, George Miller's autobiography, 12 October 1816.

books were essential, as is amusingly revealed in a poetical 'catalogue' of the Dalkeith Subscription Library, composed by one of their members, Peter Forbes, which dates from 1803:[212]

> Read first the history o' the nation,
> Frae Caesar till the reformation,
> Syne ye'll be wiser, I'll be caution,
>   An' farer ben,
> An' fit to mak a bra[ve] oration,
>   An' crack like men.
>
> ...
>
> There's Rollin's hist'ry nane can ding,
> The first fair feather in our wing,
> Where Cyrus, wi' triumphant swing,
>   Gars nations rattle;
> The dart and jav'lin he does fling,
>   In weel plann'd battle.
>
> In Rollin, likewise, ye may trace,
> Great Nimrod, master o' the chase,
> The first o' royal bluid an' race;
>   But lads that's douce,
> May read kirk hist'ry, wi' lang face,
>   Or else Stackhouse.
>
> There's Plutarch's Lives, and Women's Rights,
> There's Prince Le Boo, an' Rollin' Lights,
> There's Heron's Tour, there's 'Rabian Nights,
>   An' the *Spectator*,
> An' Franklin, wi' some funny flights,
>   On drinkin water.
>
> There's Goldsmith, Godwin, Raynal, Cook,
> Ray, Radcliff, Robertson, an' Brooke,
> An' Zimmerman, that lik'd a neuk,
>   To muse and think,
> Young, Thomson, Cowper, an' a Buik,
>   Ca'd Baron Trenk.
>
> Rob Ferguson, Auld Reikie's ranter,
> And Jamie Alves's sweet saunter;
> The next comes up, at a roun' canter,

---

[212] [Peter Forbes], *Poem* (Edinburgh, 1803); reprinted in his *Poems* (Edinburgh, 1812), pp. 9-17. Only extracts have been printed here.

Blyth Robin Burns,
And Inverleithen's bran new Chanter,
	Has canty turns.

There's Monk and Marlborough, fetchers twa,
There's Wallace wight, cou'd lick them a'
There's Lithgow, wha gaed far awa,
	An' gat sic crieshin
About some kirk court that they ca'
	The inquisition.

There's Cromwell, Mahomet an' Neckar,
For rulin roasts there's few mair sicker;
But Bonaparte gets battles quicker,
	He's ay sae cunnin,
For ilka time he draws the tricker,
	He's sure o' winnin.

There's Voltaire, Volney, but, beside,
There's Fuller, wha does trim their hide,
An' Addison, wha deep does wide,
	An' reasons strong,
An' whirls them roun' an' lays their pride
	An' shows their wrong.

There's Books by Bishops, Deans an' Rectors,
Some gay an' true, and some conjectures,
Wi' Novels walth, an' Select Lectures,
	By some great guns,
An' some cram'd fu' o' ghaists an' spectres,
	An' bleedin Nuns.

To name ilk Book, I manna fa';
There's scores an' dizens, in a ra'
'Bout chiels wha sail'd far, far awa'
	Round a' the world,
Through fields o' ice an' hills o' sna',
	An' seen whales barrel'd.

Encyclopædia, volumes ten,
Wi' pictures bra' o' beasts and men,
Read it, if ye wad a' things ken,
	Wi' care an' patience;
Hume, Smollet, Whitefield, Life o' Pen,
	An' *Wealth of Nations.*

> There's Books by Pope and Fontenelle
> And Travels lang, by Manderell [sic];
> There's Sterne's works, an' Marmontell
> > An' *Humphry Clinker,*
> An' ane that does ilk Parish tell,
> > By Sir John Sinclair.
>
> ...
>
> There may be some will think I'm wrang,
> For this dull, doited, dry harangue,
> Wi' scribbling too, sae driegh an' lang,
> > I'm haflins starvin,
> Bedsies [sic], my muse has lost the fang,
> > Your humble servant,
>
> > Finis

The books listed in this 'catalogue' would not disgrace any much larger subscription library (though the presence of the freethinker Voltaire might be questionable in more conservative libraries) and provide almost a duffer's guide to basic Enlightenment texts. Indeed, this listing would tend to confirm the view that many subscription libraries were aiming to collect the 'canonical' writers of the time. The presence of fiction shows that the library was not catering solely for those seeking education, but the works chosen are clearly the better sort of fiction.

Dalkeith's stock selection might be compared to that of the Beith Library, which had acquired just sixty-two titles by the time of its 1818 catalogue. It had presumably only recently been formed. The stock included works of Maria Edgeworth, George Crabbe, Edward Gibbon, Samuel Johnson, and Tobias Smollett, as well as *Waverley,* Alain Le Sage's *Gil Blas,* and Laurence Sterne's *Tristram Shandy,* a much different fare to that at Dalkeith. But the inclusion at Beith of the *Encyclopedia Britannica* (third edition in eighteen volumes), Daniel Neal's *History of the Puritans,* and Charles Rollin's *Ancient History* does at least point to some higher aspirations.

An anonymous English traveller who visited Scotland in 1815 has left a useful, if condescending, account of a library in Covington, Lanarkshire, founded in about 1800:

> My host and his neighbours were well informed, and well bred. B. wished to pass them off to me as samples of the Scottish country people; but I found out that they considered their parish as much more enlightened than any which surrounded it. ... About fifteen years since, some spirited young men formed a society for the purchase of books, and their library now contains a well-selected

collection of the most valuable standard works of the English language. A glance at the catalogue at once shows that the books have been chosen by Scotsmen, from the prevalence of Scottish authors. The first purchases were the works of these great men who raised the Scotish [sic] literary character so high in the last century: [Allan] Ramsay, [Adam] Ferguson, [David] Hume, [Adam] Smith, [Hugh] Blair, [William] Robertson, [Lord] Kames, &c. and the recent purchases exhibit an equally brilliant combination of great names: [Thomas?] Campbell, [James] Grahame, [Walter] Scott, [Dugald] Stewart, [John or Alexander?] Wilson, [Archibald] Alison, [James] Hogg &c. I spent some time in the library, in converse with the worthy *Dominie*, who has been 'master' nearly 40 years. He told me that there was scarcely an adult in the parish, even to the ploughman and mechanic, who was not acquainted with the writings and the authors I have enumerated; and that the population was so far literary that there was one winter a club instituted, the members of which, ploughmen, weavers, &c. were each in succession to read an essay of their own composition – and a respectable M.S. volume was *produced* by these rustic literati.[213]

The establishment of small – and sometimes longer-lived – subscription libraries by working men became more frequent after 1800. The Paisley Trades Library (1806) competed against the Paisley Library Society, but only cost six shillings per year and had no shares; it lasted about forty years and possessed about 1,000 volumes by 1823. The exclusive Ayr Library, too, was challenged by an upstart workers' library, the Ayr, Newton, and Wallacetown Library, also founded in 1806. Unusually for a workers' library, its subscribers signed a contract for five years at a time, just as members of the middle-class Kelso and Duns libraries had done, though in their case for ten years. Its members contained cabinet-makers, shoemakers, the head constable of Ayr, a brewer, a beer-dealer, hairdresser, coal merchant, and the minister of The Tabernacle. But this library was less successful than its more upper-class neighbour, with only 35 members and 100 titles by 1814 and 300 volumes in 1826, when it dissolved. Also of limited success was the Peterhead Subscription Circulating Library, established in about 1799 for the working classes. It charged a subscription of five shillings for six months but was 'about to be given up' in 1815, when the more expensive (at one guinea per year), but more successful, Peterhead Reading Society had existed for seven years.[214]

The Dunfermline Tradesmen's Library was established in 1808 by four young journeymen weavers, William Carnegie, Richard Gosman, and Charles

---

[213] *Letters from Scotland*, pp. 149-50.

[214] James Arbuthnot, *Historical Account of Peterhead* (Aberdeen, 1815), pp. 78-79.

Anderson, all from Moodie Street, and William Anderson of Nethertown (there were over 900 handlooms in the town). They pooled their own books, perhaps not at first an inspiring collection. One of its detractors recalled its early aims:

> The leading members of our little body were rather of an exclusive caste. With them poetry found little favour, novels were at a discount, and the drama was out of the question. Hume's *England* had to be approached with great caution. Our first librarian had a copy of Sterne's *Sentimental Journey* in his chest, but so convinced was he it was not fit for vulgar eyes that nothing would convince him to give us a glimpse even of its exterior.[215]

The few books were originally only lent out on the first Monday of each month, and afterwards their librarian, Charles Anderson, 'was left with a surplus, which, in a single row, reached about half across his mother's drawershead'. But because the mother objected to books cluttering her house and apparently also to late-night meetings held there by the members, the library had to be moved frequently through the streets to temporary locations, including the Victoria Lodging House. One such removal was described by a participant, James Aitken, who recalled how the members had

> brought with them for the purpose of expediting the work a new *backet*. The books were carefully removed and packed into this portable machine, and the remainder, for which there was not room in the backet, were borne in their aprons. A stranger procession never marshalled in the streets of Dunfermline than walked on that night from Moodie Street to Nethertown. Comparatively unobserved the backet and the tucked-up aprons went steadily on, the chief actors thinking not that there was anything grotesque in this utilitarian method of adapting means to ends. They had only one end in view – the success of their little library, and thereby the diffusion of knowledge.[216]

The Tradesmen's Library grew slowly, and its cheaply (and execrably) printed catalogue of 1823 only shows 107 titles, of which thirty-three were novels. Twenty-five were history and biography. (The catalogue was the handiwork of a local teacher, William Meldrum, who practised printing in his spare time.) One unforeseen obstacle was a rule that after ten years' membership, a subscriber need only pay sixpence per quarter; this rule was never abolished and was to restrict the finances for many years. Yet by 1826 it

---

[215] Andrew S. Robertson, *History of Dunfermline Tradesmen's and Mechanics' Library* (Dunfermline, 1914), pp. 12-13.

[216] Robertson, *Dunfermline Tradesmen's ... Library*, pp. 19-20.

boasted ninety-five members and took over the Mechanics' Institute in 1832, and the Subscription Library of 1789 (which itself had ninety-two members by 1815), before amalgamating with the Municipal Library in 1883. The Tradesmen's Library brought 4,000 volumes to the new Municipal Library, which was opened in 1883. The foundation stone had been laid in 1881 by the widow of William Carnegie, co-founder of the Tradesmen's Library. The new public library had of course been donated by their son, the philanthropist Andrew Carnegie.

The key to the Tradesmen's Library's success was put down to the overnight acclaim of *Waverley* in 1814, and the extraordinary enthusiasm that greeted the succeeding volumes in the series, as has already been seen in the case of circulating libraries. Many proprietary libraries (and not just workers' libraries) put in blanket orders for future novels by 'The author of *Waverley*', and a shift away from wall-to-wall non-fiction begins. In 1815 the committee of the Kirkcudbright Library minuted:

> Having observed in the Newspapers a Book advertised for sale titled *Guy Mannering* said to be wrote by the same person who was the Author of *Waverley* and understood to be a publication of great merit, and considering that Books of that description are of more value to the Subscribers if purchased at an early period, they do hereby instruct the Librarian to purchase the said Book and to take credits in the accounts for the same.

The committee of the Wigtown Library ordered their treasurer in 1820 to continue ordering the works of 'The author of *Waverley*', as published. In the 1820s and '30s, 'reading parties' became popular, where families or workmen clubbed together to buy Scott's novels to read aloud and then sell to the highest bidder.[217] In Dunfermline, local weavers formed reading clubs to borrow the novels from a bookseller at sixpence per volume for two days. A member would be appointed as official 'reader'; one such person was a William Houston, 'who appears to have possessed rather superior abilities in this direction'.[218]

As in the Dunfermline Tradesmen's Library, small acorns could lead to extremely robust and long-lived oaks. Such was the Kinross Tradesmen's Library (1824) membership of which cost only a shilling per share and sixpence per quarter. Books hostile to Christianity or the constitution were banned. 423 titles had been acquired by 1841, and 2,400 volumes by 1910; it still existed in the 1930s. Other 'trades' libraries are found in Saltcoats, Langholm, Dysart, and Greenock, as well as in Hawick and Paisley. A similar workers' library was

---

[217] Bertram, *Some Memories*, pp. 103-4.

[218] Robertson, *Dunfermline Tradesmen's ... Library*, p. 22.

the Banff Literary Society, begun in 1810 by a handful of young men with lofty aims:

> To pursue with steadiness the paths of literature is a praiseworthy design. Sensible of the advantages which result from such a pursuit some young men wished, if possible, without much expense to acquire a fund sufficient for that purpose and the formation of a library, sensible also that such a design only required a beginning and then it would glide on in prosperity. These Five viz. Lewis Wm Forbes, Alex^r Smith, James Ogilvie, James Robertson & William Bartlett, met, in a room generously given for the purpose by Mr Thos Ogilvie, on October 6th [1810] at Banff.

A contract was signed by the founding members, and by one new recruit, and each paid a few pennies. Admission was not automatic: 'Alex^r Gordon was proposed but some scruples arising the motion for his admission was deferred'. He was later admitted, but James Tulloch, clerk of the Banff brewery, was decisively rejected. The first book for the library was a donation of poetry by George Forbes, Esq. The library increased steadily through gifts, but the club had other aims as well. During its early years there were discussions at its weekly meetings, some of which were held in Aberdeen. Regular 'harangues' were delivered, but in 1811 the rules were clarified to make it clear that the club was intended to be a permanent library society, and not just a debating club. The cost was now twopence per week and three shillings *per annum*. New members included a surgeon, the sheriff substitute, and the rector of the academy; and the Earl of Fife became Patron. Their room was provided by the town council.

The 'harangues' soon began to cause trouble. In 1811 the President was accused, but acquitted, of writing a speech for someone else to deliver, while two members delivered discourses copied *verbatim* from a book – unfortunately they had both copied from the identical essay. Their papers were burnt, and they were reprimanded. But the offence was repeated, and the criminal was fined as well: 'After this sentence', according to the minutes, 'a most irregular conversation ensued in the course of which Mr Findlater [the perpetrator] used such expressions as rendered it necessary to order him to lodge written excuses with the secretary before Wednesday at 12 noon'. He was judged to have committed a malicious libel against the officers, but was allowed to continue as a member.

The seriousness with which the members took their society was demonstrated in 1812 when Alexander Chambers, who had been expelled from the society during the previous year, requested that he be regarded as having resigned rather than expelled. The reason was that he wished to join a medical society in Aberdeen and so did not want a black mark against his character. The response was that he was putting the affairs of another society first, and that his offer to pay unpaid fines was a bribe. The Banff society did agree to consider his case further when it was pointed out that Chambers, a medical student, was therefore expected to join medical societies.

The debates covered all manner of topics, including painting, female education, nature, philosophy, and solitude versus society (solitude won, 13-7), but after several years the discussions were dropped as the library became more significant. As early as 1813 it was agreed to borrow books from the local circulating library, run by James Imlach, for the benefit of society members. This may be the earliest example of a Scottish subscription library using its funds to borrow current literature, rather than purchase the same for posterity. This was to become a common practice later in the century. Also by 1813 the society possessed a reading room, and thought was being given to permit subscribers to that room only. By 1819 the library possessed 1,400 volumes and was a success, partly because of the enthusiasm and beneficence of its noble patron, the Earl of Fife. Eventually the library was kept in the Town House and had acquired 6,000 volumes by 1891. It then merged with the public library.

The role of John Millar in encouraging and publicizing workers' libraries has already been noted. But he was not the only promoter of such libraries. Another Millar, James Millar, was an Elgin industrialist who had been involved in aiding beggars in Edinburgh. He devised a scheme for book societies which he circulated several years before it first appeared in book form in 1818.[219] James Millar believed that libraries of books on useful arts 'would contribute much to diminish the number of those deluded persons who frequent tippling clubs'. He suggested that twenty people should unite and contribute sixpence a week, a paltry sum for a drinker. The resultant £26 per year would produce: £6 as rent for library rooms; £6 for three weekly newspapers, one of which would be from London; £10 for magazines and other periodicals; and £10 for useful books. He presumed that the members would possess books of their own to initiate a common stock, and that donations could be solicited. The newspapers could be sold off at half-price, and non-members could be admitted for twopence to pay for coal and candle. Also, the members could probably afford 6s.6d. as entry money, which could be used for further purchases. Indeed, he computed that twenty persons paying just threepence per week would be sufficient to start a viable book society.

Members of such a society would, claimed Millar, have risen above their neighbours by the end of a year, unlike the Bacchanalians, and they would certainly impress their wives and children with their increased knowledge.

---

[219] James Millar, *The Funding System*, 1st edn. (Stirling, 1818), 3rd edn. (Glasgow, 1824), pp. 57-62, 'Plan of a Literary Club'.

Millar went further than other library promoters by advocating the provision of beds. He envisaged the libraries as operating like a club, with members of one being permitted to use the facilities of another. He proposed a 'diploma' that members would carry with them:

> The bearer hereof, Mr ---, member of the library club, No. ---, of the town, village, or parish of ---, intends to travel on business to ---, and being honest and respectable in his sphere, is entitled to the best bed in your apartments, for lodgings, at 4d. each night: He is also entitled to amuse himself with your books and newspapers, and to have pen, ink, and paper, supplied him, on paying for the latter. Your housekeeper is bound also to furnish him with a bason of water and clean towel, to clean his boots for one penny more, and to put a comfortable fire in his bed-room, should the season require it, at 2d. or 3d. as the circumstances of your place will permit.
>
> N.B. The passenger is expected to impart all his news, and to give an account of any books, scheme, or improvement, which may be calculated to promote the interest of your club and neighbourhood.

A similar 'diploma' would be available to members who paid a lower subscription and who would be entitled to

> the second best bed in your apartments for lodgers, and also to the privileges of your library, at half the charge aforesaid. ... The honest soldier, who lost his leg in the late war, and who lives rent free in your premises for the trouble his wife has in keeping your apartments clean and in good order, can supply him with bread, butter, cheese, &c. ... and he can have his tea infused from their kettle ... till such time as he gets into permanent employment and lodgings.

A third diploma would enable the 'honest veteran' to receive a free bed and allow him to send out for a gill of spirits or one bottle of ale (but no more). James Millar evidently wished to combine his interest in tackling mendacity with a desire to disseminate knowledge. There is no evidence that such clubs came into being, and yet it would be unwise to dismiss the influence that such writings may have had in their time.

Some manufacturers provided libraries for their workers, as at Rothesay, mentioned above, or in Renton, Dunbartonshire, where William Stirling established a library for the workers at his calico-printing works. Robert Owen, too, included a library in his plan for a school and factory at New Lanark.[220] An example of a factory library for workers run on similar lines to a subscription

---

[220] *The Times*, 29 May & 9 August 1817.

library was the Glasgow Gas Workmen's Library in Kirk Street. This began on 29 October 1821 and cost 7s.6d. entry plus one and a half pence per week; the entry money was refundable if a member quit or died. Books were initially for reference only, but after two years borrowing was allowed at weekends. The rationale for encouraging working men to read improving books was laid out interestingly, if effusively, in its regulations:

> It is universally admitted, that Ignorance is the greatest source of all the crimes and all the misery with which human nature is disgraced. Man cannot always be engaged in labour: relaxation is necessary to renew his strength, and to prepare him again for labour. In these hours the ignorant man, whose mind is vacant and unoccupied, cannot remain alone; solitude is to him unbearable; he seeks society, and of course the society of such as himself; they have nothing to engage their attention, nothing to supply them with conversation: the tavern, therefore, and the gaming table, are their only resources; and to these, and to every species of dissipation and debauchery, they fly for relief.
>
> But if ignorance is thus productive of evil, assuredly knowledge, crude or ill digested, or a love of it ill directed, is equally so.

The Glasgow Gas Workmen's Library was proposed by the works' manager, James Beaumont Neilson (1792-1865), who provided a room for the workers to read and converse instead of going to the tavern, with occasional lectures which members' sons could attend. About half of the workforce of sixty to seventy became members, the remainder claiming that they could not read. A well-directed institution was the key to improving the morals and intellect of the working man, according to its promoter, and its sentiments informed the efforts not just of well-meaning employers but of self-help institutes, as most workers' libraries were. This particular library was praised by Timothy Claxton in his *Hints to Mechanics* (1839), which provided further publicity about the virtues of libraries to mechanics interested in self-help. The most influential promoter of workers' libraries, however, was Lord Brougham, whose popular pamphlet, *Practical Observations upon the Education of the People*, inspired the rapid spread of mechanics' institutes throughout Great Britain after 1825. Brougham was particularly interested in bringing the benefits of libraries to working men, and he lauded the creation of book societies as well as the example of Rev. Samuel Brown's itinerating libraries scheme (of which more later).[221] Nevertheless, he was the recipient of considerable antagonism for his support of mechanics' institutes; education for the workers was unwelcome to many.

---

[221] Henry Brougham, *Practical Observations upon the Education of the People* (London, 1825), pp. 6-7.

The coming of mechanics' institutes led to an increasing demand to found libraries for the working classes. There had been forerunners, such as the Glasgow North Quarter Library, founded in or about 1819, which claimed to be the only library in Glasgow to allow access to books for mechanics; it enjoyed free use of a schoolroom.[222] An enormous success story was the Edinburgh Mechanics' Subscription Library, established as a library rather than a mechanics' institute in March 1825 by three dissatisfied members of the Edinburgh School of Arts, which contained a library for mechanics. They were supported by donations from several booksellers, who obviously saw future profit for themselves since they urged, successfully, that the library, intended for the working men of the city, should include all literature, not solely science. Originally only open for an hour or two a week, it acquired 352 members within five years and soon opened throughout the day and evening. Costing a mere five shillings for a share and six shillings *per annum*, it had 18,000 volumes by 1850. It was located in a back street basement:

> The library which is attained by a back stair, dimly lighted, and ever thronged, owes much of its success to its economical management, if not to its unobtrusive and silent operations. Its chief defect is the want of a reading-room, or convenience for examining the works known only by the titles, before they are conveyed from the premises; but as novels and light literature form two-thirds of the issues, this desideratum has not been obtained, although frequently demanded.[223]

It merged with the Edinburgh Literary Institute in 1892, when it possessed 22,000 volumes, but was dissolved in 1899. In contrast the Perth Mechanics' Library (1824) had only acquired 130 volumes by 1830, but a creditable 11,000 volumes had been amassed by 1897; the books passed to the Sandeman Library in 1900, though not the many worn-out novels which by then had become the staple fare of the library.[224]

Rules and Regulations

Whether a library was a commercial circulating or a proprietary subscription library, rules had to be observed to protect the investment from damage or dispersal. In the Orkney Library (1815), anyone trying to dissolve the library was to be resisted by legal means by any individual in

---

[222] *Glasgow Herald*, 17 July 1820.

[223] W. Hudson, *The History of Adult Education* (London, 1851), pp. 200-1.

[224] Aitken, *Public Library Movement*, pp. 309-10.

Orkney or by the Procurator-Fiscal in the rest of the country.[225] In the Falkirk Library (1792), anyone who proposed selling the Library, or 'mutilating' it by partial sale, was to be expelled; books could only be sold if they were to be replaced. The Arbroath and Penicuik (both 1797) libraries could only be dissolved in the event of an unanimous vote. At Peterhead (1808) a proposal was made as early as 1812 to dissolve the library, while a counter-proposal was put that members wishing to retire should receive a proportion of the books; but these moves were resisted.

Books were for the exclusive use of subscribers and their families, which applied equally to circulating and subscription libraries, though, as has been shown above, some libraries relaxed their rules to accommodate more casual users, such as French prisoners of war at Selkirk and servants in Duns. Books could not be lent to non-subscribers: 'it is not thought reasonable that others should profit at the expence of the generous few' was the rule at Montrose. There were fines for late return of books; at Montrose it was sixpence per day. (The original rules of the Montrose Library are printed as Appendix 1.) At Dundee Public Library in 1798,

> Alex[ande]r Simson was impeached by the Librarian for lending a book [viz. to a non-member] but it appearing that the person to whom he had entrusted to carry it to the Library had stolen a reading of it without his knowledge or consent the committee agreed to acquit him.[226]

But another member in the same year had to pay a penny for each of the thirty-two nights a friend had been reading library books. In the Greenock Library, the fine was half-a-crown for lending to a non-subscriber, and one shilling for receiving a book from any person other than the librarian.

Arrears were always a problem; many people joined a library to show support but failed to maintain their interest. In 1773, after less than five years of existence, the Duns Library was owed £25.12s. by laggardly subscribers. In 1780 summonses were issued against members of the Kirkcudbright Library who had not paid their dues; nine were struck off in 1781. Book purchases had to be curtailed until their income was recovered; in 1790 £32.2s.6d. was owing, a significant sum. Prosecution was threatened against any non-subscriber found with one of the library's books in their possession.[227] The problem never went away; in 1822 £35.5s. was owing to the same library, while in 1808 over £46 was owed at the Kilmarnock Library, where fifteen subscribers were struck off in 1816 for non-payment. Similar problems were encountered in Wigtown

---

[225] Orkney Library catalogue (1816).

[226] From the minute book of the Dundee Public Library (Dundee Central Library).

[227] *Dumfries Weekly Journal*, 18 March 1794.

Subscription Library, where in 1798 a majority of subscribers had not paid for the previous year, while fines for overdue books had been incurred but none paid. Several subscribers were written off in 1799; and in 1807 no books could be bought for lack of income. When their treasurer resigned in 1813, he was pressed to remain because of his zeal for the library, despite his uneasiness at the state of the finances.

Most libraries in rural towns drew their membership from people who lived some distance away, though limits were often set. The Greenock Library in 1808 decreed that no new subscriber should live more than six miles away 'or in places to which water carriage is necessary'. However, an exception was made on health grounds for Dr Morrison; he lived on the Isle of Bute. At Stirling's Library, Glasgow, membership was open to anyone residing within ten miles. The rules of Kilmarnock Public Library insisted that no books could be removed outside Ayrshire. In the Kirkcudbright Library members who lived more than ten miles away were allowed an extra week's reading time (though this was soon reduced to three miles), and its committee included a balance of town and country members. Members of this library living at a distance also caused problems if they failed to pay their subscriptions on time. In 1779 four members had still not paid for 1777, and twenty were outstanding from 1778. The cashier, Thomas McMillan (who was also rector of the school for twenty-seven years), complained that he could not collect money from those far away.

Missing books were another serious issue. Frequently the librarian took the blame. In most libraries books would be called in for an annual inspection. At Greenock the librarian was sacked in 1794 over missing volumes but was permitted arrears of salary because of his distressed condition. In 1816 the Renton Subscription Library's committee blamed their previous librarian, who had left five years earlier, for eighteen books lent out but now considered irrecoverable; his account was ordered to be debited. The Duns Library catalogue of 1789 listed no less than forty-five volumes which members had not returned, including the apposite *Memoirs of a Social Monster,* written by the forger, Charles Price; by 1798 seventy volumes and a number of periodicals were missing. Occasionally the loss of books was advertised in local newspapers, as when several books went 'amissing' from Tain Public Library in 1823, while the 1820 catalogue of Rothesay Library included a list of strayed items. In Arbroath more than 200 volumes were lost over the years.

Rules for circulating libraries were just as detailed as those for subscription libraries, of course, and the regulations of Alexander Davidson's library in Inverness have already been given (see p. 63). Loss of stock was just as common a problem as for subscription libraries. The following dire warning appeared from William Brown of Dundee, who was trying to sell his library in 1794 but had failed to persuade customers to return overdue books:

the proprietor will take the necessary steps to compel a restitution of his property, and to expose a species of depredation which, in whatever light it may generally be viewed, has certainly nothing to distinguish it from the crimes of the pickpocket or the highwayman.[228]

When James McLeish retired from his circulating library in Edinburgh in 1808, he deplored the number of books which had not been returned, including Sir Robert Douglas's *Peerage*, William Maitland's *History of Edinburgh*, Hugo Arnot's *Criminal Trials*, and a set of François Rabelais in four volumes, adding that he was

> now under the necessity of intimating, that should any of those who may have Books in their possession fail to return them ..., they will only have themselves to blame for any disagreeable measures he may be compelled to adopt in order to recover their value.[229]

A somewhat more discreet tack was adopted by Alexander Mackay, the heir to Allan Ramsay's circulating library, who in 1825 wrote to an army officer who had failed to return a book after leaving Edinburgh Castle with his regiment for Fort William:

> Sir, On the 16th curr[en]t. you got from this Library a Copy of the '*Pirate* 3 vols. by the Author of Waverly', which, as application has been made at your lodging in the Castle, and at the different Officers of your regiment who read at the Library without finding it, I suppose you must have had packed up by mistake in the hurry of moving. I therefore beg as your subscription to the Library <u>expired on the ni[ne]teenth Curr[en]t.</u> that you will order the book to be returned <u>free of expence</u> [to] conform to the printed conditions that you signed on the ni[ne]teenth August.[230]

William Hunter, who ran a library in Edinburgh by 1824, warned that he would request a deposit if he deemed it necessary: 'When Subscribers are resident in lodgings, this regulation will require to be strictly enforced; for, in such circumstances, from the bustle of departure and other causes, books are always liable to be mislaid and lost'.

Deliberate theft was equally a problem. In 1825 a woman and boy visited various circulating libraries in Edinburgh and borrowed valuable books after presenting slips ostensibly signed by respectable citizens. The books were then sold on. The thefts were not discovered until the librarians began making enquiries from those whose names had been used. Eventually a boy,

---

[228] *Caledonian Mercury*, 4 September 1794.

[229] Ibid., 24 March 1808.

[230] NLS Acc. 6411, Mackay's letterbook, 29 November 1825.

Gilbert Macrae, was apprehended in the act of practising this deception in a library, and his sister was arrested shortly afterwards. Macrae was sentenced to six months in Bridewell after being found guilty on six charges, while a second-hand bookseller was fined two guineas for buying books from the lad in suspicious circumstances.[231] Later in the same year a six-year-old boy was employed to borrow books from a library. On leaving he was induced to enter a nearby building by a woman who took the books, his money (fivepence), and his clothes. Leaving him stripped naked, she tried to sell the book to a stationer, but he saw the library stamps and called a constable. The woman was sentenced to sixty days in Bridewell, and the magistrate regretted he could not sentence her to longer.[232]

Damage was another concern. In Dunfermline Library an enquiry was ordered in 1794 into the turning-down of leaves in books, while George Yule refused to attend a meeting at which he was convicted of damaging James Boswell's *Life of Johnson*; he subsequently left the country. At Arbroath in 1798 Provost Hay and Mr Henderson, the laird of Parkhill, were summoned before the directors for injuring books. The former pleaded guilty and had to repair the book; the latter refused to appear and was fined 2s.6d. In the same year Sir James Lindsay Carnegie, the laird of Kinblethnot, tore a copy of Ann Radcliffe's *The Mysteries of Udolpho* and was ordered to replace it or pay its cost of nineteen shillings.[233] In the Jamestown miners' library in 1794, John Beattie was fined one penny for a blot in a book; six other members had been fined for similar offences in the previous year, which might suggest that the malefactors were using their borrowed books for intensive study. In Stirling's Library, Glasgow, Rev. James Pate, who became librarian in 1796, examined every returned book leaf by leaf, repairing any damage immediately. According to Robert Reid (alias the local Glasgow historian, 'Senex'), 'I have seen ladies stand trembling from top to toe under the scolds of Mr Pate, for having returned books a little spoiled, or with a slight spot of ink'.[234] At Duns, a Mr Bell was ordered to replace *Don Quixote* which he had damaged in 1808. In the following year he compounded his offence by damaging John Adolphus's *George III*, while Lady Betty Gavin had to replace Jean Marmontel's *Memoirs*, which she had lost.

Alexander Mackay of Edinburgh complained in 1824 to a subscriber, Andrew Robertson, along these lines:

---

[231] *Caledonian Mercury*, 21 & 24 March 1825.

[232] Ibid., 24 November 1825.

[233] M'Bain, *Arbroath Public Library*, pp. 11-12.

[234] Mason, *Public and Private Libraries*, p. 64.

> Mr Mackay presents his compliments to Mr Robertson and loses not a moment in noticing to him the great injury he is doing to the books by writing upon them. Mr M. has as yet only examined *St Ronan's Well*, Dr Johnston [sic], and the *Abbot* on all of which he finds writings of Mrs Robertson in blotches with red Ink. On the *Monastery* there is writing with black Ink and Mr R.'s initials signed to it. In consequence of this Mr Robertson is referred to the conditions of the Library at the beginning of the Catalogue particular article 6th thereof.[235]

Many circulating libraries were open for up to twelve hours a day. Smaller working-class libraries usually opened only in the evenings. Kilsyth Reading Society had 200 titles at its opening in 1818, and opened on Mondays and Thursdays, from one hour before to one hour after sunset. The Perth Reading Society opened on Wednesdays from 2 to 3 p.m. and Saturdays from 6 to 8.30 p.m. The Denholm Library originally opened only on Wednesdays from 7 to 9 p.m., and its treasurer was once embarrassed to discover he 'had received a quantity of base money from some members unknown on account of their paying the quarter fees under night; to remedy this evil members residing in the village shall be bound to pay their money sometime in the course of the day, and not under night'. In 1819 the Library decided to open on Wednesdays and Saturdays from 3 to 5 p.m.[236]

Kyleakin Library on the Isle of Skye (1820) opened on Mondays only, while Lochmaben Library opened on Saturdays from 1 to 2 p.m. Opening hours were often restrictive, even when a library possessed its own building. During the whole of its existence the Kelso Library opened only on three days per week for three hours at a time. The Duns Library, which survived into the 1920s, was open for only two and a quarter hours per week by the late nineteenth century; at its foundation it had been open on Wednesdays and Saturdays from 11 a.m. to 2 p.m.[237] However, when the Montrose Library began in 1785 in a hired room, members were permitted to have a key cut at their own expense. The older-established libraries tended to open in the middle of the day, often on market days, since many members found it most convenient to visit when they had other business to attend to. Since a number of libraries might keep their books in a schoolhouse or even a private home, extended opening hours were not always feasible.

---

[235] NLS Acc. 6411, Mackay's letterbook, 18 May 1824.

[236] W. F. Cuthbertson, 'An Old Denholm Book', *Hawick Archaeological Society Transactions* (1933), 19-24.

[237] *Transactions & Proceedings of the 3rd Annual Meeting of the Library Association of the United Kingdom ... Edinburgh, 1880* (London, 1881), p. 159.

Stock Selection and Ordering

Although the character of subscription libraries was to change during the early nineteenth century, when more and more fiction was acquired, the intention of all the eighteenth-century foundations was, as at Perth, to acquire non-fiction, both newly-published and works of 'proven' value. The Perth Library's stated 'brief' was to acquire, in general, books on trade, commerce, and manufacture, English translations of the classics, local histories, and the best modern poets and dramatic writers. The rules of the contemporary Montrose Library (1785) did allow one concession: 'No Romances to be admitted, unless presented, or when a particular exception is made in favour of a work of superior excellence, such as Miss Burney's *Cecilia*'. In 1814, its year of publication, the library purchased Jane Austen's (anonymous) *Mansfield Park*.

The Peterhead Reading Society (1808) also insisted that its members should only suggest works of true value and resolved additionally that 'only English Books are to be admitted; That Novels and other triffling [sic] books, which excite only a temporary Interest, are exceedingly improper'. The rule against novels was, though, soon amended in practice, though not until 1821 were the rules altered to permit 'works of imagination' to be bought; but foreign books were still excluded, as were mere reference works, such as dictionaries, books on law and medicine, and anything that was profane or immoral.

The Peterhead Society also had an original rule 'that very high priced editions, bindings and other unnecessary causes of Expence to the Society are most scrupulously to be avoided'. It must be remembered that libraries had to budget not just for buying books but for binding – or re-binding – them. At this period, books were often published unbound. In the Edinburgh Subscription Library, all books had to be half-bound, lettered and numbered, and any plates stamped, before they could be issued. At the Penicuik Library (1797) books were to be bound and covered with pasteboard. In Edinburgh the prices charged for binding books with calf backs for circulating libraries (which probably would have applied to private subscription libraries too) were fixed in 1814: demy folios 4s.8d., demy quartos 2s.7d., thick octavo magazines 1s.6d., common octavos 1s.2d., 'Demy Twelvemos' eightpence, and 'Demy Eighteenmo.' sevenpence. The same prices also applied in Glasgow and Paisley, and probably elsewhere.[238]

John McAdam, future propagandist for Italian unity, recalled that in the mid-1820s he was indebted for 'an early perusal of the newest publications ... to poor old Thomas Templeton, bookbinder to a large circulating library – boy hearted, foolish old man. Years after, he was executed for killing his

---

[238] *Edinburgh Binders' Prices ... 1814*, p. 12; *Glasgow and Paisley Binders' Prices ... 1815*, p. 12.

wife in a drunken frenzy'.[239] Templeton's business was located in Hutcheson Street, Glasgow, and this anecdote suggests that he might have worked for John Smith's library in the same street and whose extensive collection would have meant plenty of employment for a binder.

Ordering books was a formal matter, sometimes reserved for a monthly or quarterly general meeting, or else suggestions could be agreed by a committee. In many cases, a library's president (or preses) might be delegated to order books in consultation with other committee members. At the Renton Subscription Library in 1801, the librarian was criticized for buying several books without authorization, including Mungo Park's *Travels*. These purchases had to be approved subsequently by its committee, whereas at Duns in 1807 George Chalmers's *Caledonia*, rejected at a selection meeting but ordered anyway, had to be returned to their bookseller. In the Peterhead Reading Society, members were entitled to request books up to the value of their subscription; if they failed to do so within three months (subsequently reduced to one month), the library's committee could do so instead. Furthermore, it was impressed on the members that it was their duty 'to propose for purchase such Books *only* as are known to be, or at any rate, such as there is every probability of being valuable'.

In most libraries, books were available on arrival to the member who had requested them first, but might 'lie on the table' for a month for inspection by others. In 1800 at Arbroath it was decreed that no person should have a preference in choosing a book simply by speaking to the librarian first; instead, it depended on who entered the room first before speaking to the librarian. This was to prevent unseemly scenes if a book in demand was returned while several people were already in the room! In the Montrose Library, if a member found a book was out, he could write his name and the date in the register to ensure he had the preference when the book was returned. Subscribers had to collect books themselves and not send servants, though a book could be delivered by a fellow-member. This rule was eventually relaxed, because in 1821 it was resolved that the Montrose Library should open from 12 noon to 2 p.m. instead of from 1 to 3 p.m., since it was inconvenient for the servants and carriers of country subscribers to wait in the town until 1 p.m. In 1820 it was reported at the Selkirk Library that 'on many occasions a kind of warfare was kept up at the Library door by individuals sent by subscribers, and even amongst subscribers themselves, as to who should first gain admittance'.[240] The same problem of precedence affected circulating libraries: in 1823 Isaac Forsyth

---

[239] *Autobiography of John McAdam (1806-1883)*, edited by Janet Fyfe, Scottish History Society, 4th ser. 16 (Edinburgh, 1980), p. 3; cf. *Morning Chronicle* (30 May 1840) for the execution.

[240] Quoted in: Alan Carter, *The History and Development of the Library Services of Galashiels and Selkirkshire* (unpublished MA thesis, Strathclyde University, 1975), p. 64.

of Elgin insisted that he used a separate register to record who had ordered new books first to ensure *'impartiality* and *dispatch* in their circulation'.[241]

In the Paisley Library Society, books were voted on at general meetings held every two months, and the committee of twelve had to ensure that the list of books for consideration amounted in value to one third more than the available funds. Books were then voted on and bought according to the votes received, until the funds were exhausted. Ladies could vote by proxy, as was the custom in all libraries; but they were not prevented from voting in person.

Books were usually supplied from Edinburgh but sometimes from London. In 1798 James Lackington offered the Arbroath Library a discount of over 10%. Lackington was also supplying the Montrose Library by 1811, particularly with French books, though many other books were provided by a local bookseller, George Murray, at trade price. In 1814 it was computed that the saving in buying books at trade price was about £14, equivalent to the librarian's salary plus heating. Perth Library used its local booksellers, the Morisons, as well as Archibald Constable in Edinburgh. Some booksellers went to extraordinary lengths to satisfy their customers. In about 1821, the Dysart Subscription Library in Fife ordered a copy of John Moore's *Travels in Italy* from Robert Chambers in Edinburgh. However, the copy supplied was deficient in four leaves. Having only just started in business, Chambers was anxious not to lose the sale and supplied the deficiency himself: 'With a crow pen he wrote in a manner to resemble print the missing eight pages. The pages supplied by him are quite as easily read as the rest of the text, and the whole transaction offers a good example of the energy of purpose and perseverance which characterised his successful career.'[242]

Although many booksellers undoubtedly strove hard to keep their library customers, equally many libraries presumed upon their suppliers and expected favours to retain their custom. Charles Elliot of Edinburgh supplied both Selkirk and Hawick libraries in the 1770s and 1780s. In September 1774 Elliot wrote diplomatically to the Selkirk Library:

> The Deadness of this Season of the year, when every body is out of Town, and the Backward payments in General of the Times makes me often apply to my freinds [sic], when I could wish not to do it, if it was convenient to you to settle the old account or part of it would greatly oblige, having very large sums to pay this vacation & very little prospect of getting any money in during a Time which

---

[241] *Aberdeen Journal*, 8 October 1823.

[242] Chambers, *Memoir*, p. 173.

most of People are out of Town. Your Complying with the above if it suits you will very much oblige.[243]

A few weeks later, Elliot sent a list of books he could supply for £9.10s., including Lord Bolingbroke's *Works* in eleven volumes, Gilbert Stuart's *English Constitution*, Conyers Middleton's *Life of Cicero*, and Marcus Antoninus's *Meditations*. He also offered an edition of Voltaire in twenty-four volumes which was cheaper and more complete than the London edition of thirty-six volumes. He explained that the former was 'one of the finest Irish editions', with the saving being £2.5s.[244]

As for the Hawick Library, in 1773 they settled a bill for £17, for which Elliot gave a discount of eighteen shillings; he also printed their catalogues.[245] Writing to them in 1775 Elliot explained that 'I have added all the new which I think will be much read both by Clergy and Laity. I shall with the first opportunity send you a present of Lord Chesterfields *Letters* 4 Vol which I hope will be accepted off'. And in 1776 Elliot immediately deducted 9s.8d. from his bill for a book by Beaven (probably Thomas Beaven on *Primitive Christianity*), to which an objection had been raised, 'which [I] hope will satisfy all concerned, it being my outmost [sic] wish to please, and greatest happiness when all my friends are pleased'. Clearly Elliot aimed to be as amenable as possible, and he even suggested more books which the library should order, such as 'Dr Smith's new book' (i.e. *Wealth of Nations*), the *Border History* by George Ridpath, and Edward Gibbon's *Decline and Fall*.[246]

Relations turned frosty in 1779 when Elliot came to feel ill-used by the Hawick Library. Their custom was to send him lists of books with the lowest prices marked which they had gathered from Edinburgh sale catalogues; Elliot himself claimed not to have read all the catalogues and so objected to being told what prices the library was prepared to pay. Elliot insisted that he provided a better service than his rivals. His position was that when libraries started up, they would naturally order a lot of books, but afterwards they would only request a small number each year. Elliot's accounts suggest that the Hawick and Selkirk libraries sometimes ordered less than £15 worth of books in a year each. Further, those books ordered would be popular works published in London for which Elliot paid London prices and made little profit.[247] What upset him most was that the Hawick Library demanded he should print their catalogue for free in order to retain their custom. He would not accept these

---

[243] NLS, MS. 43090, C. Elliot's letterbooks, 15 September 1774.

[244] NLS, MS. 43090, C. Elliot's letterbooks, 9 December 1774.

[245] NLS, MS. 43098, C. Elliot's ledgers, 21 July 1772, April 1773, etc.

[246] NLS, MS. 43090, C. Elliot's letterbooks, 20 February 1775, 11 April 1776.

[247] NLS, MS. 43092, C. Elliot's letterbooks, 13 January 1779.

terms, but indicated that he might present some books 'being very unwilling to Differ with the members of the Hawick Library'. Eventually peace was made, and in April 1779 Elliot could write to James Sibbald that 'I am again installed Bookseller to the worshipful Hawic [sic] Library after no little altercation'.[248] At that time Sibbald was working in London as Elliot's agent, and a letter from Elliot shows him giving instructions about what not to buy: 'I have a [William] Guthrie's *World* unless Foxe's is Dog Cheap don't buy[;] it is the Cheapest copy of Hollingshead [viz. Raphael Holinshed's *Chronicle*] complete but not the Black letter copy I want for the Hawic Library[;] also the cheapest of [Philemon] Holland['s] *Pliny* could you not get them in Exchange ...[;] unless they are bargains I think it would be foolish in the Library to buy such books'.[249]

Elliot also supplied the Hawick Library with periodicals, for whose non-appearance he was chased from time to time, writing for instance to the library in January 1780: 'The *Annual Register* 1778 is not yet arrived although I have mine coming by land at a very great expence, which is not the case w[ith] most of my Neighbours so soon as possible you shall have yours'.[250] But relations deteriorated again when Elliot sent the Hawick Library a threatening letter in 1786: 'This accompanies a circular letter which I now find necessary to send to all my bad Debtors which I consider the Hawick Library one of the most ungrateful'. He demanded payment with interest at once, or else they should supply him with the names of committee members, presumably so that he could threaten them. It would appear that they owed him the grand sum of £3.6s., though he was also niggled that he had spent £1.12s. out of his own pocket in printing their catalogue.[251]

The Duns Library (1768) originally employed Alexander Donaldson of Edinburgh as their bookseller, but, after comparing prices, decided that Kincaid & Bell were cheaper. By 1783 they were employing James Dickson of Edinburgh. They pointed out to him that Donaldson had made a very handsome gift of books when he ceased to be their supplier and suggested that Dickson do the same if he wished 'a further Continuance of the Library's business'. The business of the Duns Library had migrated to Bell (later Bell & Bradfute, successors to Kincaid & Bell) by 1787,[252] and the same firm served the Wigtown Library by 1800.[253]

---

[248] NLS, MS. 43092, C. Elliot's letterbooks, 17 & 25 February, & 8 April 1779.

[249] NLS, MS. 43092, C. Elliot's letterbooks, 26 April 1779.

[250] NLS, MS. 43093, Elliot's letterbooks, 4 January 1780.

[251] NLS, MS. 43096, Elliot's letterbooks, 13 December 1786.

[252] NLS, Dep. 317/1, Bell & Bradfute correspondence, 2 May 1787.

[253] NLS, Acc. 10662/17, Bell & Bradfute correspondence, 29 January 1800.

The Jamestown miners' library used the Edinburgh bookseller Peter Hill in the 1790s and received 8% discount for cash.[254] Hill also served Wanlockhead Library and was employed by Robert Burns on behalf of the Monkland Friendly Society, a permanent subscription library (in intention if not in name), established at Dunscore in 1789 by Captain Robert Riddell of Glen Riddel. Burns acted as 'treasurer, librarian, and censor to this little society',[255] and his letters to Hill provide a fascinating and rare view of how a small subscription library commenced. On 2 April 1789 Burns wrote to Hill:

> The library scheme that I mentioned to you is already begun, under the direction of Capt[n]. Riddell, & ME! There is another in emulation of it, going on at Closeburn, under the auspices of M[r] [viz. Rev. James Stuart] Mentieth of Closeburn, which will be on a greater scale than ours; I have likewise secured it for you [i.e. as a customer]. Capt[n] R. gave his infant society a great many of his old books, else I had written you on that subject; but one of these days I shall trouble you with a Commission for the 'Monkland Friendly Society'.[256]

An account was duly set up,[257] and on 2 March 1790 Burns sent a further commission, requesting their orders as soon as possible:

> *The Mirror – The Lounger – Man of feeling – Man of the world* [all by Henry Mackenzie] (these for my own sake I wish to have by the first Carrier) [John] Knox's history of the Reformation – [Peter] Rae's history of the Rebellion 1715 – Any good history of the Rebellion 1745 – A display of the Secession Act & Testimony by Mr [Adam] Gib – [James] Hervey's Meditations – [William] Beveridge's thoughts – & another copy of [Thomas] Watson's body of Divinity – This last heavy Performance is so much admired by many of our Members, that they will not be content with one Copy, so Capt[n] Riddel our President & Patron agreed with me to give you private instructions not to send Watson, but to say you could not procure a Copy of the book so cheap as the one you sent formerly & therefore you wait farther Orders.[258]

Clearly the wishes of the majority in matters of book selection were not always observed. A year later Burns is requesting more:

---

[254] McCracken, 'Glendinning Antimony Mine', p. 147.

[255] *OSA*, vol. 3 (1792), pp. 597-8, for letter from Riddell to Sir James Sinclair.

[256] *Letters of Robert Burns*, edited by J. De L. Ferguson, 2nd edn. (Oxford, 1985), vol. 1, pp. 391-2.

[257] *Letters of Robert Burns*, vol. 2, p. 9.

[258] Ibid., vol. 2, pp. 19-20.

> *The Adventurer* – *Joseph Andrews* – *Don Quixotte* [sic] – *The Idler* – *Arabian Nights entertainment* D[r] [Richard] Price's dissertations on Providence, prayer, Death & Miracles – *Roderick Random* – & – the 5th Volume of the *Observer* – for these books take your fair price, as our Society are no judges of the matter, & will insist on having the following damned trash, which you must also send us, as cheap as possible – *Scots Worthies* [by John Howie] – [Thomas] Boston's 4fold State – *Marrow of Modern divinity* [by Edward Fisher] – [Elisha] Cole on God's Sovereignty – [Isaac] Newton's letters – [Philip] Dod[d]ridge's thoughts – [Adam] Gib's *Act & Testimony* – *Confession of faith* – & Capt[n] Rob[t] Boyle. I forgot to mention among the valuable books, [Hugh] Blair's Sermons & the latest edition of [William] Guthrie's *Geographical grammar*, which two books be sure to send us.[259]

The original members of the Monkland Society were tenant farmers of Riddell's who entered into a three-year contract to buy books, each paying five shillings entry and sixpence per month. But the contract was not renewed, and so the society ceased after three years, by which time they had gathered about 150 volumes; the books were sold off by auction amongst the members who shared the money raised as well as the books. This was a rare instance of a library known to have closed down voluntarily after a very short period. To encourage others and doubtless provide some self-advertisement, Burns sent an account of the Monkland Friendly Society to Sir John Sinclair who published the letter of 'a peasant' (though Burns is named in a covering letter from Riddell) in the first *Statistical Account*.[260]

Burns was also involved in the management of the Dumfries Public Library, founded in 1792 as a cheaper alternative to the more exclusive Gentleman's Society. He had been made an honorary member at its foundation and duly responded by donating a volume of his poems. He also donated a copy of Jean De Lolme on the British constitution, and added the inscription: 'Mr Burns presents this book to the library, and begs that they will take it as a creed of British liberty until they find a better'.[261] Peter Hill also supplied their books, though relations were a little strained, as is evident in a letter from Burns in February 1794:

> I am half angry with you, that you are not [at] any pains to keep squares with our Library here. They complain much of your not attending properly to their orders; &, but for the exertions of M[r]

---

[259] Ibid., vol. 2, p. 66.

[260] *OSA*, vol. 3 (1792), pp. 599-600.

[261] *Caledonian Mercury*, 14 August 1865; *Glasgow Herald*, 4 July 1896.

> Lewars ... they had applied elsewhere. A propos, the first volume of [Sir John] Dalrymple's *Memoirs*, Mr Lewars had the ill-luck to get spoilt in his possession; which unless he can replace, will bring him in for the whole book.[262]

Damaging a library book, albeit accidentally, was a serious matter, and Burns was asking for a replacement of a single volume to spare his friend the expense of a full set.

Burns was associated with libraries supplying essentially popular literature. By contrast, the 1851 catalogue of the Gentleman's Society of Dumfries (possibly founded a century earlier) contains scholarly authors such as William Camden, William Maitland, Tacitus (1737 edition), and Niccolò Machiavelli (1720), and works such as Archibald Bower's *History of the Popes*, Sir Richard Baker's *Chronicles*, Sir Walter Raleigh's *History of the World* (1687), Sir Hans Sloane's *Voyage to Madeira* (1707), and Sir John Chardin's *Travels in Persia* (1686). Only English books could be acquired, and the lightest work was a 1742 edition of *Don Quixote*; no other fiction appears. The library then contained about 2,300 volumes and only cost £1 *per annum*; members of the Dumfries and Galloway Club could also use the library. This reveals what solid fare the subscribers of a proprietary library preferred. But it could clearly not attract enough new users and was sold off in 1875.[263]

When the Orkney Library Society was set up in 1815, it solicited donations, as many other libraries did to secure a foundation collection. In the case of Orkney, the library received a large collection of books from the Synod of Orkney, including 188 volumes of mainly seventeenth and eighteenth century theological books, and about 80 other volumes of assorted classics; a weighty collection indeed. The Cupar Library was bequeathed about 650 volumes by John Gray of Paddington Green, and this presumably explains the presence in its 1813 catalogue of such weighty tomes as *Baconi Opera*, Aristophanes, Bertius *De Aggeribus et Pontibus*, Boethius, Caesar *De Bello Gallico*, Cicero and Nepos (in Latin), Cato, Grotius, Juvenal, Plato, and Xenophon. These volumes shared shelves, rather improbably, with the likes of the *Arabian Nights*, *Celia in Search of a Husband*, Maria Edgeworth's *Leonora*, *Old Nick: a Novel*, and *Queen-Hoo-Hall: a Romance*. When it comes to donations, there may well be a suspicion of donors wishing to clear their own shelves.

The very first books ordered for the Perth Library in 1786 on the other hand included the most significant works of the eighteenth century, such as Adam Smith's *Wealth of Nations*, David Hume's *History of England*, the Comte

---

[262] *Letters of Robert Burns*, vol. 2, pp. 277-8.

[263] G. W. Shirley, 'Old Public Libraries in Dumfries', *Dumfriesshire & Galloway Natural History & Antiquarian Society Transactions*, 18 (1907 for 1905-6), 39-44; reprinted with amendments as *Dumfriesshire Libraries* (Dumfries, 1932).

de Buffon's *Natural History*, and works by William Guthrie and William Robertson, soon followed by Lord Kames, John Millar, Sir James Steuart, and Tobias Smollett.[264] Likewise, the first orders of the Edinburgh Subscription Library (1794) represent an Enlightenment reading list, with several books listed above and additionally Captain James Cook's *Voyages*, Samuel Johnson's *Lives of the Poets*, Edmund Gibbon, and many travel books. The reading tastes of the Dalkeith Library have already been seen in poetical form.

It is relevant to note that an examination of forty-four subscription library catalogues by Dr Mark Towsey has shown that the most popular history authors acquired were, in order, David Hume, William Robertson, Adam Smith, and Adam Ferguson, all of whom appear in over thirty catalogues, followed closely by Baron de Montesquieu, Kames, Voltaire, and John Gillies. In the realm of philosophy, the works of Hugh Blair, Adam Smith, James Beattie, Lord Kames, David Hume, Thomas Reid, George Campbell, Archibald Alison, and Dugald Stewart feature in that order in over twenty catalogues, while the most popular scientific books were by the Comte de Buffon, William Smellie, Adam Ferguson, and Kames. As for works of imagination, *Humphry Clinker*, *Man of Feeling*, and Burns's *Poems* appear in thirty or more catalogues (as does *The Mirror*, followed by Ossian, *The Lounger*, Henry Mackenzie's *Man of the World*, and, from a later period, Walter Scott).[265] It must, of course, be remembered that these figures represent the popularity of titles which libraries had determined to acquire rather than their popularity in terms of loans. The perceived popularity of certain titles is often only a matter of personal opinion. The story is told that when Alexander Ranken enquired of the librarian of Stirling's Library: 'Pray, Mr Pate, is Ranken's *History of France* in?', the latter, Rev. James Pate, replied sarcastically: 'It never was out'.[266]

The Peterhead Reading Society was somewhat different in its procedures. Each member was entitled to spend up to the amount of his subscription of eighteen shillings (and each entitlement could be pooled), and so the first orders, approved on 1 October 1808, reveal both requester and request:[267]

---

[264] David Allan, 'Provincial Readers and Book Culture in the Scottish Enlightenment: the Perth Library, 1784-c.1800', *The Library*, 7th ser. 3 (2002), 367-89.

[265] M. Towsey, '"All Partners may be Enlightened and Improved by Reading them": the Distribution of Enlightenment Books in Scottish Subscription Library Catalogues, 1750-c.1820', *Journal of Scottish Historical Studies* 28 (2008), 20-43.

[266] Mason, *Public and Private Libraries*, p. 44. Volume 1 of Ranken's *History* was published in 1801.

[267] The authors cited are: William Paley, George Crabbe, Joseph Priestley (viz. *The Life* by John Corry), William Roscoe, Alexander Tilloch [sic], John Adolphus, Archibald Cochrane, Earl of Dundonald, Thomas Gray, and Vicesimus Knox.

Dr Moir:	Paley's *Elements of Moral and Political Philosophy*	14s.
Mr Greig:	Crabbe's *Poems*	10s.6d.
Dr Anderson:	Priestley's *Life*, vol. 1	10s.6d.
Peterkin:	Priestley's *Life*, vol. 2 and Roscoe's *Considerations on Peace*	10s.6d. 2s.6d.
J. Argo / J. Arbuthnot / Laing / Anderson:	Tulloch's *Philosophical Magazine* and *Nicholson's Journal*	3.0.0.
Harlaw:	Adolphe's *Biographical Memoirs of the French Revolution*	18s.
Arbuthnot:	Lord Dundonald's *Chemical Introduction to Agriculture*	10s.6d.
Donald:	Paley's *Views of the Evidences*	14s.
Moir / Adamson / Donald:	Paley's *Natural Theology*	9s.
Adamson:	Gray's *Poems and Correspondence*	14s.
Gray:	Knox's *Elegant Epistles*	14s.
Dr Jamieson:	*Tradesman's Magazine*	18s.
Forbes / P. Murray / R. Gray / G. Arbuthnot:	Smith's *Works*	£2.2s.

And the list continues until the full amount available had been committed. Other volumes ordered included a *Life of George Washington* (probably by John Corry?), Thomas Malthus on population, and a *Life of Cowper* (both William Hayley and John Corry wrote biographies). But when James Arbuthnot requested Samuel Richardson's *Sir Charles Grandison*, this was disallowed since it infringed their rule against novels. There then ensued a lively debate on whether the rule was an 'absolute prohibition' or merely an expression of disapprobation. The committee decided that the rule should be disregarded, and so *Sir Charles* was ordered.

Despite its early success, the next few years found the Peterhead Reading Society in difficulties, and by 1813 only six shillings per subscriber was available for purchases. In 1816 there were complaints that members did not have enough time to read the review journals, such as the *Edinburgh Review* and the *Monthly Review*, and so the loan period for these was increased, with the president enjoying first perusal. Most libraries circulated the literary magazines, vital for stock selection, and one of the prime reasons for belonging to such a society.

A most curious permanent subscription library was the Inshewan Reading Society, founded in 1796 in Middle Inshewan, a hamlet near Dunkeld, Perthshire. It met quarterly but seems to have done little business, though it possessed a committee comprised of preses, librarian, and four inspectors to examine the books each quarter. The library had transferable shares. Books were selected by pulling names of titles out of a hat until the money available was exhausted. No one must assume 'the character of a director' at their meetings, and fines of a halfpenny were levied for every turned-down corner or spot or soiled margin. There was a twopenny fine, double for a repeat offence, for any member 'convicted of raising factions or tumults or disturb[ing] the society with idle discourse'.

Few books are mentioned in the minutes, and although catalogues were printed they do not survive. In 1812 the members, with £1.11s.6½d. sterling in their funds, contemplated buying a good history of Britain, but not until 1814 did they reach a decision (their choice was Dr Robert Henry's). In 1815 they invested in David Hume's *History of England* with Smollett's continuation, but no other books are recorded; in 1818 they only had 14s.3d. available. From 1819 members only paid threepence per quarter. In 1822, when entry money was eight shillings, *Waverley* and *Rob Roy* appear as choices, and sixteen volumes were purchased altogether. In 1824 it was proposed that the books be transported to Wester Inshewan, and a 'chaplain' was appointed to lead 'the procession carrying Dr Dodridge [sic] *Family expositor* and to consecrate the books after being placed in the new library with a prayer'. In fact, with characteristic delay, the removal was postponed until 1825, when it was reported:

> Many appropriate toasts were drunk in course of the evening and the members inspired by the enlivening spirit of genuine Glenlivet sang many national airs with real Scotch glee.[268]

When, in 1827, they decided to buy a life of a remarkable character following the Reformation, they wrote first for advice to a minister in Perth as to which character they might choose. Surprisingly, this slow-moving, if convivial, society lasted until 1854.

Most subscription libraries were conservative in their tastes and merely flirted with radical political, social and moral ideas. Censorship arose when the authorities judged Thomas Paine's writings to be seditious. In 1793 Stirling's Library, Glasgow, ordered that *The Rights of Man* should not be given out,

---

[268] Minute book in Bell Library, Perth; cf. W. R. Aitken, *Public Library Movement*, pp. 311-5.

but Ayr Library ordered its destruction, as did Selkirk. This was a far cry from the situation in 1789 when Selkirk cancelled its Annual General Meeting so that members could attend a 'thanksgiving' service for the French Revolution. The Duns Library had cancelled the *New Annual Register* in 1796 because of objections, but discovered they had never ordered it anyway. At Greenock, William Godwin's *Political Justice* and *Caleb Williams*, the radical Thomas Holcroft's *Hugh Trevor*, the *New Annual Register*, *Monthly Review*, and other works were turned out in 1799. The young John Galt, the future novelist, and his friends were appalled at the news:

> The [Greenock Library] collection was formed with judgment, for although not then calculated to promote any specific study, it was yet admirably adapted to afford the best information which a mercantile community could require. The original institution did credit in this respect to the founders, and their principles had been adhered to by their successors.
>
> But during the French revolution, when party spirit ran high, the committee who had the management partook of the excitement, and, at their suggestion, at a public meeting, the library was purged in some degree of the tainted authors: namely, Holcroft, Godwin, &c. and the books were transferred from the library room to the custody of Mr John Dunlop, the grandfather of my friend the Doctor. From this unheard-of proceeding in a Protestant land, great wrath was nursed in the bosoms of the young men connected with the library: mine was inflamed prodigiously, and I never spoke of Mr Dunlop by any other name than the kaliph Omer.[269]

After the indignation had died down, though, Galt and friends encouraged a liberal-minded member to stand for the chairmanship of the committee. Eventually enough liberals joined to overturn the ban, and 'it ended in triumphantly recalling the heretical books, and raising the rate of the annual subscription to get more. ... From that era, the liberals of the town have, I believe, had the ascendancy in the management of the library'. Nevertheless, as Galt continued, 'I will ever consider myself as greatly indebted. The fracas of banishing "the pestiferous books" had the effect, as might be expected, of bringing them into notice and Godwin's *Political Justice* attracted my attention; in consequence, I read it'. In the event, he was completely unsympathetic towards Godwin's writings and found them obnoxious and diabolical, but banning such books was not the right response, he felt. Galt was always a conservative, and Greenock was always a patriotic town.[270]

---

[269] John Galt, *Autobiography* (London, 1833), vol. 1, pp. 38-39.

[270] Galt, *Autobiography*, vol. 1, pp. 40-42.

A similar controversy is evident in the oldest subscription library in Jedburgh. Agnes E. Hall (it is unclear whether she was a member of the library), complained in 1800 that subscription library regulations never guarded against clerical intervention. Liberal opinion should be protected, she urged, because the clergy were subservient to the ruling party and only promoted party opinions. She explained what had occurred at Jedburgh:

> *The Rights of Man* soon fell a sacrifice to sacerdotal zeal, and was expelled, as I have been informed, upon a motion from Rev. Member who, a few months before, had presented it to the society. The assertion of a Noble Lord high in command at Toulon, that in the *New Annual Register* an inaccurate statement had been given of the expulsion of the English from that place, was urged, by a *ci-devant* preceptor of his Lordship, as a sufficient ground for discontinuing that publication; and the valuable works of Dr [Erasmus] Darwin were rejected, because the same, or some other *great man*, had conceived a bad opinion of that author. Mrs [Charlotte] Smith's *Desmond* is even now, I believe, kept from circulating among the members, by the exertion of individual alarm and caprice; the *British Critic* has been preferred to the *Monthly Review*, and the flimsy and equivocal productions of the Abbé Barruel and Professor [John] Robison have superseded works valuable for historical and scientific accuracy.[271]

The writer's point was that a list of books rejected by the library during the previous six, revolutionary, years, would reveal the rise of alarm amongst the privileged classes. Libraries, though, she argued, should keep a place for the 'small, still voice of reason', and that the best response was to set up rival libraries, as had happened at Jedburgh.

These episodes serve to show how magazines could fall under suspicion when library members found offence in their political or moral views. Sir Richard Phillipps's *Monthly Magazine*, for instance, was always regarded as a Jacobin publication. In 1821 the Kelso Modern Library ordered the discontinuance of *Blackwood's Magazine* because of its 'filth and frivolity'. 'Might a still stronger reason for expulsion', thundered *The Scotsman*, 'not have been found in its practical hostility to every principle of the Christian religion?'[272] At the Kilmarnock Public Library in 1806, Rev. John Robertson, the local kirk minister, moved that no 'infidel, immoral, seditious, or ... objectionable' books

---

[271] Agnes E. Hall, 'Disputes in Book Societies', *Monthly Magazine*, 10 (Dec. 1800), 402-3. The authoress is apparently referring to the Jedburgh Company Library, whose date of foundation is given in the Listing as by the late 1770s. She herself states it dated back to about 1760, though this date may only be speculation on her part.

[272] *Freeman's Journal*, 22 February 1821, reprinted from *The Scotsman*.

be admitted. James Thomson moved that all except 'objectionable' be struck out of the motion, but he was defeated, and at a further meeting in 1807 the minister's original motion was confirmed and was duly printed in the library's 1811 catalogue. Censorship was not to be an issue to disappear: in 1835, for instance, a kirk minister belonging to the Kirkcaldy Subscription Library cut out references to Unitarianism from a library book; another member bound up the torn-out pages to preserve as an example of bigotry in his town.[273]

This raises the question of whether libraries existed which specifically collected 'revolutionary' literature. In London during the 1790s many radical book clubs were operating, though understandably little or nothing is known about them (the London Corresponding Society just fits into this category). Radical societies were suppressed by the Seditious Societies Act of 1799, though in other countries at this period, particularly Germany and Austria, even ordinary circulating libraries were banned outright.[274] Probably radical book-buying societies existed in Edinburgh and Glasgow, but the only clear evidence for a library purchasing potentially seditious books for its members comes from a much later period. In November 1822 a group of police, led by the Sheriff of Edinburgh and the Procurator Fiscal, raided Cordiners' Hall, Potter's Row, where they surprised a group of free-thinkers calling themselves the Zetetical Society. Similar free-thinking Zetetical (or Zetetic, denoting the quest for knowledge) reading societies, with libraries, existed in London and other parts of England, formed under the influence of Richard Carlile.[275] The Edinburgh society's president was a wood turner, and most of those attending were youths or journeymen tradesmen. They denied the divinity of Christ and even the existence of a deity, and had been meeting every Sunday since 1820 for discussions. But they also possessed a library, to which all members paid for weekly access. The books discovered included the works of Thomas Paine and Richard Carlile (then being prosecuted in London for blasphemy), as well as (Thomas?) Evans's *Sketches of all Religions*, Percy Shelley's *Queen Mab: a Poem*, Lord Byron's *Cain*, Thomas Rickman's *Life of Paine*, and David Hume's *Essays*.[276] It would be difficult to imagine a more dangerous collection of books, or so the authorities believed, for the books were seized.

Several months later, the matter was raised in the House of Commons. No less than 110 members of the free-thinking society had petitioned

---

[273] *Caledonian Mercury*, 3 October 1835.

[274] Cf. K. A. Manley, 'Libraries and Infidel Books, 1790-1850', forthcoming.

[275] Iain McCalman, *Radical Underworld: Prophets, Revolutionaries and Pornographers in London, 1795-1840* (Cambridge, 1988), pp. 185-6; Joel Wiener, *Radicalism and Freethought in Nineteenth-century Britain: the Life of Richard Carlile* (Westport, Conn., 1983), pp. 114-5.

[276] *The Times*, 22 November 1822, quoting the *Caledonian Mercury*; cf. *Glasgow Herald*, 22 November 1822.

Parliament for the return of their books; the petition was presented by Joseph Hume. The petitioners claimed that they met on Sundays when otherwise they would be tempted to spend the day in drinking and dissipation, and that they believed in expressing their views collectively and openly. They had started a library for 'their common use and instruction', and more titles of books were named, offering a rare insight into the reading world of a group of 'revolutionaries', including Richard Watson's *Apologies for the Bible*, Uzal Ogden's *Deist Unmasked*, George Toulmin's *Eternity of the Universe*, Voltaire's *Philosophical Dictionary*, Baron Odeleben's *Campaign in Saxony*, and Robert Owen's *Essays on the Formation of Character*. It was pointed out that many of these works could be found in many other libraries and most bookshops. This was at the heart of the petition, namely that the actions of the sheriff were oppressive, and that the members had been engaging in quiet debate. They wanted Parliament to change the law and guarantee free speech. Recourse to Parliament by those arrested had arisen because under Scots (but not English) law, anyone who denied the Trinity or committed blasphemy could be put to death. The petitioners did not deny that the sheriff had the right to investigate their alleged blasphemy, but they were protesting against the severity of the law. They refused to be considered a sect because no two members could ever agree on any one point (which raised a laugh in Parliament).[277]

    The Lord Advocate of Scotland, Lord Eskgrove, accepted responsibility for advising the sheriff to take action and stated he could not believe that there were men so full of wickedness and folly in Edinburgh. But he pointed out that under the law a person could only be put to death for blasphemy after a third conviction (shouts of 'hear, hear' from the Opposition). Since the Edinburgh free-thinkers (and a similar society in Glasgow) had now agreed to disband and were suitably contrite, the Lord Advocate decided that the best course of action was to let the matter drop; unless these blasphemers preferred to go to court, he added, in which case they would undoubtedly be convicted. The so-called Edinburgh Zetetical Society may not have been at the forefront of radical opinion, and were clearly and readily cowed into submission, but the evidence of their reading reveals the importance of books for the formation of their opinions. Their leader, James Affleck, subsequently published a pamphlet advocating a union between the Zetetical Society and the Church of Scotland and was later imprisoned for blasphemy.

    There is sometimes a thin line between stock selection and censorship. Many libraries banned controversial divinity, while the Selkirk Library forbad books on divinity, law, and physick for six years, renewed for a further six years at a time. But here the reasoning seems to have been that the professional classes could provide their own literature for themselves; the purpose of a

---

[277] *The Times*, 17 April 1823; for more detail see: *Hansard Parliamentary Debates*, new ser. 8 (16 April 1823), coll. 1014-9.

proprietary subscription library was essentially to provide 'general' literature, suitable for and acceptable to all readers. This was expounded by the Montrose Library, which set out to spend most of its income on 'buying books adapted to general reading' and only a small part on 'professional' books: 'Books in defence of Christianity, illustrations of the Sacred Writings, and Sermons, are not professional books, because it belongs to every man, more or less, to know the grounds of our common religion, to understand the Scriptures, and to be put in mind of the important duties enjoined in them'. The rules further laid down that subscribers should not take it amiss if not all books purchased for the library suited their tastes.

A tangential dispute over the purpose of a library did break out in Edinburgh in 1815. It concerned newspapers. Many libraries had reading rooms if they were fortunate to have sufficient space, and would supply newspapers and magazines. In 1812 the Edinburgh Subscription Library's annual general meeting agreed that some of the London and Edinburgh newspapers be taken, and that members should pay an extra five shillings yearly if they wished to avail themselves of the service. It was noted that Mr Charles Buchan of the General Post Office was present 'and never opened his lips on the subject'. In the event all the subscribers voluntarily paid an extra one guinea a year for 1812, 1813, and 1814 – except Mr Buchan; but it was accepted that members could not be forced to pay. Then, at a special general meeting in 1815, Dr John Murray moved that newspapers should not be admitted, but an amendment was made that newspapers be regarded as one of the original purposes of the library. The latter was carried by forty-two to twenty-four amidst protests from Murray that newspapers could never be considered as part of the original design and that spending money on them was 'injurious to the Interests of the Institution, and a violation of the objects for which it was formed'. The upshot of Murray's defeat was that it was agreed that the library should spend £15 a year on newspapers to which anyone could subscribe separately for 7s.6d. yearly. This material would be available to all library members in the newsroom. Whatever the avowed intentions of any library's founder members, there was no doubt that the provision of a reading room would inevitably lead to calls for subscriptions to journals and newspapers.

The Work of the Librarian

The office of librarian was always subject to strict rules. The office-holder usually had to provide security and in many libraries was responsible for collecting the fees and fines as well as ordering books; in some, as at Greenock and the Edinburgh Subscription Library, the librarian was entitled to keep part of the fines. This practice was stopped at Greenock in 1810 because the librarian, a clergyman, felt it was indelicate for him to demand fines which would line his own pocket; his committee decided that fines should be paid entirely into the funds of the library and he should 'exact them in the most rigourous [sic] manner'. Fines were demanded not just for the late return of volumes, but also for non-attendance at meetings, since a quorum was necessary to transact business. At Wigtown the fine was two shillings in 1798, but only twopence at Denholm in the 1820s.

The librarian was usually anyone who was willing, particularly if he had space to house the books, and was often a local minister or schoolmaster. Greenock Library's first librarian was John Wilson (1720-89), a strong Presbyterian, who had been master of the Grammar School since 1767. He was also a poet, known for the descriptive poem, 'The Clyde'; his tombstone records his 'exquisite humour, and profound learning'.[278] Many librarians were local booksellers (such as David Morison, librarian to the Perth Library) who supplied the library themselves and occasionally rented out a room or a few bookcases at the back of their shop to a library. The librarian of the Paisley Library Society, Gilbert Smith, was not a bookseller but kept a coffee room.

In Duns, the existing librarian in 1788 asked to be paid £3 a year; another man, who was prepared to accept £2 a year, was promptly appointed in his place. George Clark, bookseller, was the first librarian to the Peterhead Reading Society, in 1808, and was paid two guineas annually. When he complained that his expenses on behalf of the library were really five guineas, he was threatened with dismissal. He continued at the existing rate. A few years later Clark demanded that the library pay him two guineas for storage of their books until they could transfer them to another room, but his demand was ignored. He was eventually sacked in 1813 when he failed to pay his subscription and so no longer had an interest in the library; his share was bought back.

At Arbroath the first librarians were, successively, a bookbinder, preacher, schoolmaster, and a minister; the last was their first paid librarian. At Ayr, David Tennant, librarian from 1776 to 1783 (and subsequently the library's treasurer), was also Master of the Ayr Academy from 1772 to 1796, continuing as classics master until 1811. John Roxburgh, a divinity student, became librarian in 1804 and was paid £10 per year to attend for two hours each working day. He was the first librarian to be paid. In 1791 the librarian of the Dunfermline Library was appointed at £3 *per annum* for attendance of three hours a week, increased in 1811 to £6.

In many libraries, the librarian was clearly regarded as subordinate to the committee, and his actions were circumscribed. The 1773 rules (which still applied in 1792) of the Hawick Library specified:

---

[278] Hamilton, *Greenock Libraries*, p. 48; cf. John Leyden (ed.), *Scottish Descriptive Poems* (Edinburgh, 1803) for Wilson and 'The Clyde'.

Books or pamphlets commissioned for the Library, shall not be opened out of their packages after their arrival, by the library-keeper, except at least in the presence of three of the committee, who shall be obliged, before they leave the library, to see them added to stock.[279]

One of the librarian's tasks was to keep the catalogue up-to-date and order new editions to be printed when funds permitted. At the Duns Library – and this would have applied in similar libraries – the librarian was instructed to fill in members' catalogues with lists of new acquisitions. Catalogues were often printed with blank lines, or even several pages, for additions, and subscribers were obliged to purchase them. For instance, the 1805 catalogue of the Edinburgh Subscription Library cost one shilling, while subscribers to Thom's Library in Govan had to pay twopence. Subscribers to the Duns Library objected in 1793 to being made to pay twopence, and it was agreed that they should receive one catalogue free, but pay threepence for a second, if requested.

Payment was likewise required for the catalogues of circulating libraries. John Hill of Dumfries charged fourpence for his catalogue in 1803, while John Smith of Glasgow asked sixpence in 1786 for his obviously much larger catalogue. When Alexander Angus of Aberdeen brought out a new catalogue in 1787, subscribers could receive a copy free if they returned the previous edition. Catalogues varied enormously in quality. Most were alphabetical by author; some were classified (roughly) by subject; while others were merely lists of books according to date of acquisition. The Glasgow Public Library catalogue of 1810 contained detailed analytical entries but no subject indexing; it was apparently compiled by their librarian, James Kennedy (1784/5-1851), who later commenced an unfinished author bibliography of British medicine.[280] Many circulating library catalogues were undated. This was common practice because it enabled the proprietor to bind supplements at the rear so that the catalogue was always current from one year to the next.

Fetching books from the shelves was probably the librarian's most constant job. It was a customary practise to send a servant to collect books, whether from a circulating or a subscription library. This did not necessarily reflect a borrower's class; workers were often too busy to carry out such chores themselves. Willy Carruthers, the Melrose shepherd who has been met with before, would send his youngest son, 'the only ane that's hame', to collect books from the circulating library.[281] Even if a customer visited a library in

---

[279] Hugh K. Mackay, 'Hawick Subscription Library', *Hawick Archaeological Society Transactions* (1992), 33-41 (here p. 33).

[280] For a discussion of Scottish catalogues, see: Crawford, 'Bibliography of Printed Catalogues'; cf. *ODNB* for Kennedy.

[281] *Memoirs of Susan Sibbald*, pp. 168, 200.

person, they would be unlikely to be allowed access to the shelves; the librarian, or bookseller, needed to safeguarded the stock.

There may have been compensations for acting as a librarian, as the poetical office-holder in the Dalkeith Library suggested:

> Some says I ha'e a fickle job,
> Both troublesome an' fashious O,
> To keep the books, but sweet's the looks,
> That I get frae the lasses O.
>   Green grows the rashes O, [etc.] [282]

But his sentiment may have been poetic licence. Librarians were usually men, though in England many were women and were often booksellers. One Scottish exception was Miss Mary Smith, who became librarian of the Kirkcudbright Library in 1817. Her father had been a Muscovy merchant who had been burned out in 1812, and she was also apparently a relation of Adam Smith. She subsequently married John Nicholson, a bookseller who ran the only circulating library in the town.[283] Mary Findlater was for a few years librarian of the Peterhead Reading Society but was already keeper of the local news room. In 1805 a Miss Reid became librarian to the Ayr Library.

Even in the days when librarianship was not yet a profession, Alexander Somerville discovered that not just anyone could become a librarian. He was a self-taught farm-boy and labourer from near Haddington, and also an omnivorous book reader. He recalled how, in 1831 when he was twenty years old,

> some one told me of a public library and reading-room, which were in process of formation for the use of working men, and that it was possible that I might obtain the situation of librarian. This was a grand idea. It seemed to be the 'open Sesame' of all the world; that it needed only to be pronounced, and all would be accomplished – the world's doors would fly open. Alack! when I tried it, the raw looking 'Lothian lout' was rather an object of derision to those town-bred artizans who were collecting from the public the elements of the public library, than their fellow-equal, with intellectual sympathies like their own. I was pronounced to have formed a very absurd opinion of what a librarian should be, when I thought that a person of my *class* could fulfil its duties.[284]

---

[282] Peter Forbes, *Poems* (Edinburgh, 1812), p. 150.

[283] From notes by James Nicholson inside Mary Smith's diary for 1809 (Hornel Library, Broughton House, Kirkcudbright).

[284] Somerville, *Autobiography*, pp. 109-10.

The Physical Form of Libraries

Once books had been acquired, they had to be stored. Circulating libraries were inevitably closed-access, and so the stock would often be crammed into very tall bookcases. The difficulties encountered in gaining access to the shelves at Peterhead (noted on p. 48) serve as a reminder that in most subscription libraries members demanded a book through a written order to the librarian. At Stirling's Library, the first librarian (appointed in 1791), Rev. (later Dr) William Taylor, the local minister, was, as Robert Reid recalled,

> always glad to give out a load of books at once, as it saved him the trouble of frequent application to the shelves. The doctor in particular was very reluctant to take the ladder and mount aloft to the upper shelves of the library in search of old, dusty, cob-webbed volumes so enticing to our antiquaries, this operation causing the necessity for the application of a clothes-brush to his clerical blacks. I have known the doctor to give out books by armfuls, and he was not very particular about the period when they were returned, for the longer they were kept out so much less trouble was it to him. I must say, however, that Dr Taylor was a polite and obliging librarian.[285]

In the Edinburgh Subscription Library, subscribers could fetch books themselves, but if they did not replace them in the right position, they would forfeit one penny; this also applied at Penicuik. At Kilmarnock, the committee regretted the confusion caused when members left returned books in their librarian's bookshop instead of returning them to the library's own shelves.

For growing subscription libraries, the physical size of the library was often a problem. Many such libraries occupied rented rooms, depending on who was prepared to allow them space; if a library grew too large, it had to move on. Many libraries were kept at the rear of a bookshop, but Perth Library opened in 1786 as one book-press in a back room of the Academy; this was the physical 'space' of the library for many years. Subscribers were permitted to use the Perth Academy's 'Old Library' books, and eventually all the books were moved to the Session House. When a new book-press was commissioned in 1789, it cost £1.19s.6d – £1 for larchwood, 4s.6d. for hinges, 1s.6d. for nails, three shillings for pelmets, and 10s.6d. for the workman. (The Kirkcudbright

---

[285] Mason, *Public and Private Libraries*, p. 62.

Library had paid a joiner £2.10s. for their first press in 1777, specifying that it should be at least seven feet by five feet; the Duns Library only paid 19s. for shelves in 1769, plus 1s.8d. to glaze the windows.[286])

Some libraries kept books in schoolhouses (as at Wanlockhead, Beith, Alloa, Greenock, and elsewhere) or town halls (as at Duns, Montrose, Arbroath, and Selkirk); Kilmarnock Library (1797) was kept in both in succession. One reason for the longevity of some libraries was the generous terms which they secured for their tenancies. The Montrose Library kept its books free of charge in the Academy until 1821 when it moved to the new Town Hall. The room was to be rent-free, but because of increased municipal costs the library agreed to pay £5 *per annum*. When the Council proposed an increase in 1873, the library argued successfully that it would be a breach of good faith, because of the original intention to provide a rent-free room; the library won. Books from the Kirkcudbright Library were still kept in the local town hall in the 1950s.

Dundee Public Library employed a local bookseller, James Martin, as librarian; he kept the bookstock and of course supplied orders. But this caused inconvenience when, in 1800, the librarian left town in a hurry. Fortunately 'His Majesty's servants had in their great wisdom put his Majesty's seals on his property including the Dundee Public Library'. The library was safe, but his creditors needed to secure an order to recover the library. After that experience the committee decided to rent a room in future.

The largest libraries inevitably required their own buildings. Legal protection became necessary when a library owned property: Edinburgh Subscription Library (1794) became incorporated in 1815, the Ayr Library (1762) in 1808, and Glasgow Public Library (1804) in 1811. Most libraries did not legally become companies, though that was the normal pattern in North America. It is probable that more small Scottish subscription libraries built their own buildings than their English equivalents because convenient plots of land were easier to find. This was also true in North America. But raising money could present problems. The Ayr Library spent the significant sum of £330 on erecting a new building in 1804 when it had barely 100 members; the money could only be raised by increasing the subscription and borrowing money from individual members. On the other hand, Sir Patrick Murray of Ochtertyre built a room for the Fowlis Library, near Dundee, completely unsolicited. Thomas Telford and a wealthy manufacturer, Alexander Reid, bequeathed £1,000 to the Langholm Library (1800) in 1834, on condition that a similar sum be raised by public subscription for a building; in the event no new library building was opened until 1877.[287] Although the library still

---

[286] Borders AO, DL/3/2, Duns Library account book, 23 August 1769.

[287] According to the Langholm Library catalogue (1888).

exists as a reference and local history library, it closed as a lending library in 1974 for lack of funds.[288]

The Greenock Library occupied a variety of homes over many years, including the local schoolroom and then rooms rented from the Town Council. Not until 1837 did it find a permanent home in a new building (designed by Sir Edward Blore, the architect of Abbotsford) erected to house a monument to the town's most famous son, James Watt; and the costs were entirely defrayed by Watt's son. Watt himself had donated £100 to the library in 1816 'to form the beginning of a science library, for the instruction of the youth of Greenock'. Library subscribers and schoolchildren paid 1s.6d. yearly to use the 'Library of Arts and Sciences', while non-subscribers paid 2s.6d. Although £50 was spent immediately, the remaining £50 was not touched until 1848. In fact, in 1824 the Greenock Library's members considered transferring Watt's donation to the new School of Arts, but in the end decided to keep it.[289]

Religious and Children's Libraries

Of specialist subscription libraries, the most common were the theological. No general commercial circulating or proprietary subscription library could satisfy all the interests of the minister or the theological student, and many people of strict religious convictions may well have felt qualms at subscribing to a common circulating library, especially if they shared the same views as did Robert Wodrow towards Allan Ramsay (see p. 10-11). Although many ministers belonged to private subscription libraries, those repositories of knowledge rarely included works which might prove challenging to the average orthodox kirk minister. Neither would such libraries collect books which might appeal to people of differing religious opinions. On the other hand, many purely theological libraries were particularly associated with ministers who did not belong to the established church and looked for an opportunity to have access to a wider collection of theology.

An interesting example of a theological subscription library was started at Alloa in 1777. This was not a proprietary library as such, and its purpose was to provide books for Presbyterian students of divinity and philosophy. The property was vested in the president and managers, who could appoint a 'Liberary Keeper' and move the collection elsewhere. An entry fee of five shillings was charged, with a yearly subscription of 2s.6d., but the rules were

---

[288] R. McQuillan, 'Langholm Library', *Akros* 9 no. 25 (1974), 44-47.

[289] George Williamson, *Old Greenock* (London, 1888), vol. 2, p. 258; Watt's own copies of Greenock Library catalogues are now in NLS; *Greenock Advertiser*, 2 April 1824.

extremely complex and foresaw too many problems. The president was Walter Moncrieffe, local minister and Professor of Theology under the General Associate Synod (or Antiburghers); other committee members included Alexander Pringle, a preacher from Kelso.[290] The first year's accounts show that £42.12s. was subscribed by divinity students and £4.2s.6d. by philosophy students, while donations produced the strangely precise sum of £31.0s.8 5/6d. Around 200 titles had been acquired. In 1781 all managers who lived outside Alloa were made to resign. On the death of Moncrieffe, the library moved to Whitburn in 1787 but finally found a home in Edinburgh in 1807, where it became the Divinity Hall library 'under the inspection of the General Associate Synod'. Though not a proprietary library, it was not immune from the kind of disputes which afflicted some subscription libraries. In 1812 there was an acrimonious meeting over a new catalogue, when the librarian complained of a 'clandestine' meeting of a committee set up to produce just that. He claimed that he served on another committee intended to produce a catalogue, but he was expelled from the meeting for refusing to accept the authority of the president and for failing to explain just exactly what the committee he was supposed to be a member of had ever done.

A similar library, but for students of divinity of the Burgher sect, operated at Selkirk from 1787 under Rev. George Lawson (1749-1820), a Secession church minister there who had been appointed Professor of Theology under the Associate Synod. He had studied under the noted Rev. John Brown (1722-87) of Haddington, and on the latter's death the Associate Synod's divinity hall, including their books, had moved with Lawson to Selkirk. The library was described as 'by no means extensive, though it contained a fair collection of good books', but students were encouraged to use Lawson's own personal library of 2,000 volumes. Lawson kept a close eye on the students' library and refused to permit Thomas Paine's *Rights of Man* (which had already been purchased for the library) to be added to the stock since the government had banned it, but retained the copy himself. When the fuss had died down, Lawson returned the volume: 'I think it may now be restored, without any offence being taken'.[291]

The Paisley Theological Library, unlike those at Alloa and Selkirk, was a more accessible public subscription library, though it had been begun for the Burgher Congregation. Founded in 1808 with fifty-four members paying half-a-guinea a year, it had collected 700 volumes by 1825 and still existed in 1850. Another example of a successful venture was the Robertsonian Theological Library, a subscription library founded in 1814 and located in Mitchell Street,

---

[290] NRS, MS. CH3/11/1.

[291] John MacFarlane, *The Life and Times of George Lawson, D.D.* (Edinburgh, 1862), pp. 292-3, 301; cf. *ODNB* for Lawson and Brown.

Glasgow. It originated as the private collection of Rev. James Robertson, a secessionist minister of Kilmarnock, and operated as a regular subscription library, with shares which cost £5, though annual subscribers were admitted at 10s.6d. a year. The library had attracted no less than 165 members by 1816, and possessed 4,000 volumes in 1818. It was subsequently taken over by the United Secession Synod for the benefit of its students, though their congregations were reluctant to pay for it.[292]

Another library based on a private collection was – and still is – the McIntosh Library of Dunkeld (now held in the Bell Library, Perth), bequeathed by Rev. Donald McIntosh, a Jacobite, member of the Old Episcopal Church, and the last non-jurant clergyman in Scotland. His library was established in 1811 with 1,200 volumes, to which 200 further volumes were soon added. Though only open for an hour on Saturdays, subscribers paid £1.5s. entry for a transferable share, and twelve shillings a year after the first year. There were many tracts and pamphlets, particularly explaining 'difficult passages' in matters of civil and ecclesiastical history, and even a handful of novels.

In Edinburgh a group of people met in 1811 to inaugurate a library devoted to books on sacred philology and the study of the Scriptures; much of this literature was, of course, too expensive for many individuals to purchase. Common commentaries and purely doctrinal and polemical works would be excluded. The resulting Edinburgh Biblio-critical Library was a subscription library, with entry at £5 for a share in the property, and a subscription of fifteen shillings a year. There were fourteen original members, including seven reverends and a doctor of medicine. The books were kept in Bristo Street Session House and one of the members was Rev. James Peddie, co-founder of the Edinburgh Subscription Library and minister of the Bristo Street chapel. The first catalogue listed 188 titles, the majority in Latin. The library later combined with the Edinburgh Religious Subscription and Circulating Library (1824), whose first president, James Douglas of Cavers, Roxburghshire, founded in 1825 the Woodside Library, a free library of 1,000 volumes for the benefit of children attending the Denholm Sabbath School.

The existence of such libraries underlines the existence of strong religious views which no ordinary 'public' library could satisfy. The Stirling Society for Promoting the Knowledge and Practice of Christianity was not a subscription library, but in the absence of any other suitable library, it gave access to a religious library for members and those recommended by them; ninety volumes had been collected by 1798. Theological subscription libraries of which little is known beyond their name include the Biggar Evangelical Library (1807), Glasgow Theological Library (1808), Stranraer Theological Library (1820),

---

[292] Robert Chapman, *Picture of Glasgow*, 3rd edn. (Glasgow, 1818), p. 231; *Caledonian Mercury*, 18 September 1824, 14 May 1827.

and the Newtyle Library (by 1822). The Glasgow Friendly Library Society was founded in 1802 to unite the benefits of public libraries and book clubs: immoral books, such as novels and plays, would be excluded, along with controversial divinity. There were transferable shares at £3 and a fee of one shilling per quarter. 259 volumes had been collected by 1805 and still existed after twenty-five years. In addition, the Preshome Catholic Circulating Library in Banffshire (established in 1818 and apparently run as a subscription library) was the first known Roman Catholic congregational library in Scotland, though a circulating library existed at St. Peter's Chapel, Aberdeen, by 1821 and probably for a few years earlier.

Many religious libraries were run along the lines of a Sunday School library or a small lending library for a congregation, providing moral tracts, especially for the young, rather than weighty tomes of learned theology. These were not usually run as proprietary libraries – though some probably were – and belonged to the congregation rather than to individual shareholders; but they flourished in dissenting chapels. A typical example was the Canal Street Relief Library in Paisley, established in 1815 for the congregation of a dissenting church and kept in the Session House. The library cost two shillings to join and one shilling per quarter thereafter; there was also a juvenile section, available for half the price. Similarly, the Evangelical Library of Inverkeithing, established in 1802, cost 1s.6d. entry plus threepence yearly, and by 1822 contained 430 volumes of moral tales, sermons, and other religious works.

In Campbeltown, Argyllshire, a small religious library was set up in the early 1790s 'for the purpose of reading between sermons', charging one shilling a year, with the intention of allowing the poor to have free use. A local minister, Rev. Dr John Smith, commented:

> Books of controversy, (which are read with such avidity by the common people in Scotland,) are carefully excluded from this collection, as the fruit which they produce is bitter. The ancient martyr said, he could either live or die for Christ, but could not dispute for him. In our times the reverse of this is more commonly the case.[293]

Concerted efforts were made by a handful of individuals to spread religious libraries. In Haddingtonshire, Rev. Samuel Brown, the progenitor of 'itinerating' libraries, also furnished for ready money divinity libraries of thirty volumes of religious works. Books could be lent for a penny per volume for the first year and *gratis* thereafter. For three guineas he would provide sixty-two Kildare Place Society pamphlets bound into thirty volumes, which could

---

[293] *OSA*, vol. 10 (1794), pp. 561-2.

be circulated according to his scheme by the librarians of standing religious libraries; this was separate from his famous itinerating scheme.[294]

The Bothkennar Library in Stirlingshire was established in 1824 by Mr [John?] Walker of Orchardhead as a religious library for youths; the schoolmaster was librarian. The library relied mostly on donations and contained fifty-nine titles for adults and a further twenty-three for children, including Charles Rollin's *Ancient History*, Ezekiel Blomfield's *History of the World*, James Cook's *Voyages*, the *Statistical Account*, *Farmer's Magazine*, *The Rambler*, Philip Doddridge, and the *Juvenile Plutarch* of John Saville. The Paisley Juvenile Library (1814) and Rothesay Youths Library, established on the Isle of Bute in 1818, were probably similar in scope. The Melrose Parish Library was formed in the 1820s by a group of ladies of the town for the benefit of the poor. The ladies paid 1s.6d. yearly, or a shilling if they did not want a vote in its proceedings, and 317 volumes of improving literature were available for loan on Saturdays by 1828.

Religious libraries tended to be virtually the only libraries which catered specifically for juvenile readers, though the fare on offer may not have been particularly appealing. The Glasgow Public Library, though, did possess a Juvenile Library of about a hundred titles by 1810, from which subscribers could borrow one at a time for four days. The selection included Henry Blair's *Advice to Youth*, Edward Baldwin's *History of Rome*, *Cheap Repository Tracts*, *Book of the Ranks and Dignities of British Society*, John Gay's *Fables*, *Gulliver's Travels*, *The Complete History of England by Question and Answer*, *The Vicar of Wakefield*, *Wonders of the Telescope*, and an adapted version of *Robinson Crusoe*. The Greenock Library, too, established a Juvenile Library in 1812, using £3 from their funds.

Circulating libraries rarely catered specifically for children, but occasionally an effort was made. James Miller of Dunbar ran a juvenile circulating library for a short time, while Alexander Watson of Aberdeen opened a Juvenile Circulating Library in 1827. Miss Johannah Tansh of Edinburgh devoted three pages of her 1826 library catalogue to listing books suitable for juvenile readers extracted from her full catalogue. These included George Anson's *Voyages*, J. Cook's *Roman History*, Plutarch, *Arabian Nights*, Mrs Barbara Hofland's *Good Grandmother*, *The Young Misses's Magazine*, *Paul and Virginia*, Thomas Day's *Sandford and Merton*, *The Female Academy*, and Jean Marmontel's *Belisarius*.

---

[294] Samuel Brown, *Cheap Itinerating Libraries for Villages* (ca. 1817).

Special Libraries: Law, Foreign Books, Music

Subscription and circulating libraries were essentially general collections, catering for the wide tastes of all members. Specialist libraries emerged in the nineteenth century. However, a forerunner can be seen in a library near Crieff which was supplied in 1774 by the bookseller Charles Elliot, and whose purpose was 'that all the Books should Relate to Farming or Improvements of that kind'.[295] The Dumfries Law Library is another example of a specialist professional library run along subscription lines. Founded in 1819 with twenty-two initial subscribers paying one guinea entry and five shillings per quarter, its membership was defined as 'unlimited', though members had to be connected with the county's courts, but including clerks and apprentices; law firms could not join, only individuals. The purpose was obviously to acquire expensive law books which many individuals could not afford, and the first order was for an ongoing publication, begun in 1801, William Morison's *Dictionary of Decisions of the Court of Session* for £41. When a cheaper copy was offered, the members debated over which copy they should accept. They then debated the propriety of changing a decision once it had been reached, deciding that their rules were deficient. As with all lawyers, the members required exact laws and precedents for their own library. And as with any other subscription library, the rules had to be obeyed. In 1823 several were expelled for not having paid their dues for nine quarters, and their interest reverted to the society. By then they possessed twenty-nine titles in 157 volumes, of which seventy-three volumes were *Statutes of the Realm* and twenty-two volumes were of Morison's *Decisions*. Some books were found to be missing in 1824, but, unusually, all were returned. A similar law library was started in Stirling in 1828 with a donation from the Stirling Subscription Library of its law books.[296]

In England medical subscription libraries and book clubs were relatively widespread, but not so in Scotland. Although local medical societies existed, like the Aberdeen Medico-Chirurgical Society (1789) and the Fife Medico-Chirurgical Society (1825) in Cupar, both of which possessed libraries, they were essentially professional societies. The older-established national societies had far more significant libraries, such as the Royal College of Physicians of Edinburgh, the Royal College of Surgeons in Edinburgh, and the Royal College of Physicians and Surgeons in Glasgow. The only 'public' medical collections were those in the Dundee Public Library, where a library belonging to the town's medical men was deposited in 1809, and the Medical Society of the North in Inverness, established by 1821 as a subscription library for local medical practitioners.

---

[295] Information kindly supplied by Warren McDougall from the John Murray Archive (now in NLS); cf. MS. 43090, Charles Elliot to Thomas Keir, 2 December 1774.

[296] *Stirling Journal*, 25 September 1828.

Foreign books were an equally specialized taste. The largest circulating libraries of Edinburgh, Glasgow, and Aberdeen offered at least French books, and some would have included Italian; Spanish and German books do not seem to have been popular, though in 1821 John Hunter of Edinburgh lent books in all of these languages, as well as in Portuguese. Walter Berry of Edinburgh lent only French books by 1796, when he issued a catalogue of 589 titles in his 'cabinet littéraire'. Two books could be borrowed for one guinea a year, but only one new publication at a time. Much fiction was offered, such as Anne Ferrand's *Amours de Cléante et Bélise* and the ubiquitous *Paul et Virginie* by J. B. H. de Saint-Pierre, but there was also non-fiction, such as *Comédies de Terence, Histoire de Thucydide*, 'Guillaume' Robertson's *Histoire d'Écosse*, and the *Œuvres de Voltaire*. Berry's reading room provided the *Moniteur* and other newspapers for an extra guinea.

Two private subscription libraries are known to have collected only foreign books. The Greenock Foreign Library (1807) met next door to the Greenock Subscription Library, and members of the former also had to belong to the latter. There were originally fifty-seven members paying 10s.6d. a year, and its purpose was to supplement the work of teachers of French in the town. French was recognized as a useful language, but lack of available books limited its students' proficiency in the tongue. Virtually only French and a few Spanish books were bought. The catalogues list books by Pierre de Marivaux, Voltaire, Madame de Genlis, the Comte de Mirabeau, Molière, the Abbé Prevost, Montaigne, and Montesquieu, and works such as *Annales de Chemie* and *Magazin Encyclopédique*. Only about £20 yearly was raised in subscriptions, sufficient for perhaps one to two dozen new books a year, and eventually in 1834 the library united with the Greenock Library. The Glasgow Foreign Library was founded as a private subscription library in 1820 by the bookseller, John Wylie, who acted as librarian. A committee was responsible for book selection and transferable shares cost one guinea plus twelve shillings a year. There were sixty-seven subscribers in 1823, including two members of parliament and ten university professors. English works published abroad were considered to be part of the library's remit, and non-resident foreigners were admitted to read. The library was eventually moved to the shop containing Wylie's circulating library, but was dissolved in 1832. A new Glasgow Foreign Library was established in 1834.

Many circulating libraries offered a music section. Proficiency in music was always a desirable accomplishment for the cultured person, and particularly for the modern young miss. James Sibbald in Edinburgh offered music, while Domenico Corri and James Sutherland started a separate music circulating library in 1783. Neil Stewart had started another by 1786, advertising that his music was selected by the firm of Clementi of London. Other Edinburgh music libraries were run by William Whyte by 1800 and John Hamilton by 1805. In Glasgow, Archibald McGown proposed a music library in the 1780s, while John McFadyen established his musical business in 1798, and D. Macintyre in 1809. In Aberdeen James White appears to have run a music library by 1788, and Davie & Morris by 1814.

Probably the largest music library in Scotland belonged to Alexander Brown of Aberdeen, founded in 1798, with over 2,000 items.[297] He issued a separate catalogue, which, unusually, survives, with appendices in 1799 and 1805, in which he flattered himself on the service he was performing towards the interests of musical science in north-east Scotland; it was probably a justifiable boast. He charged £1.5s. yearly for two books at a time (or four for country subscribers), though lower rates were available, and non-subscribers could borrow a book or score of a value between three and ten shillings for sixpence per book for two days, or a shilling per book for works of a higher value than ten shillings. Brown's collection included almost a hundred opera scores and oratorios, including Gluck, Handel, and Thomas Arne (though none by Mozart or Haydn); over a hundred volumes of songs and arias and 165 volumes of English, Scottish, and Irish songs; collections of glees, catch-songs, sacred music, sonatas (chiefly Clementi, Dussek, Haydn, and Pleyel), and military pieces; music for violin, flute, clarinet, and guitar; and almost two dozen theoretical and instruction books. In addition he sold and hired musical instruments, and music could be copied.

The cultured young lady did not just read polite literature and study music; she also had to be able to draw and paint. And the circulating library could oblige in that respect as well. The lending of books clearly influenced tradesmen to hire out other forms of cultural goods. Esplin and Forbes established a 'circulating repository of prints and drawings' in Edinburgh's High Street in 1790 for 1s.6d. per month or 3s.6d. per quarter. They explained that theirs was 'a CAPITAL COLLECTION of PRINTS and DRAWINGS by the best Masters, both Ancient and Modern, consisting of HISTORICAL SUBJECTS, LANDSCAPES, SEA PIECES, FRUIT PIECES, FLOWERS, ANIMALS, &c., many of which are beautifully coloured, which they propose to lend out to draw after'.[298] The practice of lending prints was for copying rather than hanging on walls; Thomas Brown lent prints by 1794 at £1.4s. per year, and Sibbald had offered them since 1780. Daniel McIntosh lent prints and drawings from his Repository of the Arts by 1800, and William Swinton, too, from his Artists' Repository by 1823.

---

[297] McDonald, 'Circulating Libraries', pp. 128-9.

[298] *Caledonian Mercury*, 15 July 1790.

David Auld of Ayr lent prints and drawings by 1815; that he was also a perfumer and hair-dresser suggests he was pursuing a fashionable clientèle. In 1821 James McDiarmid opened a shop in Dumfries to sell paints, varnishes, and drawing materials. He also lent prints and drawings to copy 'upon the plan of a circulating library of books' at three guineas per year or less *pro rata*, or two shillings per week.[299] In the same year Alexander Watson of Aberdeen circulated drawings and mantle-piece ornaments. The intention was not interior decoration but to provide objects for the aspiring artist to copy. For instance, landscapes, artificial flowers and fruit, shells, etc., could be borrowed for one shilling per week; match figures and drawings on velvet, for 1s.6d. per week; and hand screens, card racks, watch stands, and so on, for one shilling each per day. An interesting variation on this theme in Aberdeen comes from Smith & Co., carvers, who in 1825 made available 'for circulation' busts, anatomical heads, oil paintings, and portfolios of flower pieces for study from their Artists' Repository at 78 Union Street. They also employed a young artist to copy portraits, landscapes, and so on – but the company did not lend printed materials.[300]

The Question of Book Clubs

An important area of book provision where Scottish and English practice diverges concerns book clubs. Dividing book clubs comprised one to two dozen members who met monthly to select and circulate books and divide them once a year amongst themselves. They flourished throughout England and Wales from the very beginning of the eighteenth century and were actively encouraged by the SPCK, which even circulated model rules for their regulation.[301] In England many clubs developed into subscription libraries and frequently were the only provision for borrowing books in rural areas. But in Scotland (as too in Presbyterian northern Ireland), references to book clubs in the eighteenth century turn out to be to societies with permanent collections. The Mauchline Conversation Society and the Monkland Friendly Society, both connected with Robert Burns, are often referred to as book clubs but in reality were sociable literary clubs which, though short-lived, collected books for permanent use. Burns, his brother Gilbert, and various friends had initiated the Bachelor's Club of Tarbolton, Ayrshire, in 1780 as a debating club. When the two brothers moved to Mauchline, they set up a similar club,

---

[299] *Dumfries & Galloway Courier*, 6 November 1821.

[300] From the 1821 catalogue of Watson's library; copy in Aberdeen University Library. See: *Aberdeen Journal*, 9 February 1825, for Smith.

[301] K. A. Manley, 'The SPCK and English Book Clubs before 1720', *Bodleian Library Record* 13 (1989), 231-43.

the Mauchline Conversation Society, in about 1786, but with the difference that money from fines for non-attendance was spent on books for a permanent library. Purchases included Jean-Jacques Rousseau's *Emile*, Voltaire's *Peter the Great*, Henry Mackenzie's *Man of Feeling*, the *Mirror* and the *Lounger*. Mackenzie, incidentally, was probably the most popular author of the period as far as Scottish subscription libraries were concerned. Debating, political, and literary clubs were legion across Scotland, of course, and no aspiring poetaster, wit, or man of substance could afford not to be a member of one club or another; but how many collected books as a prime purpose, rather than as a secondary consideration (as in Allan Ramsay's Easy Club), is a question for debate.[302]

There may be many reasons why dividing book clubs found little or no favour in Scotland before the nineteenth century. Travel considerations would have made regular monthly meetings impossible in many localities during winter months. Meetings of English book clubs were social occasions, often held in taverns. In the Leadhills miners' library there was provision for an annual dinner in a public house, but no more than sixpence each could be spent on liquor. After 1807 members of the Selkirk Library were permitted whisky punch at their anniversary at the library's expense, though they were allowed to pay for wine from their own pocket. In England the mainstay of book clubs were local clergy; in Scotland Presbyterian ministers held a less liberal attitude to the union of books and beer (at least outside Edinburgh and Glasgow). At the Kelso Library, business meetings were held on the same dates as the presbytery because many members belonged to both; hardly an auspicious opportunity for excessive drinking. Anniversary dinners were common for subscription libraries, and in England the Kendal Book Club's annual venison feast was a major social event. But sobriety was normally the order of the day in Scotland.

Scots, it seemed, preferred the idea of a permanent library, available (if at a fee) to all members of the community. In a dividing book club members bought books collectively, but they became individual property. Every member recovered the value of their outlay within a year; it was not an investment for the future. Book clubs and subscription libraries represented different ways of regarding the use of books and reading, essentially community versus the individual. That does not mean that dividing book clubs might not have existed. The slender evidence revolves around interpretation of phrases such as 'book society' and 'reading society', which in England could signify either a permanent book collection or a dividing book club. Tantalizing references can be found. In Banff in about 1798 a 'Book Society is at present forming, on a

---

[302] Davis D. McElroy, *Scotland's Age of Improvement: a Survey of Eighteenth-century Literary Clubs and Societies* (Pullman, Wa., 1969), pp. 97-98; cf. James Currie (ed.), *The Works of Robert Burns* (Liverpool, 1800), vol. 1, pp. 106-11.

liberal plan, to consist of twenty gentlemen'; the phrase 'at present forming' tends to suggest a permanent collection, but the restriction to twenty members might imply otherwise.[303] Many permanent subscription libraries began as societies containing just a few original members, such as the Dunfermline Tradesmen's Library. In 1793 Thomas Muir was tried before the High Court in Edinburgh for seditious libel, standing accused of distributing copies of Thomas Paine's *Age of Reason*. One of the witnesses, William Muir of Kirkintilloch, deposed that he belonged to a 'reading society', and that Thomas Muir had invited him to show Paine's writings to the club. But was this society a permanent library? Almost certainly it was, and this same society was one of those listed in the articles by John Millar cited previously; but there must remain some doubt over similar reading societies.[304]

Other clues could equally be understood to mean different things. The Glasgow publishers, Stewart and Meikle, advertised in 1799: 'Clubs supplied with Books on the most reasonable terms',[305] while John Murdoch, bookseller, offered to supply libraries and book clubs.[306] As has been seen above, the Glasgow area contained a network of workers' book societies; but contemporary evidence shows that they were all small, permanent libraries kept in workmen's cottages, and not dividing clubs.

In Dunkeld, the minister recorded in 1793 in the first *Statistical Account* that 'several clubs have been formed, who purchase the *Statistical Account of Scotland*'.[307] Clubs which were established to buy periodical publications, beyond the pocket of many workers, became common in the nineteenth century and may have collected books as well; but what happened to the works they acquired is unclear. Similar clubs may well have existed for a considerable time. David Hume belonged to such a club in Edinburgh by 1770, as he wrote to a friend: 'I am of a Club here that get down News papers and Pamphlets from London regularly: So that you wont need to send me the *[London] Chronicle* any more'; however this may have been a debating society rather than purely a book or newspaper club.[308]

It is highly likely that dividing book clubs were commonplace after 1800, but the documentary evidence is lacking. One club for which some evidence

---

[303] *OSA*, vol. 20 (1798), p. 369.

[304] *The Trial of Thomas Muir* (Edinburgh: printed by Alexander Scott, [1793]), pp. 35-36; *Scots Chronicle* (30 December 1796); on Muir, see: Nigel Leask, 'Thomas Muir and *The Telegraph*: Radical Cosmopolitanism in 1790s Scotland', *History Workshop Journal* 63 (2007), 48-69.

[305] *Glasgow Courier*, 11 July 1799.

[306] Ibid., 7 December 1799.

[307] *OSA*, vol. 6 (1793), p. 369.

[308] J. Y. T. Greig (ed.), *Letters of David Hume* (Oxford, 1932), vol. 2, p. 218.

has survived is the Dunfermline Pamphlet Club, established in 1810 to buy periodicals and pamphlets. Seventeen members each paid twelve shillings per year and were grouped into districts to help the circulation of the books. Items were selected at quarterly meetings and circulated according to a prescribed order. Periodicals ordered included the *Edinburgh Review*, *Quarterly Review*, *Monthly Magazine*, and *Cobbett's Political Register*. Pamphlets included Lord Melville's letter, Henry Grattan's speech (presumably on Catholic office holders), William Huskisson on currency, *Letters of Publicola* (by Robert H. Evans), *Legend of Guineviere*, *The Bachelor's Wife*, and David Lindsay's dramas. But the records cease after a year, and it must be presumed that the club had as well. A similar club in Lanark was said to have terminated after a year, apparently in the 1820s.[309]

Writing in 1809 of newspapers in Paisley, a local author commented: 'It is through this channel and book societies that the "Paisley weavers" improve in politics, and can converse with propriety on "many subjects"!'[310] John Millar had recorded ten book societies in Paisley for the working classes by 1796; these were small, permanent libraries and were probably the same as those existing in 1809. John Urie, writing of Paisley in the 1820s and 1830s, wrote:

> The want of circulating libraries was filled by numerous book clubs. Each member contributed one book to the common stock. The books were exchanged monthly at the club meeting-place, where discussions on their contents and current topics were indulged in.[311]

John Urie also recalled how at the age of eight (i.e. 1828) he had carried a volume of the *Encyclopedia Britannica* to a meeting of an Encyclopedia Club in Paisley to which his father belonged, and where the members kept up continual discussions about the Reform Bill and other topics of the day.[312] This club, which met every three months to exchange volumes, seems to have existed by about 1771; succeeding editions were purchased as they appeared.[313] A private subscription library in Kincardine, which existed by 1828 and possibly before, apparently began with a few people clubbing together to buy the *Encyclopedia Britannica*.[314]

---

[309] Davidson, *Lanark*, p. 78.

[310] William Taylor, *An Answer to Mr. Carlile's Sketches of Paisley* (Paisley, 1809), p. 33.

[311] John Urie, *Reminiscences of 80 Years* (Paisley, 1908), p. 27.

[312] Urie, *Reminiscences*, p. 28.

[313] David Semple, *Poems and Songs and Correspondence of Robert Tannahill* (Paisley, 1876), p. xxxvii.; cf. *A Cyclopaedia of Canadian Biography*, edited by George M. Rose (Toronto, 1886), p. 342, and Crawford, '"High State of Culture", forthcoming.

[314] *Stirling Journal*, 15 January 1829.

By 1837, a contributor to the *New Statistical Account* was able to report that there were innumerable dividing book clubs in Paisley: 'They have long been in high repute; and their periodical sales have been the means of introducing many valuable literary works into the houses of the members'.[315] But the minister of Lochwinnoch, Renfrewshire, commenting on its parochial library established in 1823, presented an opposing view:

> book-clubs interfere with the prosperity of the parochial institutions. Some people prefer these clubs not merely from their dislike of public libraries, but because, after they have existed for some time, the books are sold, and divided amongst the members, which enlarge and improve their private libraries.[316]

In about 1825 John McAdam, future propagandist for Italian unity, was a member of a book club in Glasgow. 'The members', he recorded, 'mainly Calton weavers and warpers, were very indulgent, giving me often first choice of books';[317] this description suggests a dividing book club, though could still refer to a small permanent library. The Calton Public Library certainly existed by 1825. By the 1820s dividing book clubs were obviously found more frequently throughout Scotland, but it had been a slow development.

Later History

The rapid expansion of subscription libraries between 1800 and 1825 can be seen in the *New Statistical Account of Scotland* published in 1845 in fifteen volumes, which is the prime source for knowledge of their development. In East Lothian, for instance, no subscription libraries are known before 1800, but fifteen appear by 1825. In Renfrewshire, sixteen subscription libraries are noted before 1800, the majority being small working class libraries; another sixteen were founded by 1825. Libraries spread throughout the bigger islands, too, beginning with Rothesay in Bute (1792) and reaching Lerwick in Shetland in 1809, Kirkwall in Orkney (1815), and, during the 1820s, the isles of Skye, Mull, Lewis, and Arran. The subsequent history of subscription libraries, however, is a tale of mixed fortunes.

A number of the smaller subscription libraries are sometimes described as parish or parochial libraries, which can confuse understanding of the kind of library they were. In England the term 'parish libraries' is used in connection with libraries attached to a local Anglican church. Although a

---

[315] *NSA*, vol. 7 (1845), p. 300.

[316] *NSA*, vol. 7 (1845), p. 108.

[317] *Autobiography of John McAdam*, p. 3.

subscription might be charged, ownership was usually vested in the church or its congregation. This distinction is not so clear in Scotland, where the term parish or parochial library could refer to a library which existed for the benefit of all members of the parish, regardless of whether they were members of the Church of Scotland. Ownership might be vested in individuals rather than in the church authorities. An example is the Tranent Parish Library established in 1792 by Rev. Hugh Cunningham and containing mostly divinity and history. Parishioners were invited to join for a shilling a year, but from 1800 anyone from inside or outside the parish could pay four shillings entry and two shillings annually. Books were selected by ballot rather than majority voting to overcome any prejudice.[318] Despite this resource, the Tranent Library, a competing proprietary subscription library, was founded in 1820.

Confusion arises because the individual ministers who compiled parochial reports for the *New Statistical Account* in the 1830s and early 1840s frequently refer to 'parish libraries' without necessarily meaning a library attached to a kirk. Undoubtedly some of these 'parish' libraries really were libraries set up by the minister, and several will have been included in the present Listing for want of further information. Parish libraries such as those in East Saltoun, Haddingtonshire, and Kirkwall in Orkney (both seventeenth-century foundations), have been excluded.[319] Most parish libraries of the nineteenth century contained improving books aimed at children and juveniles. Alexander Somerville (1811-85), the journalist, recalled:

> About this time [1824/5] a parish library was established at Innerwick [Haddingtonshire], and we got books from it. But the larger part of them were silly stories, of that silliest kind of literature – religious novels. Intermingled with these, however, were a few useful works of divinity, history, and biography. Since that time the library has been much improved.[320]

One interesting and unusual example of a 'parish-cum-subscription' library was the Comrie Parochial Library in Perthshire. This was a subscription library established for the benefit of the parish in 1820, and whose books were held in the school. The library was set up following a public subscription, which raised £29.3s., of which £12.17s.6d. was spent by the local United Secession minister, Rev. Samuel Gilfillan (1762-1826), on books bought in Edinburgh. For many years the library's annual income was below £10, and usually less than £5. But it managed to survive, and, thanks to a local benefactor, Lady

---

[318] *Cheap Magazine* (1813), p. 376.

[319] Aitken, *Public Library Movement*, pp. 2-4; for Saltoun see: 'Extracts ... Relating to Dr Gilbert Burnet, and the Library of the Kirk of Salton [sic]', in: *Bannatyne Miscellany III* (Edinburgh, 1855), pp. 389-402.

[320] Somerville, *Autobiography*, p. 47.

Lucy Dundas, a new building was built in 1901. This still survives as a branch of the county library service.

Proprietary subscription libraries were important in their time, but times changed rapidly, and competition contributed to their decline. The growth of circulating libraries – especially in Edinburgh and Glasgow – meant that the latest books could be made available more quickly, and it became easier – and cheaper – for individuals to borrow books from them, especially as rail and postal services developed. Increasing numbers of books were borrowed by proprietary subscription libraries from commercial circulating libraries to satisfy their members' needs for the books of the day. The rise of the free municipal library naturally affected subscription libraries, which could hardly compete.

Circulating libraries were more resilient, and flourished throughout the nineteenth century. In Edinburgh at least eleven new libraries were started between 1820 and 1825, and seven in Glasgow. But this kind of library too had to change, and by the end of the nineteenth century the dominance of the large circulating libraries was threatened by the arrival of chain stores – such as W. H. Smith and Boots, which flourished during the first half of the twentieth century – and the 'long-distance' services of Mudie's and other such firms, which used the postal and railway systems to dispatch books to individual homes. The small, local circulating libraries were doomed by the time of the Second World War, though a handful of libraries survived into the 1960s, especially those belonging to chains, such as Argosy Libraries.

A competitor rather different from subscription libraries arrived with Rev. Samuel Brown's scheme for itinerating libraries, which began in Haddingtonshire in 1817. One of the earliest derived from a private subscription library in North Berwick, which by 1816 had acquired a mere 155 volumes. The proprietors were induced to hand the books over to Brown who used them as the basis of a much more viable collection. Brown divided the county into divisions which received a collection of books for two years, after which they were passed on to another area. Local volunteers ran the scheme, which became very successful and provided books for all classes of society.[321] Brown avowedly intended his libraries to promote the cause of religion, but books of history, travels, and other popular works were included. By Brown's death in 1839, 3,850 volumes were divided amongst forty-seven divisions, all in East Lothian.

---

[321] Aitken, *Public Library Movement*, pp. 30-39; L. G. Durbidge, 'Itinerating Libraries', in: *Encyclopedia of Library and Information Science* (New York, 1975), vol. 13, pp. 154-60.

Samuel Brown's itinerating scheme was widely praised and imitators introduced similar schemes in Berwickshire and Roxburghshire,[322] while in 1819 a group of ministers, including Samuel Gilfillan of Comrie (see p. 136), planned and erected fourteen lending libraries in the Highlands.[323] This may be the same scheme devised by Rev. John Brown of Whitburn in 1818 to form small evangelical circulating libraries in the Highlands (Brown was the son of Rev. John Brown of Haddington and the half-brother of Samuel, both mentioned previously). The provision of small evangelical libraries had been pioneered by the itinerant preacher, William Brown (no relation), who had founded 14 religious libraries for adults and 14 for children in Aberdeenshire between 1809 and 1818.[324] Although the number of collections had much declined by 1850, itinerating libraries were influential on the thinking of the members of the 1849 Parliamentary Select Committee set up to consider the desirability of public libraries. One witness called by the Committee was Samuel Smiles, progenitor of 'self-help', who as a teenager was an enthusiastic user of the itinerating library in Haddington.[325] The Committee's report also surveyed the state of private subscription libraries: many still survived, but few were flourishing.

The example of the Kelso Library, one of the better-documented private subscription libraries in Scotland, once again can serve as an example of what befell this kind of library service provider. Although the Kelso Library had seventy-one subscribers with approximately 1,300 titles by 1793, by 1857 it had sixty-five subscribers and around 2,000 titles in about 6,000 volumes; it had hardly changed in size at all. There was by then much more competition for the supply of books, and Kelso was a small town. But private subscription libraries could not compete with circulating libraries such as Sibbald's and later libraries in Edinburgh for size and accessibility; they also enjoyed long opening hours, unlike the Kelso Library, open only for nine hours per week. In 1860 came a move to borrow books from Mudie's in London. Traditionalists opposed this proposal on the grounds that the basic purpose of the Kelso Library was the purchase and preservation of books, not their hiring. The counter-argument was that more books could be procured for readers by borrowing from a commercial library, and that the library's income could be spent on buying books of proven worth. In 1863 it was decided to spend £10 with Mudie's, which would entitle them to twenty volumes of new books

---

[322] 'Itinerating Libraries', *Bristol Mercury* (21 Mar. 1825), reprinted from *The Scotsman*.

[323] Cf. *ODNB* for Gilfillan.

[324] *Inverness Journal*, 14 January 1820, for J. Brown; R. Penman, *Memoir of William Brown* (Aberdeen, 1830), p.18; cf. J. C. Crawford, 'Denominational Libraries in 19th-century Scotland', *Library History* 7 (1985), 33-45.

[325] Thomas Mackay (ed.), *Autobiography of Samuel Smiles* (London, 1905), pp. 29-30.

and twenty volumes of last season's, to be exchanged every three months. The library would also spend £30 on purchasing books of 'ascertained worth'. The reasoning was that the library had only been able to afford £40 per year on books, enough perhaps for 80 titles of which one-quarter would turn out not to be worth keeping, thus 'losing' the library ten pounds per year. Ten pounds spent at Mudie's would mean a hundred books in a year, to be returned and replaced. The committee also suggested that extra money be spent on hiring books as an experiment, and that no new books be purchased for several months until they were available at half-price.[326]

The experiment was tried but cancelled in 1864; another attempt was defeated in 1865. The traditionalists, led by a local minister and his brother, had won in the short term, but by the 1870s the use of a commercial circulating library in Edinburgh, Edmonstone & Douglas, was approved, and this method of satisfying readers became widespread in similar libraries: for example, from 1882 Hawick Library borrowed books from Edmonstone and Douglas's successors, Douglas & Foulis.[327] People wanted the latest books as soon as possible, and the old form of subscription library was not geared up to rapid supply. Statistics of a library's size are not particularly meaningful when books may be brought in from outside, and Kelso Library's aims had to adapt to changing times. Only in 1886 were annual subscribers admitted, at a guinea a year but by 1901 there were only twenty-three proprietors, debts of £138, and heavy legal expenses in prospect. The library closed in 1907, one year after the municipal library had opened. However, difficulties in tracing the heirs of proprietors delayed the final winding-up of the library. At least seventy-seven shares were in the hands of unknown heirs rather than known executors. Strictly speaking, those shares would revert to the library if the annual fees were not paid for two years; but the library had been unable to contact many of these shareholders, and the whole business of settlement was further delayed by the Great War. The library was finally wound up in 1927 when the books – perhaps around 8,000 volumes by then – were sold for £220 and the property for £250 to the British Legion, who remain the owners.

Many private subscription libraries were to amalgamate with other libraries and often formed the basis of a municipal library. Cumbernauld Public Library (1816) merged with the local Literary Institution in 1850, and when it was dissolved in 1933 the books were transferred to Dumbarton County Library. This was how many local libraries of the twentieth century acquired older, often 'classic', books, particularly on local history. Many other subscription libraries were as long-lived as Cumbernauld. Kelso and Duns were two, while Kirkcaldy Library (1800) lasted until 1934, and Elie (1814) until 1968

---

[326] NRS, E 870/7/1, Kelso Library minute book.

[327] *Hawick Advertiser*, 22 December 1882.

when it was taken over by Fife County Libraries. Other subscription libraries which merged with municipal libraries included Forfar, Arbroath, Montrose (which ceased only in 1975), Dundee, Airdrie (which had merged first with the Mechanics' Institute), and the Banff Literary Society. The Greenock (or Watt) Library, however, enjoyed a staggering membership of 365 in 1875 and had 682 members in 1966.[328] On the other hand, the Galashiels Library was dissolved in 1857 because, it was said, of competition from 'the many cheap serials which find their way into every family'.[329] As for the Perth Library, it was taken over by the Perth Literary and Antiquarian Society in the 1890s, regardless of its much-vaunted rule which insisted that it should remain the property of the burgh rather than of individual subscribers.[330]

The demise of the older-established libraries was often put down to their exclusivity. The minister of Ayr, writing in the 1830s for the *New Statistical Account*, claimed that the Ayr Library's entry money of £3 was too high for the general public, despite having been reduced from £5. And, he added, they would have far more than 3,000 books if the fee had only been £1: 'This affords one instance among many, that when an institution sets out at first on a wrong principle, it is exceedingly difficult afterwards to get it rectified'. The Ayr Library eventually dissolved in 1871 when it only had fifteen members and its lease was shortly to expire; but the books were offered as a gift to its new rival, the Public Library.

Many libraries simply faded away. Without sufficient new members and with no urge to continue buying new books, libraries inevitably stagnated and were eventually sold off, though the books of the Lilliesleaf Library suffered the indignity of being pulped in 1942, presumably to help the war effort, while books from Biggar Public Library (1797) ended up on a hogmanay bonfire in 1921, attested by a bill paid to a local carter.[331] Several hundred volumes from the Lamlash (formerly Kilbride) Library were still extant in 1974, when they were examined by Dr John Crawford, but disappeared after the local government reorganization of 1975. At Peterhead, the members of the Reading Society, so keen in 1808 to buy books only of high worth, had for long been ordering solely cheap fiction when in 1893 they agreed to hand over the older books to the Public Library, though this decision was only reached after acrimonious discussion. Despite this, the Society managed to stagger on until 1932, but membership had so declined by then that no librarian or treasurer was needed.

---

[328] Hamilton, *Greenock Libraries*, p. 58.

[329] Kaufman, 'Community Libraries', p. 294, quoting *The Scotsman*.

[330] Smith, *Historians of Perth*, p. 100.

[331] *Library History* 3 (1974), p. 160.

Local historians often bemoaned the fate of old libraries, as in Helensburgh, where a writer in the 1890s referred to the good library which had existed there sixty years earlier but had been sold off at auction when membership declined. The Clackmannanshire Library (1797) possessed 1,500 volumes by 1840 but dissolved by 1848 when the books were bought by the newly-founded Clackmannanshire Subscription Library; but this too dissolved, in 1860. A rather acerbic, and somewhat ungenerous, local historian recalled:

> This great literary wreck was removed from the Parish School-room to the Alloa Academy, was there broken up into many fragments, and scattered by Mr Russel [sic], auctioneer, to all parts of the country – the sale of the books, the accumulation of half a century, yielding the insignificant sum of £60. The only, and apparently the last, public library in the county.[332]

One problem which impeded some libraries was that people became more reluctant to spend time on committees or attend meetings. Many minute books complain of a lack of a quorum at management meetings. On 12 November 1834 the minutes of the Lilliesleaf Library recorded:

> This night the members of the Library present agreed that in future the fines for unattendance be regourously [sic] enforced in all time to come, that the meeting[s] are frequently so small as to prevent those present from entering on Business.

The Arbroath Library permitted annual subscribers from 1844, but a near terminal decline had set in. By 1862 many subscribers were in arrears, and no more books were bought for some time. Although the library was saved by a small legacy, that was a short-term solution. The idea of opening in the evenings to attract working-class readers was rejected because of doubts as to whether there would be sufficient interest. The Public Libraries Acts were repeatedly rejected by voters in the town, but eventually a municipal library opened, and the subscription library handed over its books in 1896.[333] The Hawick Library (1762), however, was sold off in its entirety to a bookseller in 1893.[334] Although the Cupar Library survived until about 1870, it reached a crisis in 1850 when the managers resigned as a protest against the incompetence of the librarian, who had failed to attend meetings and maintain the catalogue; 200 books were said to be missing.[335]

---

[332] James Lothian, *Extinct Clackmannanshire Societies* (Alloa, 1875), pp. 11-13.

[333] M'Bain, *Arbroath Public Library*, pp. 23-42.

[334] *Hawick News*, 24 March 1893.

[335] *Report of the Special General Meeting of the Proprietors of the Cupar Library* (Cupar, 1850); copy in Cupar PL.

As the century progressed, the social dimension of belonging to a select library also became less important. The success and significance of private subscription libraries – as opposed to circulating libraries – is difficult to assess, and certainly cannot be computed by statistics. Membership figures, where they exist, show that few libraries in small towns attracted more than one hundred members, at least before 1825. Even allowing for family members reading the books, this does not represent a sizeable proportion of any local population. Although many of the country subscription libraries clearly only catered for community 'leaders', the increasing number of workers' subscription libraries suggests that the importance of reading to acquire knowledge was not lost on the 'ordinary' person. Only in Edinburgh and Glasgow did membership of private subscription libraries reach several hundreds, and their influence – before the days of municipal public libraries – must have been immense.

The increase of mechanics' institutes from the mid-1820s onwards also played a part in the changing landscape of book provision in Scotland. Although mechanics' institutes were aimed at the working classes, and were therefore usually open in the evenings, when many private subscription libraries were not, they began to attract the middle classes away from the older libraries. (Circulating libraries were often open for eleven hours per day.) But a detailed account of mechanics' institutes, as well as of literary and scientific institutes, many of which had libraries, lies well outside the scope of the present work.[336]

The motivation behind the establishment of libraries obviously differs. The private subscription libraries of the gentry and the middle-classes were self-conscious attempts to introduce literature to provincial towns as a communal resource. Subscription libraries can perhaps be best considered as components in the drive towards civic improvements which became most marked in the nineteenth century. Circulating libraries may not have aspired so highly, but they rode the crest of a wave driven, ultimately, by a demand for escapist literature, of which Scott's *Waverley* novels formed the pinnacle. Yet, their provision of non-fiction must not be ignored. The fact that many circulating libraries lent books to distant country subscribers ensures the importance of their role in distributing literature and knowledge to the furthest points of Scotland. Taken as a whole, the country's subscription and circulating libraries represented an impressive and influential resource. They were genuinely storehouses of knowledge and disseminated widely the multifarious intellectual developments of the eighteenth and early nineteenth centuries.

---

[336] For more information, see: Hudson, *Adult Education*; Brian Burch, 'Libraries and Literacy in Popular Education', in: Giles Mandelbrote and K. A. Manley, *The Cambridge History of Libraries in Britain and Ireland: Vol. 2: 1640-1850* (Cambridge, 2006), pp. 371-87; K. A. Manley, 'From Workers' Libraries to Public Libraries', in: Mechanics' Institutes of Victoria Inc., *Building Books and Beyond...: Proceedings of an International Conference ... 2004* (Melbourne, 2004), pp. 253-66.

Appendix I

Rules of the Montrose Library (1785)

[From *Gentleman's Magazine* 55 (July 1785), pp. 535-6.]

Concordia res parvæ crescunt

I. Every subscriber to pay one guinea yearly, in the month of January: the first guinea to be paid in the month of June, as some months of 1785 are already elapsed. Subscribers are not bound to present books, as originally proposed; but all donations, either from subscribers, or others, will be thankfully received, and entered in the Journal of the Society.

II. The books to be deposited in a room in town, hired for the purpose; and any subscriber may cause a key to be made for himself, at his own expence.

III. Two managers and a secretary to be chosen annually by a majority of subscribers, who shall attend at a general meeting. These three to have full powers to purchase books, cause them to be bound, and do every thing else that may be necessary.

IV. The society to have three white paper books placed in their library; a CATALOGUE to contain a list of the books, with the prices of each; a JOURNAL, to contain minutes of their transactions and resolutions, account of donations, &c. &c.; and a REGISTER, to contain a list of books taken out of the library.

V. Every subscriber taking out any book, is to mark it in the *Register* in the following manner, "June 10, 1785, Gibbon's Roman History, vol. 1. A. B."

VI. Until a book has been six months in the library, no person to be at liberty to keep it above eight days at once, upon penalty of 6d. a day. After six months, it may be kept one month at a time. Subscribers not to send servants, but either to call themselves, or cause another subscriber to bring them books out of the library.

VII. Subscribers are not to give the books to one another, but to return them to the library after their time is out. No one to take out a new book a second time, until it has been lodged by him eight days in the library. If any subscriber finds a book out that he wished to see, he is to mark in the Register the date when he called, which will secure to him a preference when the book is returned to the library.

VIII. On the last week of the year all the books are to be returned to the library, in order that it may be seen if any of them are missing.

IX. Subscribers are not to lend the books to others out of their own families, as the expence of the subscription is moderate; and it is not thought reasonable that others should profit at the expence of the generous few.

X. The books to be bought are chiefly the best new books in History, Belles Lettres, Voyages and Travels, Antiquities, Natural and Moral Philosophy, and Theology. Some part of the money to be reserved for purchasing standard works already published.

XI. No Romances to be admitted, unless presented, or when a particular exception is made in favour of a work of superior excellence, such as Miss Burney's *Cecilia*.

XII. It is understood that the managers will employ the subscription money in such a way as to suit, as much as possible, the general tastes of the subscribers; and, on the other hand, it is hoped, that no subscriber, if the books are generally agreeable, will take it amiss, if some few are introduced that may not suit his taste, or plan of reading, the whole success of the plan depending on unanimity. The greater part of the money is to be laid out in buying books adapted to general reading, and only a small part to be devoted to professional books in medicine, Commerce, Law or Theology. Professional books of Theology are understood to be such as discuss the controversies among Christians. Books in defence of Christianity, illustrations of the Sacred Writings, and Sermons, are not professional books, because it belongs to every man, more or less, to know the grounds of our common religion, to understand the Scriptures, and to be put in mind of the important duties enjoined in them. So much of this article as provides, that professional books shall not be *totally* and in every case excluded, is to be fundamental and unalterable.

XIII. Quarto volumes, published at London, not to be bought till they come to octavos, unless in particular cases, or when, from the nature of the work, it cannot be expected to be re-printed in octavo.

XIV. If any subscriber leave the country, or withdraw his subscription, the books remain the property of those who continue the scheme; but he may transfer his property in the library to any other person, who shall then begin to be a subscriber.

XV. Subscribers, who wish any particular book to be bought, may recommend them to the secretary, who is then to consult the managers.

XVI. Managers for 1785, Rev. Mr Reay, Dr Mudie; Thomas Christie, secretary.

N.B. Next year some rule is to be fixed as to the terms of admitting those who shall become subscribers after the first year. The present number of subscribers is 36, who are persons of all stations, sects, and professions.

APPENDIX II

SIZE AND MEMBERSHIP OF LIBRARIES: STATISTICAL SURVEY

TABLE I

Number of volumes in selected subscription libraries 1790-1910

Name	1790	1810	1840	1880	1910
Alloa			1,500		
Arbroath			4,000		
Ayr		3,000			
Cupar (Fife)			4,000		
Dalkeith		1,200	2,400		
Dumbarton		2,000			
Duns	600			5,070	7,000
Edinburgh		3,000		40,000	
Edinburgh Select		1,100	10,000	30,000	
Greenock	500		10,000		
Falkirk		3,000			
Hawick			3,500		
Kelso	5,000		5,000	8,000	
Kelso Modern		1,500			
Kelso New		2,000			
Kilbride			300		
Kilmarnock	840				
Leadhills	700				4,000*
Methven			1,100		
Montrose			7,000	20,000	27,000
Paisley	3,000		4,500		
Penicuik			1,200		
Perth		2,000	5,500		
St. Andrews				1,200	
Sanquhar			1,460		
Stirling		2,000			
Wanlockhead	309		1,300	2,500	4,000*

* Total in 1900

Table 2

Number of members in selected subscription libraries 1790-1910

Figures include both shareholders and annual subscribers, if known.

Name	**1790**	**1810**	**1840**	**1880**	**1910**
Ayr	73	105	108		
Catrine United					177
Cupar (Fife)		140			
Dalry			120		
Dumfries Gentlemen's			30		
Dumfries Public			75		
Duns	54			80	
Edinburgh		180	350	400	
Edinburgh Select		110	593	306	
Galashiels			153		
Glasgow Public		300			
Greenock	70	170		365	
Hawick	41		56		
Hawick Trades		40	135		
Kelso	70	70	70		53
Montrose		70	100		
Paisley		200	200		
Penicuik			50		
Perth	54				
St. Andrews			100		
Sanquhar			178		
Stirling		127			
Wanlockhead			105	65	

TABLE 3

Number of volumes in selected circulating libraries 1770-1825

Place/Name	1770	1790	1810	1825
Aberdeen: Angus	3,000		over 50,000*	
Aberdeen: Brown		3,536		
Ayr: Dick				3,000
Dunbar: Miller		2,500		
Edinburgh: P. Buchanan		5,000		
Edinburgh: Clarke			7,000	
Edinburgh: Kinnear			7,000	
Elgin: Forsyth		1,092	3,000	5-6,000
Glasgow: Murdoch			1,400	
Glasgow: Knox	1,000			
Glasgow: Noble		4,000		
Glasgow: J. Smith	2,000		20,000	
Inverness: Dick		1,000		
Perth: Hill		1,800		1,200

*Amalgamation of Burnett's (late Angus) and Brown's libraries

TABLE 4

Number of titles in selected circulating libraries 1770-1825

Place/Name	1770	1780	1790	1810	1825
Aberdeen: Angus	1,830		3,384		
Aberdeen: Brown			3,536		
Dunbar: Miller				2,500	
Dundee: Hamilton					700
Dundee: Nicoll	1,000				
Edinburgh: Gray	1,700				
Edinburgh: Sibbald/ Mackay		4,338			7,600
Edinburgh: Tansh					1,471
Edinburgh: Hunter					1,940
Glasgow: J. Smith			3,631*	5,400	6,000
Paisley: Caldwell			442		
Paisley: Auld				1,200	

*Total in 1796

Listing

Scope

The purpose of the Listing is to document all proprietary subscription libraries, commercial circulating libraries, and book clubs known to have been founded in Scotland before 1825. The Listing is arranged topographically according to the old county names which would have been familiar at the time of the *Statistical Accounts* of the 1790s and 1840s. Under each place name, the listings are arranged according to the following order: proprietary (i.e. private) subscription libraries, circulating libraries, book clubs. Sources of information are given for each individual library where appropriate, but published references to more than one library appear at the end of the entry for that place. Unsourced information usually derives from trades directories, which have not been separately itemized; additional information about certain specific libraries will be found in Paul Kaufman's essay on Scottish community libraries, cited in the Preface. Much of the information about subscription libraries comes from the *Statistical Account of Scotland* (*OSA*) and *New Statistical Account* (*NSA*) volumes; it should be remembered that within each volume, each county section is paginated separately. For further bibliographical details of *OSA* and *NSA*, see the Abbreviations section.

Foundation dates of libraries are given when known, but in many cases are unknown and may never be discoverable. Some libraries have been included if they definitely existed just after 1825 and there appears a reasonable chance they were in operation before that date; a few libraries known to have been founded after 1825 have crept in, especially if no other earlier library in the locale has been found. The emphasis has been to record successive locations of libraries and, in the case of circulating libraries, their owners, including information relating to those libraries which continued in existence beyond 1825. Wherever possible, brief details are given of stock size, fees, and, in particular, library catalogues; locations are provided for surviving catalogues, and non-extant catalogues are indicated by an asterisk (*) after the date. In some cases locations have been taken from a secondary source, and are followed by a query (?); it has not always been possible to verify every location. Supplementary catalogues are shown by the abbreviation 'supp.' immediately before the date of that supplement. Subsequent dates given will be of whole catalogues unless otherwise stated. Archival as well as printed sources are listed.

No attempt has been made to list individual librarians of subscription libraries. In a handful of cases (e.g. Greenock and Ayr) the names of successive librarians have been recorded in the sources and can be compiled from the bibliographical references given here, but for the majority of libraries it is impossible to recover the names of their keepers.

Much of the material provided in the Listing has been derived from local directories and histories, newspapers, book labels, archives, advertisements, and, quite often, from brief, passing references in published diaries and letters and locally published books, including imprints and other sources. Undoubtedly, further similar libraries must have existed, and the compiler is always interested to learn of new finds. Because of the inexactness of terminology, a number of subscription libraries may have been included which were not strictly proprietary subscription libraries. Parish libraries have been excluded if it is known that ownership rested with the kirk rather than a group of proprietors, but sometimes the words 'library' or 'parish library' appear in a local directory, and it is impossible to establish exactly what kind of library is meant.

A *caveat* is necessary here, because newspapers and directories cannot be relied upon for strict accuracy; conflicting information sometimes appears, such as alternative spellings of the same surname; in particular, inexact, unclear, or often contradictory addresses abound. Many errors which have appeared in other publications have been silently corrected here, but at the same time some old, and possibly new, errors may have been inadvertently included. One important source for background information relating to the book trade, and therefore relevant for circulating libraries, is the Scottish Book Trade Index, compiled by the late John Morris and freely available through the website of the National Library of Scotland, though this too shares the problem above of listing booksellers with contradictory forms of names and addresses. It must also be borne in mind that the Listing includes the dates for which circulating libraries existed, where known or presumed; but many booksellers who ran a library may have been selling books for a much longer period. Only their careers as library owners are relevant to the present work.

Parts of the Listing have appeared on the internet, though in condensed form, as my contribution to Professor Robin Alston's 'List of British Libraries 1500 to 1850'. But many amendments and 'discoveries' have been added to my own database, and the Listing presented here represents a substantial revision of the material currently available online.

Aberdeenshire

Aberdeen

Subscription libraries

Aberdeen Medico-Chirurgical Society: not a private subscription library, but effectually operated as one for medical books; est. as discussion society in 1789, and added library in 1791; belonged to Marischal College; 3,000 vols. by 1839; cat. 1812 (Aberdeen UL).

Caledonian Literary Society; est. 22 Feb. 1805; cost 10s.6d. entry + 6s. p.a. and the gift of one book; library kept in bookshop of Alexander Stevenson, Castle St.; 80 members by 1805; 1,000 vols. by 1809; label in Franks clln.; cats. 1814[1], supp. ca. 1820 (Aberdeen PL; [1]also in Aberdeen UL).
Aberdeen Journal (20 Nov. 1805, 1 Feb. 1809).

Aberdeen Reading Society; est. 1805; dissolved in 1834 when had only been open for two hours per week; held at 64 Broad St.; cat. 1828*.
Aberdeen Journal (13 Feb. 1828, 26 Feb. 1834).

St. Peter's Chapel, Castlegate: by ca. 1815; chapel erected in 1803 by Charles Gordon, priest, who established a circulating library there by ca.1818 or before; cat. 1821 (Scottish Catholic Archives).
Robert Wilson, *An Historical Account and Delineation of Aberdeen* (Aberdeen, 1822), pp.125-6.

Circulating libraries

Alexander Angus (1721-1802), Castlegate; est. 1764; mainly novels; in Narrow Wynd by 1791; succeeded by John Burnett, 1795, who may have started his own library in Broad St. shortly before; Angus's library was moved to Burnett's shop; 6,000 vols. in 1796; merged with A. Brown's library, 1804 (see below); Burnett died in 1806; cats. 1764*, 1765[1,2,3], supps. ca. 1766[2] & 1771*, 1773*, supp. 1775*, ca. 1779[2], 1787*, supps. 1789-90[2], 1796[3] ([1]Aberdeen PL; [2]Aberdeen UL; [3]NLS).

John Boyle, head of Broadgate; est. 1765; this library may have dissolved during the 1770s and revived in 1797; died 1805; cats. 1765*, supps. 1766-7*, 1768*, 1797*.

James White, Broadgate, by 1788, when may have had music library.
Aberdeen Journal (1 Jul. 1788).

Alexander Brown (1766-1843), Broad St.; est. 1789; almost 7,500 titles by 1821; est. a separate large music library in 1798, which cost an extra £1.5s. p.a.; on 1 Feb. 1804 the main library was merged with Burnett's library (above) to form the United Public Library; the new library of 50,000 vols. was kept on the second floor of the Athenaeum, Castle St.; subscribers to the latter were allowed an extra book; library run by Brown and Burnett until 1806, from when Brown on own, but Burnett family continued to own a share until 1823; moved to Forbes Frost's bookshop in Broad St. in 1810 but still owned by Brown; moved to Brown's house, 38 Broad St., 1814, when Frost became Brown's partner; sometimes known as Aberdeen Public (or Circulating) Library; at 71 Union St. from 1831 (then other nos. in Union St.); business merged with David Wyllie (see A. Watson, below) in 1915; cats. ca. 1789 (Houghton Library, Harvard), supp. 1790*, ca. 1796, 1804*, supps. 1806* & 1809* and 1814* & 1815, cats. 1818*, 1821[1], 1822, supps. 1827* & ca. 1838 (Aberdeen PL;[1] also in Edinburgh PL); music library cats. 1798, supps. 1799 & 1805 (Aberdeen PL).

Aberdeen Journal (15 & 29 Oct. 1798, 25 Jan. 1804, 1 Feb. 1809, 30 May 1810, 20 Mar. 1811, 22 Jun. & 12 Oct. 1814, 15 Feb. 1815, 30 Dec. 1818, 16 Oct. 1822, 26 Nov. 1823, 17 Oct. 1827, 14 Dec. 1831).

George Moir, Gallowgate; est. 1800; excluded novels and politics; 600 vols., mostly history and religion; he was also an hosier; died 1803 and library continued by widow until about 1808; possibly a relation of Thomas Moir (see below)?; cat. 1800, supp. ca. 1802 (Aberdeen UL).

Aberdeen Journal (27 Oct. 1800).

James Davie & Michael Morris's musical library, by 1814; partnership dissolved, 1815; Davie on own at various addresses, but unknown if library continued.

Aberdeen Journal (9 Feb. 1814).

Alexander Stevenson, 60 Castle St., by 1814; bankrupt 1831 though continued, at least as bookseller; cat. 1827*.

Aberdeen Journal (14 Sep. 1814, 31 Oct. 1827).

William Robertson, 19 Broad St., by 1815; known as Aberdeen New Public Library; planned to move to the former Exchange News Rooms, 1822; bankrupt 1831 and succeeded by John Russel [sic], then William & John Russel until 1832, when William on own; became partner with - Gordon, but latter died 1857; William Russel continued on own, at least as bookseller; retired 1878; cats. 1816*, 1818*, 1822*, 1828*, supp. 1832*.

Aberdeen Journal (26 Apr. 1815, 7 Feb. 1816, 30 Dec. 1818, 7 Nov. 1821, 20 Mar. & 13 Nov. 1822, 17 Aug. 1831, 31 Oct. 1832, 2 Mar. 1878).

William Laurie, 38 Gallowgate; est. 1818; at 11 St. Nicholas St. by 1827; at 169 Union St. West by 1831; for sale, 1846, when had 6,000 vols.; cats. 1819*, 1825*, supp. 1836*; sale cat. 1846*.

Aberdeen Journal (18 Nov. 1818, 20 Oct. 1819, 26 Oct. 1825, 26 Oct. 1836, 18 Nov. 1846).

Alexander Watson, 51 Broad St., by 1821; bookseller by 1811; also lent drawings and ornaments to copy; opened a Juvenile Library, 1827; moved to 95 Union St., 1827 (the Broad St. shop was taken by George Clark, bookseller, previously of Peterhead); dissolved 1832, but 4,000 vols. bought by David Wyllie & son, who est. circulating library at his bookshop, 43 Union St.; latter were booksellers by 1814; at 51 Union St. from 1833 to 1847, then various shops in same street; Wyllie (father) died in 1844 and son in 1894; in 1915 took over the business of A. Brown (above); Wyllie & son's library still existed in 1930s; cats. 1821, 1826*, supp. 1827*, 1833, supps. 1827* & 1843* & 1867* (Aberdeen UL).

Aberdeen Journal (8 Aug. & 12 Sep. 1821, 14 Feb., 22 Aug. & 12 Dec. 1827, 12 Dec. 1832); *Aberdeen Book-Lover* (Nov. 1914).

Artists' Repository, 1 Adelphi, Union St., by 1821; circulating portfolio of 500 drawings, etc., lent out to copy.

Aberdeen Journal (21 Nov. 1821).

James Johnston, Union St.; est. as a bookseller in Dec. 1821 and planned to open a circulating library of religious & moral books in 1822; but library was sold off late in 1822.

Aberdeen Journal (5 Dec. 1821, 16 Oct. 1822).

James Ellithorne, 88 (later 89) Green, by 1825, according to SBTI.

Thomas Moir, 12 Correction Wynd, by 1825; a relation of George Moir, above?; at 45 The Green by 1825, and at 28 Upperkirkgate by 1828 until 1833.

James Elmslie, 57 North St., by 1828.

William Collie, 47 Upper Kirkgate, by 1827; bookseller by 1822; succeeded in bookshop by Lewis Smith, who ran library at 66 Broad St. by 1834.

Walter Thom, *History of Aberdeen*, vol. 2 (Aberdeen, 1811) 207-9; J. & M. Lough, 'Aberdeen Circulating Libraries in the 18th Century', *Aberdeen University Review* 31 (1945-6) 17-23; W. R. McDonald, 'Circulating Libraries in the North-east of Scotland in the 18th Century', *Bibliotheck* 5 (1968) 119-37; Pigot (1825/6-37).

Cardno

James Nicol, grocer and bookseller, planned to open a circulating library in 1801; unclear where the library was to be; Cardno is a parish near Fraserburgh, but not a town itself; he is probably the person of that name who was a merchant in nearby Strichen by 1808, later described as bookseller; person of same name also later in Turriff (see below).

Aberdeen Journal (14 Oct. 1801).

CRAIGDAM

Craigdam Library: subscription library, by 1825, when meeting held to consider its future.
Aberdeen Journal (30 Mar. 1825).

FRASERBURGH: see CARDNO

HUNTLY

George Legg: circulating library, by 1825, when for sale.
Aberdeen Journal (28 Dec. 1825).

John Geddes: circulating library, by 1825; may have been succeeded by Charles Cameron, who ran Huntly Circulating Library by 1829; joined by James Downie, 1833, who ran library on own from 1836.
Pigot (1825/6); *Aberdeen Journal* (1 Jul. 1829, 21 Dec. 1836).

NEW DEER

Two unidentified circulating libraries by 1825.
Pigot (1825/6).

NEW MACHAR

New Machar Library: subscription library; est. 1816; 470 vols. by 1842; dissolved 1849.
NSA, vol. 12 (1845) 1034; *Aberdeen Journal* (25 Jul. 1849).

OLDMELDRUM

John Montgomery, jun.: circulating library, by 1810, when bankrupt; he was also grocer and druggist; succeeded by Robert Henry, 1811; presumably bankrupt, because in 1820 Thomas Moir, writer, advertised the existence of a circulating library of 500 vols., and that he could direct intending subscribers to the person in charge.
Aberdeen Journal (19 Dec. 1810, 13 Feb. & 15 May 1811, 31 May 1820).

Peterhead

Subscription libraries

Peterhead Subscription Circulating Library; est. ca. 1799 for the working classes; cost 5s. per ½ year; dissolved ca. 1815.

Peterhead Reading Society; est. 12 Sep. 1808; 1 gn. p.a.; 300 vols. by 1815; in 1893 all pre-1889 books were donated to the Public (Municipal) Library, but the Society continued until 1932; cats. 1808, 1822*, 1832, supps. to 1846, 1859*, 1868, 1889*, 1893, supps. 1894-1900 (Aberdeenshire Libraries HQ, Aberdeen); minute books, 1808-1932 (Aberdeenshire Libraries HQ, Aberdeen).

Windmill St. Congregational Church Library, by ca. 1825; cat. ca. 1825 (Aberdeen UL).

Circulating libraries

William Farquhar, by Jan. 1794; moved to Edinburgh later in same year but does not seem to have continued his library; cat. 1794*.
   William Farquhar, *Poems on Several Occasions* (Edinburgh, 1794) 186-7; *Bibliotheck* 5 (1968) 132-3; William Walker, *The Bards of Bon-accord 1375-1860* (Aberdeen, 1887) 313-5.

John Dallachy, by 1803 when died and books for sale; bookseller here since 1795.
   Aberdeen Journal (3 Aug. 1803).

George Clark, Broad St.; est. 1805; he was a bookseller in Aberdeen and also ran library in Inverness; run by his brother, A. Clark by 1808; partner with Alexander Sangster by 1816 when A. Clark retired in favour of G. Clark; partnership dissolved, 1822, and Sangster continued on own.
   Aberdeen Journal (15 May 1805, 13 Mar. 1816, 1 May 1822); Alexander Murray, *Peterhead a Century Ago* (Peterhead, 1910) 53.

William Mortimer, Broad St., by 1814; known as Peterhead Circulating Library; for sale in 1818, when had 1,500 vols.; business bought by James Smith and John Cairns, who started a new library, but stock-in-trade for sale, 1820; this library had 'new proprietors' in 1821, when run by George Mudie, St. Andrew's St.; 1,300 vols.; Mudie was in Maiden Lane by 1825 and back in St. Andrew's St. by 1837; he still ran library in 1852; cats. before 1818*, 1818*.
   Aberdeen Journal (29 Dec. 1813, 22 Apr., 27 May, & 14 Oct. 1818, 9 Feb. 1820, 11 Jul. 1821).

James Arbuthnot, *Historical Account of Peterhead* (Aberdeen, 1815) 78-79; P. Buchan, *Annals of Peterhead* (Peterhead, 1819) 125-6.

Tillyching

Tillyching Library: subscription library; est. 1814; 400 vols. by 1843.
  NSA, vol. 12 (1845) 1095.

Towie

Towie Library: subscription library; est. 1827.
  NSA, vol. 12 (1845) 419.

Turriff

Turriff Circulating Library: probably a circulating, rather than a subscription, library; est. 1818; proprietor unknown; could possibly be James Nicol (see Cardno, above) who become a bookseller in nearby Strichen; a James Nicol was bookseller here by 1837 and also in 1876 (presumably son) at 10 High St.; cat. 1818*, supp. 1818*.
  Aberdeen Journal (15 Apr. & 21 Oct. 1818).

Angus: see Forfarshire

ARGYLLSHIRE

Campbeltown

Campbeltown Public Library: subscription library, by ca. 1790; cost 6s. p.a.

Another subscription library, consisting of religious works, est. ca. 1793; cost 1s. p.a.
  OSA, vol. 10 (1794) 561-2; Pigot (1820) 2nd edn.: *Addenda*.

Dalmally

Library for lead miners working at nearby Ben Cruachan: subscription library; est. ca. 1784; but unknown where the books were actually kept.
  Thomas A. Thornton, *Sporting Tour through the Northern Parts of England* (London, 1804) 241.

LOCHGILPHEAD

Subscription Library, by 1825.
 Pigot (1825).

AYRSHIRE

ARDROSSAN

Two unidentified circulating libraries by 1820.
 George Robertson, *Topographical Description of Ayrshire* (Irvine, 1820) 154.

AYR

Subscription libraries

Ayr Library Society; est. 1 Jan. 1762; 51 members in 1781, and 73 in 1792; 2,000 vols. by 1803; books kept by the various librarians, but settled in Fort St. in 1804; dissolved 1876 and most books passed to the Public (Municipal) Library; cats. 1781*, 1785[1,2], supp. 1791[1], 1795[1], 1802[2,3], 1817[2,3,4], supps. to 1827[2,3], 1832[1,5] ([1]Ardrossan PL; [2]NLS; [3]Ayr PL; [4]Mitchell Library; [5]Glasgow UL); minute books & accounts, 1776-1858 (formerly in Ayr PL, now in Ayrshire AO?), 1859-75 (Ayr PL).

Ayr, Newton, and Wallacetown Library; est. 9 Jun. 1806; originally 6d. per month + 2d. per meeting; 35 members and 100 titles by 1814; 300 vols. in 1826, when dissolved; cat. 1814 (NLS); sale cat. 1826*.
 Air Advertiser (24 Aug. 1826).

Ayr Mechanics' Library: really a mechanics' institute, rather than subscription library; est. 1825; cats. 1825[1], 1826[1], 1841[2], ca. 1865[1,2] ([1]Ayr PL; [2]Ardrossan PL).

Ayrshire Horticultural Library: specialist subscription library; est. 1827; held at William MacCarter's, New Bridge St. (see below); cat. ca. 1827*.

Circulating libraries

James Meuros; est. 1766; may only have lasted a short time; his main business was in Kilmarnock, where he also ran a library (see below); cat. 1766*.
 Edinburgh Advertiser (14/17 Jan. 1766).

James Jamieson, by 1808; in Sandgate St. by 1820, and Main St. by 1825; at 12 Sandgate St. by 1830, possibly as bookseller only; cat. 1808, supp. 1810 (Ardrossan PL).
Pigot (1825/6).

David Auld, perfumer and hair-dresser, lent prints and drawings by 1815 when moved to the New Bridge.
Air Advertiser (3 Aug. 1815).

John Dick, Sandgate; est. 1825 when had 3,000 vols.; at 28 New Bridge St. by 1837; still there in 1860; cat. 1825*.
Air Advertiser (10 Nov. 1825).

William MacCarter, 7 New Bridge St., by 1826.
Air Advertiser (4 May 1826).

Allan Leach, *Libraries in Ayr, 1762-1975* (Ayr 1975): reprinted from *Ayrshire Collections* 2nd ser. 11 (1975) 69-84; *NSA*, vol. 5 (1845) 72-73; local directories.

Beith

Subscription library

Beith Library, by 1818; kept in parish school; still existed in 1839; cat. 1818 (NLS).
Pigot (1820) 2nd edn.: *Addenda*; *NSA*, vol. 5 (1845) 603.

Circulating libraries

William White, by 1780; see Irvine, below, where he also had library; probably the same library as used by Elizabeth Gooch in 1789; cat. ca. 1780 (Ardrossan PL).
Life of Mrs Gooch (London, 1792) vol. 3, 102.

John Smith, Town Buildings, by 1834; unknown when library started, but he was grocer in Whang St. by 1825; still there in 1860, then as Smith & son until about 1878; cat. 1834 (NLS).

Catrine

Subscription library for working classes by 1796, according to *Scots Chronicle* (10 Feb. 1797).

Catrine Public Library: subscription library; est. 1814; 70 members, paying £1 entry and 2s.3d. p.a., and 600 vols. by 1837; dissolved 1849.

Catrine Philosophical Library: subscription library; est. 1825; 24 members and 90 vols. by 1837; 2s. entry + 6d. per quarter; in 1858 merged with Catrine New Public Library and Catrine Book Society to form the Catrine United Public Library; 4,500 vols. by 1897; cats. 1858, supp. 1862 (Ardrossan PL).

NSA, vol. 5 (1845) 145-6.

Dalmellington

Dalmellington Library: subscription library; est. 1823; 60 members and 800 vols. by 1837; still existed in 1852.
NSA, vol. 5 (1845) 320.

Dalry

Dalry Library: subscription library; est. 1811; postmaster was librarian; 1,000 vols. and 120 members by 1836.
Pigot (1820) 2nd edn.; *NSA*, vol. 5 (1845) 238.

Darvel

Darvel Library: subscription library, by 1825?; est. 'many years' before 1842.
NSA, vol. 5 (1845) 852.

Dunlop

Dunlop Library: subscription library; est. 1828.
NSA, vol. 5 (1845) 306.

Fenwick

Subscription library for working classes by 1796, according to *Scots Chronicle* (30 Dec. 1796).

Fenwick Library: subscription library; est. 1808; re-formed, 30 Dec. 1826; cost 1 gn. + 4s. p.a.; still existed in 1908 but may have dissolved shortly afterwards; cat. 1827 (NLS); records, 1833-1908 (Ayrshire AO).
J. C. Crawford, 'Recovering the Lost Scottish Community Library: the Example of Fenwick', *Library History* 23 (2007) 201-12.

Galston

Galston Library Society: subscription library, by 1806; probably same library as here in 1837; rules (1806) in NLS.
    Pigot (1825); *NSA*, vol. 5 (1845) 189.

Girvan

Girvan Library: subscription library; est. ca. 1810; still there in 1840s.
    NSA, vol. 5 (1845) 405.

Irvine

Subscription library

Irvine Library; est. 1795.

Circulating libraries

William White, by 1780, when had 3,000 vols.; he also had a shop at Beith, above; cat. ca. 1780 (Ardrossan PL).

Maxwell Dick, High St., by 1825; he invented a suspension bridge in 1829; library still in business in 1860; died 1870.

Pigot (1820-37); *Edinburgh Almanack* (1827): *Western Kalendar*.

Kilbirnie

Kilbirnie Library: subscription library; est. 1820; 500 vols. by 1840, when cost 2s.6d. entry + 2s.6d. p.a.; minute books, 1853-92 (NRS).
    NSA, vol. 5 (1845) 723.

Kilmarnock

Subscription libraries

Subscription library for working classes by 1796, according to *Scots Chronicle* (30 Dec. 1796).

Kilmarnock Public Library; est. 30 Nov. 1797; originally held in Grammar School; used room in Town House from 1811 when had 840 vols.; at 18 Cheapside by 1837, and 5 Portland St. by 1860; took over the libraries of the Philosophical Institution and the Athenaeum in 1862; moved to Corn

Exchange Buildings by 1880; merged with Public Library, which opened in 1895; cats. 1811, 1835, 1865[1], 1880, 1895, 1901 (Dick Institute, Kilmarnock; [1]also in Ardrossan PL); minute books, 1797-1874 (Ayrshire AO).

    Archibald M'Kay, *History of Kilmarnock* (Kilmarnock, 1880) 309-10; *Glasgow Herald* (21 Oct. 1893, 18 Feb. 1895).

Kilmarnock (New?) Library, by 1820.

Circulating libraries

James Meuros's Ayrshire Circulating Library, by ca. 1760?; also ran library in Ayr (see above); bookseller here until 1821, but unknown how long library continued; a defendant in the landmark perpetual copyright case in 1774; cat. ca. 1760 (fragment in BL).

John Wilson (d. 1821), by 1782; at 23 High St. by 1790; moved to Ayr to commence *Air Advertiser*, 1803.

    Glasgow Mercury (18 Apr. 1782).

Robert Mathie, 1 King St., by 1816; run by Elizabeth Mathie by 1825, and by James Mathie by 1837; still there in 1860.

    Air Advertiser (24 Oct. 1816).

Hugh Crawford, The Cross, by 1820; joined by son by 1837 at 2 King St., possibly same address; still here in 1851; cat. 1820*.

    Ayrshire Collections 2nd ser. 12 (1976) 33.

Robert Nelson, by 1826, when died and library for sale.

    Glasgow Herald (24 Mar. 1826).

James Paterson (1805-76), 53 King St., est. 1826; opened a reading room in 1827 in addition to his 'public library'; edited *Kay's Edinburgh Portraits* (London, 1837-9 & 1885).

    Air Advertiser (27 Sep. 1827); *ODNB*.

George Robertson, *Topographical Description of Ayrshire* (Irvine, 1820) 380; Pigot (1820-37).

KILWINNING

Subscription library for working classes by 1796, according to *Scots Chronicle* (30 Dec. 1796).

Largs

Subscription library

Largs Library; est. 1815; next to the baths in Bath Buildings, Bath St.; 400 books by 1836.

Circulating libraries

James Morrison, by 1825; at 6 Main St. in 1837; person of same name ran library in Greenock (see below).

Robert Harriston, by 1825.
 Largs Magazine (1826) imprint.

Pigot (1820) 2nd edn.: *Addenda*, & (1821-37).

Mauchline

Mauchline Conversation Society: discussion society with library; est. by Robert Burns and others in ca. 1786.
 Robert Burns, *Works*, vol. 1 (Liverpool, 1800) 111, & subscription list.

Maybole

Maybole Library: subscription library, by 1822; subscribed to John Goldie, *Poems & Songs* (Ayr, 1822); cats. n.d. (Ayr PL), 1822 (Glasgow UL).

Muirkirk

Subscription library for workers, by 1797.
 Monthly Magazine 4 (Oct. 1797) 275-7.

New Cumnock

New Cumnock Subscription Library: subscription library; est. 1828.
 Pigot (1837).

Newmilns

Newmilns Library: subscription library, by 1825?; est. 'many years' before 1842, when had 500 vols.
   NSA, vol. 5 (1845) 852.

Newton-upon-Ayr:
see under Ayr for Ayr, Newton, and Wallacetown Library

Saltcoats

Subscription Library, by 1825.

Tradesmen's Library: subscription library, by 1825.

Pigot (1825).

Stewarton

Stewarton Library: subscription library; est. 1810; open to annual subscribers for 6s. p.a. from 1825; still existed in 1900; cat. 1816[1], supp. 1825 (Ardrossan PL; [1]also in New York PL).
   NSA, vol. 5 (1845) 739.

Tarbolton

Subscription Library; est. ca. 1813; still existed in 1837.
   Pigot (1825/6-37).

BANFFSHIRE

Banff

Book Society: unclear whether a book club or a subscription library; est. ca. 1798 by 20 gents.
   OSA, vol. 20 (1798) 369.

Subscription libraries

Banff Literary Society; originally a discussion society, with permanent library; est. by five students, 6 Oct. 1810; some members also met in Aberdeen for a time; from 1811 paid 3s. p.a. and 2d. per week, and met in room provided by the town council; subscribed to Imlach's circulating library from 1813; 1,400 vols. by 1819; eventually became an ordinary subscription library, kept in Town House; 2,000 vols. by 1836; only 23 members by 1886; 6,000 vols. by 1891; taken over by Public Library, 1899; cat. 1896 (NLS); minutes & accounts, 1810-34 (Grampian Archives).

    William Cramond, *Annals of Banff*, vol. 1 (Aberdeen, 1891) 249-50; *Aberdeen Journal* (20 Oct. 1819); *Aberdeen Weekly Journal* (7 & 9 Jan., 6 Jul. 1899).

Independent Chapel Library; est. 1814; 320 vols. by 1836.

Circulating library

James Imlach and James Smith, by 1770; Imlach on own by 1786 and died in 1820, age 79; Banff Literary Society, above, subscribed to the library from 1813, according to its minutes, 15 Dec. 1813; this may be the Banff Circulating Library which was to be sold off in 1831; his son, James Imlach, was still in Low St. in 1837, at least as bookseller; cats. 1786*, 1796*.

    Bibliotheck 5 (1968) 131; Pigot (1825/6-37); *Aberdeen Journal* (18 Apr. 1832).

NSA, vol. 13 (1845) 52-53.

CABRACH

Cabrach Library: subscription library; est. 22 Mar. 1815; originally excluded novels and plays and cost 4s. (later 6s.) entry + 1s. p.a.; only open on last Friday of month; kept at Mains of Lesmurdie (home of first librarian, James Taylor) and from 1823 at the United Presbyterian Church, Oldtown; 60 members by 1826 when split; main library continued in lower village, while part of the books were moved to Upper Cabrach; latter dissolved by ca. 1900, though books still existed in 1915; main collection moved to Milltown of Lesmurdie, 1844, then to new school, 1865; 500 vols. and 20-30 members by 1920; dissolved ca. 1925?

    'Lower Cabrach Library Centenary, 1815-1915', *Banffshire Journal* (27 Apr. 1915); James Taylor, *Cabrach Feerings* (Banff, 1920) 106-11.

DUFFTOWN

J. Eyval's Dufftown Circulating Library: circulating library, by unknown date, but probably by mid-1820s; known from book label; presumably same as

James Eyvel [sic], who was merchant here by 1824 and listed as a linen-draper in Convel St. in 1837.
   Henry W. Fincham, *Artists and Engravers of British & American Bookplates* (London, 1897) under W. Gordon, engraver; Pigot (1837).

Grange

Grange Reading Society: subscription library (or book club?), by 1826 when dissolved and books divided amongst members; a parish rather than a town, and unknown where books held.
   Aberdeen Journal (27 Dec. 1826).

Keith

Keith Library: subscription library, by 1820; subscribed to Lachlan Shaw, *History of the Province of Moray* (Elgin, 1827).

Two evangelical and one juvenile subscription libraries by 1820.

Pigot (1820) 2nd edn.: *Addenda*.

Preshome

Preshome (Enzie) Catholic Circulating Library: subscription library; est. 1818; may have existed earlier; the first Roman Catholic congregational library in Scotland; Preshome was a house rather than a village, the seat of the first Roman Catholic see in Scotland; over 400 vols.; surviving vols. are in NLS; cat., n.d., & minute books, loans books, etc., 1819-31 (Scottish Catholic Archives).
   J. C. Crawford, in: *Library History* 7 (1985) 41.

BERWICKSHIRE

Ayton

Subscription library est. ca. 1825.
   NSA, vol. 2 (1845) 146.

Chirnside

Chirnside Library: subscription library, by ca. 1805; 500 vols. by 1834.
> *NSA*, vol. 2 (1845) 129.

Cockburnspath

Cockburnspath Library: subscription library; est. ca. 1815; 1,228 vols. by 1866; cost 6d. per month.
> *NSA*, vol. 2 (1845) 315-6; Sally Smith, *Cockburnspath* (Cockburnspath, 1999).

Coldingham

Coldingham Library: subscription library; est. 18 May 1810; 400 vols. by 1834 and 1,244 vols. in 1906; probably dissolved soon after.
> *NSA*, vol. 2 (1845) 289; Andrew Thomson, *Coldingham* (Galashiels, 1908) 48.

Coldstream

Coldstream Library: subscription library; est. 1801; merged with Mechanics' Institute (est. 1852); 2,000 vols. in 1914; still existed in 1930s; cat. 1914 (Borders Library HQ, Selkirk).
> Eneas Mackenzie, *Historical View of Northumberland* 2nd edn., vol. 2 (Newcastle, 1825) 450.

Two other subscription libraries by 1834.

NSA, vol. 2 (1845) 212.

Duns

Subscription library

Duns Subscription Library; est. 1768; initially cost £2 entry + 6s. p.a.; 54 members and 387 titles by 1789; originally kept in town house, but then in a succession of private homes, including Mr. Whyte's, the schoolmaster, in 1801; moved to Town Hall, 1820, but may have moved elsewhere later; in New Town St. by 1876; 80 members and 5,000 vols. by 1880; dissolved ca. 1925?; cats. 1771*, 1780 (St. Andrews UL), 1789 (NLS), 1793 (University of Virginia Library), 1801*, 1822*, 1850*; rules, 1801 (University of Virginia Library); minute book, 1768-1850 (Borders AO, Hawick).

Transactions & Proceedings of the 3rd Annual Meeting of the Library Association of the United Kingdom ... Edinburgh, 1880 (London, 1881) 159; *OSA*, vol. 4 (1792) 391.

Circulating libraries

David White: circulating library??, by 1813; subscribed to James F. Stanfield, *Essay on the Study & Composition of Biography* (Sunderland, 1813); he may not have run his own library but was possibly buying book for the Duns Library.

Two circulating libraries by 1834.

NSA, vol. 2 (1845) 258.

Eyemouth

- Patterson, Market Place: circulating library, by 1806; he was also master of the kirk school.
   Directory and Concise History of Berwick-upon-Tweed (Berwick, 1806) 169.

Greenlaw

Greenlaw Library: subscription library; est. 'long before' 1834.
   NSA, vol. 2 (1845) 47.

CAITHNESSSHIRE

Thurso

Donald MacKay: circulating library, by 1810; later known as Thurso Circulating Library; in Main St. in 1825 and Traill St. by 1837.
   Glasgow Bibliographical Society Records 6 (1916/18) 87; *Edinburgh Almanack* (1824-34): *Northern Counties Supp.*; Pigot (1825/6-37).

According to John Henderson (see ref.), a 'circulating library' was est. here in May 1811 from where agricultural publications would be disseminated; uncertain whether MacKay's library, above, is meant, or a private subscription library.
   John Henderson, *General View of the Agriculture of the County of Caithness* (London, 1812) 261.

WICK

Wick Subscription Library, by 1814; probably ceased before the following library.

J. Young & Co., *Supplement to the Almanacs for 1814.*

Wick and Pulteneytown Juvenile Library: subscription library; est. Mar. 1826; the word 'Juvenile' was soon dropped; cost 6s.6d. entry + 1s. per quarter; see also following; rules (1830) in Mitchell Library; still existed in 1850s; cats. 1843 (Wick PL), 1851 & supp. ca. 1854 (Mitchell Library).

Wick and Pulteneytown Reading Club: subscription library, by 1830; almost certainly the previous library is meant, but unclear; cat. 1830 (Wick PL).

Edinburgh Almanack (1824-34): *Northern Counties Supp.*; *NSA*, vol. 15 (1845) 170.

CLACKMANNANSHIRE

ALLOA

Subscription libraries

Theological Library, for students of divinity and philosophy; est. 24 Oct. 1777; not proprietary but ran as a subscription library vested in a committee of Presbyterians under William Moncrieffe, Professor of Theology, who died in 1786; books moved to Whitburn, 1787, and to Edinburgh, 1807, where placed under the General Associate Synod; see Edinburgh for subsequent history and sources.

Clackmannanshire Library; est. 1797; 1,500 vols. by 1840 when cost 10s. p.a.; kept in parish schoolroom; dissolved by 1848 when the books were bought by the newly-founded Clackmannanshire Subscription Library, but this dissolved 1860.

NSA, vol. 8 (1845) 62; *Alloa Advertiser* (19 Oct. 1850); James Lothian, *Extinct Clackmannanshire Societies* (Alloa, 1875) 11-13, 18.

Circulating library

Mary Charles, New Market St., by 1825; in Mill St. by 1837.

Pigot (1825/6-37).

Alva

Subscription library for working classes est. Jan. 1797, according to *Scots Chronicle* (21/24 Feb. 1797).

Tillicoultry

Tillicoultry Reading Society: subscription library; est. Jan. 1793; 23 members by 1797.
Scots Chronicle (21/24 Feb. 1797).

Dumbartonshire: see Dunbartonshire

Dumfriesshire

Annan

Subscription library

Subscription Library, by 1825; still there in 1837.

Circulating libraries

John Maconachie, by 1806; he was also a cooper; used by Thomas Carlyle when he attended Annan Academy in 1806/9; mostly novels and romances.
  Edwin W. Marrs, Jr., *The Letters of Thomas Carlyle to his Brother Alexander* (Cambridge, Mass., 1968) 7.

Peter Forrest, High St., by 1825; may have been succeeded by Wellwood M. Richardson, who the only librarian here by 1837 and was a bookseller in Langholm in 1825; latter still here in 1852; label of latter in Franks clln.

Pigot (1825/6-37).

Canonbie

Canonbie Library: subscription library; est. 1813; still existed in 1836.
  NSA, vol. 4 (1845) 497.

Closeburn

Closeburn Library: subscription library; est. 1789 in imitation of the nearby Monkland Society (see Dunscore, below).

J. De L. Ferguson (ed.), *Letters of Robert Burns* 2nd edn. (Oxford, 1985) vol. 1, p. 391.

Dumfries

Subscription libraries

Dumfries Presbytery Library: not a proprietary subscription library, but opened to the public in 1736 on payment of a subscription, so similar to Leightonian Library, Dunblane, below; originally founded in 1706; the books were removed in 1885 and are now in New College Library, Edinburgh; cat. 1784 (NLS; Ewart Library, Dumfries); loans register, 1732-1800 (Ewart Library, Dumfries).

Dumfries Gentlemen's Library, possibly by ca. 1750 but definitely by 1767; subscribed to Thomas Short, *Comparative History of the Increase and Decrease of Mankind in England* (London, 1767); known as Dumfries Society Library by 1832; 30 members in 1845; in Irish St. by 1860; dissolved 1875; cats. 1835, 1851 (Ewart Library, Dumfries).

Dumfries Public Library; est. 3 Sep. 1792; held in High St.; 72 members in 1845; 700 titles by 1853 when cost 8s. p.a. and was open 2 hours per week; merged with Mechanics' Institute which eventually became the Ewart [Public] Library; cats. 1819, 1853 (Ewart Library, Dumfries).

New Church Sabbath School Library; est. Nov. 1816; intended for all denominations; 5s. p.a.

Dumfries & Galloway Courier (19 Nov. 1816).

Dumfries Law Library; est. 2 Nov. 1818; cost 1 gn. + 5s. per quarter; open to people associated with the county's courts; kept in the Court House, Buccleuch St.; still there in 1860; taken over by the Facutly of Procurators of Dumfriesshire (est. 1865) and still existed in 1900s, with over 500 vols.; cat. 1824*; records, 1818-37 (Dumfries AO).

Dumfries Weekly Journal (16 Feb. 1819).

Circulating libraries

William Boyd, opp. the Cross, by 1777; cat. 1778*.

Dumfries Weekly Journal (13 Jan. 1778).

- McLachlan and William Chalmers, by unknown date; label in Franks clln.; Allan McLachlan was bookseller here in 1780s (died 1785/6), while Robert

and Cuthbert McLachlan were booksellers here from 1790s until 1800 and ca. 1817 respectively; Robert McLachlan was bankrupt in 1791, when goods sold off (inventory in NRS); Chalmers died in 1813; succeeded by J. Preacher & John Dunbar, who began a new circulating library on 1 Jan. 1814, but bankrupt 1815.
Dumfries & Galloway Courier (3 Aug. & 14 Dec. 1813, 30 Jan. 1816).

John Hill, opp. the Fish Cross; est. 15 Dec. 1803; library run by George McCartney; cat. 1803*.
Dumfries Weekly Journal (24 May & 13 Dec. 1803).

John Wood, High St.; est. 1816; for sale in 1818; cat. 1816*.
Dumfries & Galloway Courier (23 Jan. & 14 May 1816, 15 Sep. 1818); *Dumfries Weekly Journal* (26 Nov. 1816).

John Anderson, 74 High St.; est. 1818; still existed in 1890s, when had 15,000 vols.; cats. 1842, 1861, ca. 1890 (location uncertain).

Allan Anderson, 69 High St., by 1820; at no. 70 by 1837 and no. 75 by 1860; cousin of John Murray of Dalbeattie (see below).

John Johnstone, 33 High St., by 1820.

James McDiarmid, High St.; est. 1821; he sold paints, etc., and lent prints and drawings to copy at 3 gns. p.a. or 2s. per week.
Dumfries & Galloway Courier (6 Nov. 1821).

Five circulating libraries in 1833.
NSA, vol. 4 (1845) 24.

New Edinburgh Almanack: Western Supp. (1845) 163; Pigot (1820-37); G. W. Shirley, 'Old Public Libraries in Dumfries', *Dumfriesshire & Galloway Natural History & Antiquarian Society Transactions* 18 for 1905-6 (1907) 39-44; reprinted with amendments as *Dumfriesshire Libraries* (1932); see also *Transactions ...* 19 (1908) 176.

Dunscore

Monkland Friendly Society: subscription library; est. 1789; Robert Burns was librarian; see under Closeburn for an imitator; members signed a 3-year contract which was not renewed; so dissolved in 1792 and books divided amongst the members; no permanent library was formed, which may have been the intention had the society continued.
J. De L. Ferguson (ed.), *Letters of Robert Burns* 2nd edn. (Oxford, 1985) vol. 1, pp. 391-2; C. Angus, 'Burns and the Circulating Library', in: *Burns Chronicle & Club Directory* 2nd ser. 18 (1943) 26-29; see also 2nd ser. 7 (1932) 120; *OSA*, vol. 3 (1792) 597-600.

Johnstone

Johnston Library: subscription library; est. 1828; dissolved 1941 and more valuable items transferred to County Library, Dumfries.
Third Statistical Account of Scotland: ... Dumfries (Glasgow, 1962) 383.

Langholm

Langholm Library: subscription library, not proprietary; est. 1800; 36 members paying 10s. p.a. by 1835; held in High St.; benfited from will of Thomas Telford; new building, 1877; 12,000 vols. in 1910; dissolved 1974 but still exists as a local studies library; cats. 1856, 1864, supps. to 1868, 1878, 1888, supps. to 1923, 1969 (NLS; Langholm Library); minute books, 1833-1975 (Langholm Library; microfilm in NLS).
    R. McQuillan, 'Langholm Library', *Akros* 9 no. 25 (1974) 44-47; *Library History* 3 (1974) 160; J. C. Crawford, 'The Langholm Library Project', *Library Review* 44 (1995) 36-44.

New Langholm, or Tradesmen's, Library: subscription library; est. 1815; held in the parochial school, New Langholm, by 1837; dissolved 1853 and absorbed by the Langholm Library, above; minute books, 1838-53 (Langholm Library; microfilm in NLS).

Pigot (1821-37); *NSA*, vol. 4 (1845) 427.

Lochmaben

Lochmaben Library: subscription library; est. 14 May 1819; still existed in 1837; cat. 1828 (Glasgow UL).
    Pigot (1825/6-37); *NSA*, vol. 4 (1845) 396.

Lockerbie

Lockerbie Library: subscription library, by 1820.
    Pigot (1820) 2nd edn.: *Addenda*.

Thomas Walker, High St.: circulating library, by 1825; still there in 1837.
    Pigot (1825/6-37).

Moffat

Moffat Library: subscription library; est. in ca. 1788 or 1821, according to different sources; 3,000 vols. by 1910; dissolved ca. 1930; cat. 1890 (?).
  John J. Ogle, *The Free Library* (London, 1897) 288.

Peter Begg: circulating library, by unknown date; probably later than 1825; label in Glasgow UL.

Moniaive

Glencairn Library: subscription library; est. 1812; dissolved 1894.

Monkland: see Dunscore

Roberton

Roberton Village Library: subscription library; est. 1809; dissolved ca. 1940; many books moved in 1974 to Gladstone Court Museum, Biggar, as a reconstruction of the library; loans register, 1904-27 (Gladstone Court Museum); cat. 1910 (The Museum ?).
  Library History 3 (1974) 160.

Sanquhar

Sanquhar Library: subscription library; est. 1800; 178 members and 1,460 vols. by 1835; dissolved 1935; cat. 1901 (??); loans registers, 1833-6 & 1894-1934 (Dumfries AO).
  NSA, vol. 4 (1845) 312.

Thornhill

Thornhill Library: subscription library; est. 1814; dissolved 1900.
  NSA, vol. 4 (1845) 101.

Wanlockhead

Wanlockhead Society for Purchasing Books: subscription library; est. 1 Nov. 1756 for local miners; 32 original members; held in school until 1787, when new building built; 105 members, paying 5s. entry + 2s. p.a., and 1,300 vols. by 1835; another library building erected, 1850; 2,500 vols. by 1876, and 4,000 vols. by 1901; only 56 members by 1890; ceased as an active library in 1938, but re-opened as a mining museum and library in 1978 under the Wanlockhead Museum Trust; cats. 1819[1], 1821 (in MS.), 1829, 1848, 1854, 1868, 1888, 1901[2], 1979[2] (Wanlockhead Museum Trust; [1]only in Glasgow UL; [2]also in NLS and Ewart Library, Dumfries).

NSA, vol. 4 (1845) 313; John C. Crawford & Stuart James, *The Society for Purchasing Books in Wanlockhead, 1756-1979* (Glasgow, 1981); S. James, 'Restoration and Conservation of the Wanlockhead Miners' Library', *Library Review* 36 (1987) 191-4.

Westerkirk

Westerkirk Library: subscription library; est. 1792 for local antimony miners at Jamestown; moved to Kirktonhill, 1800, and to the New School House, Old Bentpath, in 1841; new building built here, 1860; given 5,000 vols. and £1,000 by Thomas Telford; the bequest was vested in the minister and kirk session; still exists; cats. 1853, 1925, supp. 1930, 1998 (Westerkirk Library; NLS); rules (ca. 1843) in Westerkirk Library & NLS; minute books, 1792-1974, & register of members and loans, 1813-42 (Westerkirk Library; microfilm in NLS).

Transactions & Proceedings of the 3rd Annual Meeting of the Library Association of the United Kingdom ... Edinburgh, 1880 (London, 1881) 162-3; *NSA*, vol. 4 (1845) 435-6; A. McCracken, 'The Glendinning Antimony Mine (Louisa Mine)', *Dumfriesshire & Galloway Natural History & Antiquarian Society Transactions* 3rd ser. 42 (1965) 140-8; *Westerkirk Parish Library Restoration Project 1992-1997* (The Library, 1997).

Dunbartonshire

Alexandria

Subscription library for working classes by 1796, according to *Scots Chronicle* (20 Jan. 1797).

CUMBERNAULD

Cumbernauld Public Library: subscription library; est. 1816; 1,200 vols. by 1839; merged with the local Literary Institution, 1850, and the library was revived in 1860; dissolved 1933 and books transferred to Dumbarton County Library; minute books, 1828-74 (formerly in Cumbernauld PL).

DUMBARTON

Dumbarton Library: subscription library; est. 1796 or 1797; 2,000 vols. by 1839.
 Edinburgh Almanack (1827): *Western Kalendar*, NSA, vol. 8 (1845) 13.

HELENSBURGH

Helensburgh Public Library: subscription library; est. 1816; at Town Hall, Princes St. by 1834; probably dissolved soon afterwards.
 [G. MacLachlan], *Story of Helensburgh* (ca. 1894) 198; Pigot (1825/6-37).

KIRKINTILLOCH

Unidentified reading society, by 1793, when William Muir, weaver, was a member; presumably the same as the working class subscription library which existed here by 1796.
 The Trial of Thomas Muir (Edinburgh, [1793]) 36; *Scots Chronicle* (30 Dec. 1796).

RENTON

William Stirling & Sons' Calico Printfield, Cordale: general subscription library for workers, by 1797.
 Monthly Magazine 4 (Oct. 1797) 275-7.

Renton Library: subscription library; est. 1797; 1,400 vols. by 1838; cats. 1798*, 1819 (Glasgow UL); minute book, 1797-1838 (Dumbarton PL).
 NSA, vol. 8 (1845) 93.

EAST LOTHIAN: see HADDINGTONSHIRE

EDINBURGHSHIRE

BONNYRIGG

Bonnyrigg Subscription Library: subscription library; est. 13 May 1825; dated label in Franks clln.
> Walter Hamilton, *Dated Book-plates* (London, 1895) 132.

CRAMOND

Cramond Subscription Library: subscription library; est. 29 Dec. 1815; dated label in JJ.
> Walter Hamilton, *Dated Book-plates* (London, 1895) 127.

DALKEITH

Subscription library

Dalkeith Subscription Library; est. 16 Jan. 1798; originally 1s. entry + 1d. per week; 1,200 vols. by 1813, and 2,400 vols. by 1843; still existed in 1930s; rules (1798) in BL.
> Peter Forbes, *Poems* (Edinburgh, 1812) refers to the Library on pp. 9-17, 81-83, and 148-50; *Cheap Magazine* (1813) 376.

Circulating libraries

Unidentified circulating library est. 1768; may have belonged to James Megget, who succeeded by Alexander Megget (or Meggat) in 1782/3; unidentified library for sale in 1800; the library was continued and had 3,000 vols. by 1844.

Peter Lyle, High St., by 1825; bookseller here by 1798 (or his father?); he may have bought the library above, for sale in 1800; joined by David Lyle by 1852; latter still here after 1900.

NSA, vol. 1 (1845) 529; Pigot (1825/6-37).

EDINBURGH

Subscription libraries

Edinburgh Subscription Library; est. 11 Nov. 1794; originally kept in Rose St. Chapel session house; at 39 South Bridge from 1807 and 4 St. Andrew Square from 1838; cost 8½ gns. entry + 10s.6d. p.a. in 1808 when had 260 members; at 26 George St. from 1844, no. 24 by 1860, and no. 25 from 1883 (but may be errors for same address, probably no. 24); 40,000 vols. and over 400 members by 1881; dissolved 1900 and books sold; cats. ca. 1795*, 1805*, 1808*, 1816[4], 1819[5], supps. 1823-9[5], 1833[1,2,6], supps. 1834-9[2] & 1845-86[1], 1866[3], 1878[5], 1887[3,7], and sale cat. 1901[1] ([1]Edinburgh PL; [2]NLS; [3]Bodleian Library; [4]Newcastle Lit. & Phil.; [5]BL; [6]NRS; [7]NLW); rules (ca. 1826) in BL; minute books & other papers, 1794-1901 (Edinburgh PL).

Caledonian Mercury (10 Dec. 1808); *Edinburgh Gazette* (27 Nov. 1900).

Edinburgh Select Subscription Library; est. Mar. 1800; originally 5s. entry + 6d. per month; used various rooms until moved to North Gray's Close, 1810, then to Royal Exchange, 1821, and 86 Bridge St., 1826; moved to 26 Waterloo Place, 1837; 30,000 vols. and 300 members by 1881; dissolved 1882; about 1,400 were bought by Lord Rosebery and passed to Edinburgh City Library; cats. supp. 1820 (BL), 1842 & supps. 1848-78 (Edinburgh PL), 1846 (Birmingham UL).

Sketch of the Origin and Progress of the Library (1834): reprinted in 1842 cat.

Theological Library, for students of divinity and philosophy, by 1807; est. 1777 in Alloa (see above); similar library at Selkirk; placed under the General Associate Synod (or Antiburghers); in Nicolson St. by 1825 and known as Divinity Hall library; the Synod became the United Secession Church, 1820, and merged with Relief Church in 1847 as the United Presbyterian Church; see also under Glasgow for the Robertsonian Theological Library; cats. 1812, 1825, 1850[1] (Glasgow UL; [1]also in NLS); a catalogue dated 1839 (in Glasgow UL) of the United Associate Synod for theological students may be of the same library; minute book, 1777-1812 (NRS).

Edinburgh Biblio-critical Library; est. Jan. 1811; exclusively for studies of the Scriptures; £5 entry + 15s. p.a.; 14 members; kept in Bristo St. Session House; still existed in 1827 but had combined with the Religious Subscription and Circulating Library, below, by 1825; cat. 1812 (New College, Edinburgh).

Commercial Reading Rooms, 98 South Bridge St.; est. 1811; incl. a library; 300 vols. when opened in Apr. 1811.

Caledonian Mercury (9 Mar. & 27 Apr. 1811).

Hope Park Library; est. 1816; 2s.6d. entry + 3s. p.a.

Southern Districts Subscription Library; est. 1816.

Edinburgh Religious Subscription and Circulating Library; est. Jan. 1824; held at shop of John Lindsay, bookseller, 6 St. Andrew's St.; open 8 a.m. - 8 p.m.; merged with Edinburgh Biblio-Critical Library; cat. 1824*, supp. 1825*; report of meetings (1824) in Edinburgh UL.

Caledonian Mercury (31 Dec. 1825, 25 Oct. 1827).

Edinburgh Mechanics' Subscription Library; est. Mar. 1825; originally at Strichen's Close, High St.; at 7 James Court, Lawnmarket, by 1832, and at 5 Victoria Terrace from 1855; at 22 Giles St. in 1891; cost 5s. entry + 6s. p.a.; merged with Edinburgh Literary Institute in 1892, when had 22,000 vols., but dissolved 1899; cats. 1859[1], 1862, 1874[1] (Edinburgh PL; [1]also formerly in Royal Institution of South Wales).

J. W. Hudson, *History of Adult Education* (London, 1851) 200-1; *Caledonian Mercury* (25 Apr. 1825).

United Presbyterian Church Library, Rose St.; est. 6 July 1825; cat. 1850 (NLS).

United Associate Congregation Library, by ca. 1826; cat. ca. 1826 (Edinburgh PL).

Stockbridge Subscription Library; est. Dec. 1826; held at 5 Kerr St.; still there in 1832; report of inaugural meeting in St. Andrews UL.

Caledonian Mercury (23 Dec. 1826).

Circulating libraries

Allan Ramsay (1684/5-1758), Luckenbooths; est. 1725; bookseller by 1722; retired in 1740; believed to have been succeeded in the library by John Yair; latter certainly ran library in Parliament Close (where the Luckenbooths situated) by 1746; partner with R. Fleming by 1756, but run by Yair's widow, Margaret, by 1758; sold to James Sibbald (1745-1803), 1779, who claimed 20,000 vols.; he ran the library at 28 Parliament Close (presumably same address or close by) but leased it to Alexander Lawrie and James Symington in 1790 or 1791 (see below for Lawrie and Symington, successors to Berry); also lent prints (from 1783) and music; known as Edinburgh Circulating Library; Sibbald took over personally again in 1800, when lease expired; to 18 Parliament Close; he died 1803 and succeeded by brother, William, but library managed by Walter Hart Stevenson; bankrupt 1805 when sold to Alexander Mackay and moved to 10 High St. (see below for subsequent history); Lawrie subsequently moved his own library (see below) to 28 Parliament Square (formerly Close), where Sibbald's library had been; cats. 1746*, 1750*, 1761*, 1779 & supps. 1780-6 (NLS), supp. 1784 (NRS), 1790 (Newberry Library, Chicago), ca. 1800 (Edinburgh PL; UCLA).

Caledonian Mercury (30 Sep. 1746, 12 Aug. 1758, 1 Jan. & 2 Dec. 1780, 29 Nov. 1783, 20 Mar. & 4 Dec. 1790, 25 Aug. 1800, 18 Apr. & 12 May 1803, 15 Jun. & 28 Sep. 1805, 8 Feb. 1806); *Edinburgh Evening Courant* (22 Dec. 1748, 22 Nov. 1757, 24 Dec. 1760); *Edinburgh Advertiser* (17 Dec. 1779); Allan Ramsay, *Works*, ed. Alexander M. Kinghorn & Alexander Law, vol. 4 (Edinburgh, 1970); cf. *ODNB* for Ramsay and Sibbald.

William Gray, and Walter Peter, in the New Exchange, by 1756; partnership dissolved by 1758; Peter continued here, probably only for a short time; Gray moved to 'eastmost low shop in the Front of the Exchange'; run by widow, Margaret Gray, by 1788; she died 1794 and succeeded by George Gray, presumably son; given as in High St. by 1796 and at 3 North Bridge by 1799; bankrupt 1801; succeeded by Alexander Mackay, who was advertizing from 10 High St. by 1803; he also took over the Edinburgh Circulating Library, formerly of Ramsay and Sibbald, above, in 1805 and removed it to his own library; moved to 154 High St. by end of 1811; retired in 1831; most of the stock was acquired by William Wilson, who had run his own library by 1811 (see below); books said to have been sold off in 1851; cats. 1758* for Gray & Peter, 1759* for Peter alone, 1772 (Bodleian Library), 1795*, 1799*, 1804*, 1805*, 1807*, ca. 1810 [1811?] (Cambridge UL), supps. 1814* & 1816* (& yearly), ca. 1824 (Edinburgh PL).

A Present for Children 2nd edn. (Edinburgh, 1761) for advert.; *Edinburgh Chronicle* (28 Apr. & 3 May 1759); *Edinburgh Evening Courant* (24 Dec. 1760); *Edinburgh Advertiser* (4 Sep. 1764, 22 May 1795, 26 Oct. 1804); *Caledonian Mercury* (27 Nov. 1794, 7 Dec. 1799, 12 May 1803, 16 Mar. 1805, 21 Jan. & 30 Nov. 1811, 6 Jul. 1812, 31 Jan. 1814); *Edinburgh Weekly Journal* (23 Sep. 1807).

John Wood, in the Exchange, by 1764, when had 1,400 vols.; still there in 1769, when charged 3s. per quarter (according to letter in NRS); see William Wood, below; cat. 1764*.

Edinburgh Advertiser (13 Jan. 1764).

Alexander McAslan, Cross Causey, by 1765; widow here, at least as bookseller, by 1778 until 1780; cats. by 1765* & 1771*.

Renowned History of Valentine & Orson (Edinburgh, 1765) for advert.; Robert Grosthead, *The Testament of the Twelve Patriarchs* (Edinburgh, 1767) for advert. [available online].

Alexander Brown, Cowgate, by 1774; presumably the same as the person who est. a new library in 1782 in North Bridge St.; cat. ca. 1786 (NRS).

Edinburgh Advertiser (26 Jul. 1782).

James McLeish, Candlemaker Row, by 1778; subscribed to [T. Anburey], *Travels through the Interior Parts of America* (London, 1789); he and his brother or son, John, had bookshop at 12 South Frederick St., whither he moved the library in 1793; succeeded in 1808 by Robert Kinnear, when had 7,000 vols.; at 29 South Frederick St. by 1810; succeeded by John Durham by 1835, then by Rev James Laurie by 1837, and by Quentin Dalrymple by 1839; dissolved 1846, when for sale; cats. 1808*, ca. 1815 (Edinburgh PL).

Ruddiman's Weekly Mercury (23 Dec. 1778); *Caledonian Mercury* (30 Apr. 1791, 21 Jan. 1793, 24 Mar. 1808, 4 May 1839); *Edinburgh Advertiser* (15 Jan., 21 Jun. & 18 Nov. 1808); *Glasgow Herald* (23 Oct. 1846).

William Wood, Parliament Square, by 1778; son of John Wood, above, but unknown if took over the latter's library.
Caledonian Mercury (28 Sep. 1778); *Edinburgh Advertiser* (5 May 1780).

Domenico Corri & James Sutherland's music circulating library, 37 North Bridge St.; est. 1783; latter died 1790; former moved to London in 1789, where ran library, while the Edinburgh business was continued by brother, Natale Corri; in 1802 Corri opened a new music shop, incl. a musical circulating library, at 8 South St. David's St.; at head of Leith Walk by 1807; still there in 1820; cats. 1783*, 1820*.
Caledonian Mercury (30 Jun. 1783, 18 Apr. 1807, 6 May 1820); *Edinburgh Advertiser* (21 Dec. 1802, 2 Jun. 1809).

Neil Stewart & Co.'s musical library, Parliament Square, by 1786; at 37 South Bridge St. by 1795; Neil Stewart had music shop by 1761, but unknown if lending by then.
Caledonian Mercury (12 Dec. 1786); *Edinburgh Advertiser* (29 Sep. 1795); *Edinburgh Evening Courant* (24 Jan. 1761).

John & James Ainslie, 4 St. Andrew's St., by 1789; subscribed to [T. Anburey], *Travels through the Interior Parts of America* (London, 1789); see below for Mrs Ainslie; James Ainslie's stock-in-trade was for sale in 1793; the library was run by Ninian Richard Cheyne by 1797; joined by P. G. Buchanan before 1805, when partnership dissolved, and possibly by 1803; Buchanan continued on own and moved to 5 North St. Andrew's St.; for sale in 1811, when bankrupt and had 5,000 vols., but resumed at same address; temporarily moved, but back at no. 5 in 1816; bankrupt 1820; succeeded by John Hunter & Co., 1821, and moved to no. 3; label in JJ; succeeded by Richard D. Davidson and William Elgin by 1829; Davidson on own by 1832 and still here in 1850; some of Buchanan's books may have been bought by James Whyte, according to label in JJ; latter was at no. 14, but also ran circulating library at Leith (see below); Elgin also ran a library on his own at nos. 10-13 by 1832; joined by son, also William, by 1851, and still there in 1890; cat. supp. 1805*, 1821*.
Edinburgh Advertiser (12 & 22 Nov. 1811); *Caledonian Mercury* (25 Feb. 1793, 27 Jul., 15 Aug. & 14 Dec. 1805, 4 Nov. 1811, 22 Jun. 1816, 15 & 31 Mar., 2 Sep. 1821).

James Findlay, Chapel St.; est. 1789; in Castle St. in 1790, when library damaged by fire, but re-opened in Dec.; cat. by 1791*.
Edinburgh Advertiser (6 Jan. 1789); *Caledonian Mercury* (4 Dec. 1790).

Robert Jameson's British Library, 45 South Bridge St.; est. 1790; cat. 1790*.
Edinburgh Advertiser (22 Jan. 1790).

John (?) Esplin and - Forbes, High St., below the Exchange; est. a 'circulating repository of prints and drawings' in 1790 at 1/6d. per month or 3s.6d. per quarter.
Caledonian Mercury (15 Jul. 1790).

John Elder, 7, later 9, North Bridge; est. 1791; label in JJ; cat. 1791*.
Caledonian Mercury (17 Nov. 1791).

Thomas Brown, 1 North Bridge St.; planned to est. a library in Nov. 1791; by 1794 he lent prints only, at £1.4s. p.a.
Caledonian Mercury (25 Jul. 1791, 27 Jan. 1794).

James Fowler, 1 Blair's St., by 1792.
Edinburgh Advertiser (31 Jan. 1792).

Alexander Monro, 81 Nicolson St., by 1793, and at different nos. in same street, incl. no. 15 in 1801; presumably the same as 'Dr.' A. Monro, professor, who at this address in 1788; died 1813 at no. 59.

Hugh Evans' Lecture Library, Gibb's Entry, Nicolson's St., by 1793; apparently a circulating library for students rather than a private subscription library; still here in 1803.
Edinburgh Directory (1793-1803).

Walter Berry, 39 South Bridge, by 1796; lent French books only; taken over in 1797 by James Symington, who had previously run Sibbald's library (see above), and moved to 24 Parliament Square; Symington added a general library; after Sibbald took back the running of his own library in 1800, Alexander Lawrie joined Symington and continued on own after latter's death in 1801; in 1806 he moved the library to 28 Parliament Square, the same shop used previously for Sibbald's library; succeeded by William Wilson, who moved library to 21 George St., 1810, while Lawrie continued his own bookshop at previous address; Wilson moved to no. 44 by 1811 when had 8,000 vols.; 10,000 vols. by 1812; took over Mackay's library, formerly Allan Ramsay's, in about 1831 (see above); said to have sold off much of the library in 1851, but library was continued by his relation, W. Wilson Moffat, from 1851 until Moffat's bankruptcy, 1857; cats. of French books, 1796 (NLS; Houghton Library, Harvard), 1799*; cat. of English books, 1798*; general cats. 1801*, n.d. for Lawrie (UCLA), 1811*, supp. 1812*, 1813*, 1814*, supp. 1816*, 1855*.
Edinburgh Advertiser (31 Oct. 1797, 4 Dec. 1798, 19 May 1807); *Caledonian Mercury* (10 Jan. 1799, 2 May 1801, 8 Nov. 1806, 10 & 26 Jan. & 9 Nov. 1811, 29 Nov. 1813, 29 Oct. 1814, 25 Jan. 1855, 23 Dec. 1857); *Leith Telegraph* (9 Jun. 1812).

John Galbraith, front of the Exchange; est. 1796, but bankrupt in 1797 and library for sale; formerly clerk in Gray's library, see above; may have bought

stock of George Peattie of Leith (see below), as labels of both in a novel of 1796 in Aberdeen UL; cat. 1796*.
Caledonian Mercury (24 Nov. 1794); *Edinburgh Advertiser* (22 Jul. 1796, 27 Oct. 1797).

John Forbes, bookseller, 5 South Hanover St., lent newspapers for 2d. per hour, by August 1797 (printed advert. in Falkirk AO); John Hume ran library at this address by 1860.

John Macara, by 1798; a philanthropical library?; see Deuchar, below, under 1802.

William Whyte, 1 South St. Andrew St., by 1800 as a music library; formerly worked for Corri, above; at no. 12 by 1811 as a music seller and by 1825 as a general library.
Caledonian Mercury (2 Jan. 1800).

Daniel McIntosh's Repository of the Arts, 15 St. Andrew's St., by 1800; lent prints and drawings; at no. 16 by 1811, and at 49 Princes St. from 1817 to 1822.
Caledonian Mercury (20 Dec. 1800).

James Watson, 40 South Bridge, by 1800 and probably before; moved to no. 57 in 1801, but died, & library for sale.
Edinburgh Advertiser (29 May 1801); *Caledonian Mercury* (17 Sep. 1801).

James Muir, - Wood, & Co., 7 Leith St., musical circulating library, by 1801.
Caledonian Mercury (2 Jan. 1802).

John Deuchar, Cross, by 1802; may have been a free library; Deuchar was a writer; printed label of his 'Private Library' inside BL copy of David Crawford's *Poems, Chiefly in the Scottish Dialect* (Edinburgh, 1798), with inscription dated 1802; label includes an admonition 'to the reader' against turning down leaves, which shows that his books were intended to be lent; same book formerly belonged to John Macara, and was no. 166 in latter's library (and no. 47 in Deuchar's); printed label of Deuchar's library also noted, dated 1806.
Walter Hamilton, *Dated Book-plates* (London, 1895) 122.

John Buchanan, 30 North Bridge (St.); est. 1802; formerly worked for Mackay (see above); at no. 4 by 1806, then at South Bridge by 1810 and later at 11 Princes St.; cats. 1802*, 1805*, 1806*.
Caledonian Mercury (18 Mar. & 31 Jul. 1802, 31 Jan. 1805, 24 May 1806); *Edinburgh Advertiser* (23 Nov. 1802).

William Baird, 27 Parliament Close (later Square); est. 1802; formerly worked for Sibbald; still there in 1806; cat. 1802*.
Caledonian Mercury (4 Sep. 1802); *Edinburgh Advertiser* (1 Oct. 1802).

Stewart Cheyne, 22 George St., by 1804; he was bookseller in same street in 1790s; later at no. 48; A. Hogg (see below, 1816) was at latter address in 1816, but the libraries may have been different; Cheyne later moved to Union St. but unknown if library continued; label on book of 1800 in University of Virginia Library.
Caledonian Mercury (5 Jan. 1804).

John Hamilton (1761-1814), 24 North Bridge, by 1805; ran a music library; also a songwriter; moved to 26 Princes St., 1811, and included a circulating library of novels.
Caledonian Mercury (8 Aug. 1805, 27 Jul. 1811).

John Denham, 20 South College St., by 1807.

William & James Deas, 13 Princes St.; est. 1808, though had been booksellers since 1803; known as Princes St. Circulating Library and planned to be the main library in the New Town; dissolved ca. 1810 and may have been taken over by Goldie (see below); label in G. K. Scott clln.; cats. 1808*, 1809*.
Caledonian Mercury (2 Jun. 1808, 11 Nov. 1809); *The Sleeping Beauty* (Edinburgh, 1809) imprint.

John Sutherland, 27 Leith St., by 1809; at 9 Calton St. by Jan. 1812; 12 Calton St. by 1835; still there in 1860.
Caledonian Mercury (8 May 1809); *Edinburgh Advertiser* (15 Dec. 1809); *Edinburgh Weekly Journal* (15 Jan. 1812).

William Kay, 5 South Frederick St.; est. 1809; formerly worked for Sibbald, above.
Edinburgh Advertiser (5 Dec. 1809).

George Rix Clarke, 20 (re-numbered 6) South St. Andrew's St., by 1811, when had 7,000 vols.; for sale in 1813 when bankrupt; a library was run in Ipswich by a man of exactly the same name in 1800, but no connection known; latter known to be in Birmingham by 1839; cat. 1811*.
Caledonian Mercury (7 Mar. & 20 Jun. 1811, 13 May 1813); *Edinburgh Advertiser* (26 Apr. & 17 May 1811, 25 May 1813); *Leith Telegraph* (28 Jul. 1812).

George Goldie, 34 Princes St., by 1811; known as Princes Street Circulating Library and may have taken over Deas's library, above; 7,000 vols. by 1812; bankrupt 1814 and moved to London; label in G. K. Scott clln.; cat. 1813*.
Edinburgh Advertiser (2 Jul. 1811); *Caledonian Mercury* (17 Oct. 1812, 6 Nov. 1813).

William McWilliam, 427 Lawnmarket, by 1811; moved several times to different addresses, including 16 West Nichoslon St. by 1815, then 3 Salisbury Square; still existed in 1825; cats. 1811*, 1815*.
Caledonian Mercury (7 Dec. 1811, 4 Nov. 1815).

John Robertson, 132 High St.; est. 1814; apprentice of one of the Cheynes, above; succeeded by James Stillie, by 1826; with brother George at no. 140 High St. by 1829; James on own by 1833, and later in Princes St., at least as bookseller, until 1877.
Caledonian Mercury (12 Nov. 1814).

William Nivison, 2 St. Patrick Square, by 1815; also ran library in Portobello (see below); moved to 10 North Bridge St. in 1818, but possibly as bookseller only; succeeded at former address by Alexander Todd, 1818; known as St. Patrick Square Circulating Library; moved to 1 St. Patrick Square, 1820, and to 3 Clerk St. by 1858.
Caledonian Mercury (15 Nov. 1817, 14 Dec. 1818).

Miss Johannah Tansh, 24 South Hanover St., by 1814; she took over the bookshop of Mrs Ainslie, who had previously been at 42 South Hanover St.; unknown if Mrs Ainslie ran a library, but she was in business by 1793 and may have been related to the Ainslie's, above; Miss Tansh at no. 20 by 1820, no. 22 by 1825, and back at no. 24 in 1826 when moved to 1 William St., Stafford St., with 1,471 titles; James Tansh at same address by 1838 and library still existed in 1868 when moved to 23 William St.; run by Misses Margaret & Jessie Wilson by 1876, and still there in 1880s; cat. 1826 (NLS).
Caledonian Mercury (11 Nov. 1826).

Adam Hogg, 48 George St., by 1816; S. Cheyne (see above, 1810) had been at this address, but the libraries may have been different.

William Chambers, Leith Walk, by ca. 1820; moved to 23 Broughton St., 1823; brother of Robert Chambers, see below; library dissolved 1832 to concentrate on publishing.
William Chambers, *Memoir of Robert Chambers* 8th edn. (Edinburgh, 1874) 156.

William Hunter, 23 South Hanover St.; est. 1822; cat. 1824 (NLS).
Caledonian Mercury (10 Aug. 1822).

Henry Rule, Lothian Rd., by 1820; at 10 Wellington St. by 1823.

William Swinton, 60 Princes St.; lent prints and drawings from his Artists' Repository by 1823.
Caledonian Mercury (9 Jun. 1823).

David Maculloch, 13 South College St., by 1823.

Adam Stewart, 38 Howe St., by 1823; succeeded by Alexander Learmonth by 1834.

James Bourhill, 2 Infirmary St., by 1824; at 5 North College St. by 1825; succeeded by Colin Campbell, who ran library at 147 Princes St. by 1826, but soon moved elsewhere.
Pigot (1825); *Caledonian Mercury* (8 Jun. 1826).

Maria Spalding, 1 Warriston Crescent, Canonmills, by 1824; at 5 Warriston Place by 1825; succeeded by Mrs B. Philip, at least as bookseller, in about 1843.

James Taylor Smith & Co.'s British and Foreign Public Library, 3 & 4 Hunter Square, by 1824; later at various addresses.
Caledonian Mercury (13 Nov. 1824, 5 May 1825).

John Aitken, 1 Anthony Place, Port Hopetoun, by 1825; succeeded by Joseph Purdie by 1826 until about 1833.

George Brown, 58 Westport, by 1825; 66 Westport by 1835, and 32 Hume St. by 1837; bookseller by 1818.

James Kay, 1 Ronaldson's Buildings, Leith Walk, by 1825; at 2 Blenheim Place by 1828.

John & - Thomson, 3 Princes St., by 1825; known as Thomson Brothers.
Caledonian Mercury (24 Nov. 1825).

John Forbes, 6 Horsewynd, Cowgate, by 1825; also a binder; at 16 Rose St. as the latter by 1835.

- Colquhoun, 9 Abbey [Hill?], by 1826.

John Dick & Co., 3 Picardy Place, by 1826; bookseller by 1820 at 142 High St.; at 11 Broughton St. by 1829.

Charles Mackenzie, 1 Elder St., by 1827; at 2 West Register St. by 1829; for sale in 1832, when had 1,000 vols.; A. J. Blake ran library at 1 Elder St. from 1829.
Caledonian Mercury (1 Nov. 1832).

Joseph Skeaf, 3 Hanover St., by 1827; a quill-dresser by 1793, and was a stationer here by 1822.

Robert G. Aitken, 79 Queen St., by 1828; bookseller by 1825.

James Winckworth & Henry Elder, 12 South St. Andrew's St., by 1827, and at 35 George St. by 1828; bankrupt 1829.

Robert Chambers, 48 Hanover St., by 1828; he was a bookseller at 4 India Place by 1823, where his younger brother, James Chambers, ran library by 1828 (James died in 1833 and was succeeded by James Burnet Dunlop, who moved to 28 Howe St. by 1837 and to no. 24 by 1841; David MacGregor ran library at 4 India Place from 1837 until 1840 when moved to 25 George

IV Bridge, and in 1841 to 47 Hanover St.); Robert's library sold in 1832; Robert later est. *Chambers' Journal* and became better-known as a publisher; published *Edinburgh Journal* with his other brother, William, who had also run a circulating library (see above); the library in Hanover St. was run by James Inglis by 1840, and by W. & C. Inglis by 1846; at no. 46 by 1857; library continued for many decades; cats. 1829, supp. 1887 (NLS), 1852*; loans register, 1828-9 (NLS).
  James Thin, *Reminiscences of Booksellers and Bookselling* (Edinburgh, 1905) 20-21; *Caledonian Mercury* (27 Oct. 1832, 29 Nov. 1841, 24 May 1852).

William Hunter, jun., 75 Northumberland St., by 1828.

Robert A. Souter, 43 Dundas St., by 1828; formerly a partner with James Souter, who a bookseller by 1813; succeeded by Alexander McGregor by 1831; latter at no. 21 by 1836 and at 71 Hanover St. by 1843.

Edward West, 3 Albany St., by 1828; had been bookseller with James Robertson at 7 Parliament Square by 1822, then at 11 Register St., but no library known at earlier addresses.

Book club

Newspaper Club: David Hume belonged by 1770 to a club which circulated London newspapers and pamphlets; there were presumably many more such societies.
  J. Y. T. Greig (ed.), *Letters of David Hume* (Oxford, 1932) vol. 2, p. 218.

Local guides and directories; Holden (1811); Pigot (1820-37); Alan G. D. White, *Public Libraries of Edinburgh, 1800-1970* (unpublished FLA thesis, 1975).

Fala

William Paterson: circulating library, by 1825.
  Pigot (1825/6).

Fountainhall

Fountainhall Library: subscription library; est. 1812; 700 vols. by 1843.
  NSA, vol. 1 (1845) 427.

Gorebridge

Gorebridge Library: subscription library; est. 14 Dec. 1818; 80 members and 600 vols. by 1839.
NSA, vol. 1 (1845) 55, 188-9.

Inveresk

Inveresk Library: subscription library; est. 1812; 1,300 vols. by 1839.
NSA, vol. 1 (1845) 298.

Leith

Subscription libraries

Leith Public Library; est. 23 Aug. 1808; 10s. entry + 10s. p.a.; 1,700 vols. by 1818; held in Exchange Buildings from 1812; at 123 Constitution St. by 1824, at no. 116 by 1842, and no. 63 by 1866; in 1881 became the Leith Public Institute and Library at 58 Tolbooth Wynd; cats. 1812*, 1853, 1873, 1887 (Edinburgh PL).
Leith Telegraph (17 Jan. & 26 Jun. 1812); *Caledonian Mercury* (1 Jan. 1818).

Leith Select Subscription Library; est. 1815; at 46 Charlotte St. by 1822; still there in 1827.

Circulating libraries

William Coke, foot of Weigh-house Wynd, by 1764; bookseller by 1764; near Bernard's St. by 1776, probably same address, later known as 40 Shore; bankrupt and stock-in-trade for sale in 1793; died 1819; succeeded by William Reid, who still here in 1825; at no. 35 by 1841; joined by son, and business still existed in 1886; labels of Coke in Franks & G. K. Scott cllns. and of Reid in Henry W. Fincham, *Artists and Engravers of British & American Bookplates* (London, 1897); cats. 1764*, 1771*.
Edinburgh Advertiser (30 Nov. 1764, 5 Mar. 1771); *Caledonian Mercury* (6 Apr. 1776, 26 Oct. 1793).

George Peattie, New Key, or foot of Tolbooth Wynd, shore of Leith, long before 1793; known as the Leith Circulating Library; for sale in 1796; stock may have been bought by John Galbraith of Edinburgh (see above), as labels of both in a novel of 1796 in Aberdeen UL; label of Peattie in JJ.
Thomas Haselden, *The Seaman's Daily Assistant New Modelled* (Glasgow, 1788) for advert.; James Thomson, *Rudiments of Music* (Edinburgh, 1793) imprint; *Edinburgh Advertiser* (30 Sep. 1796).

Archibald Allardice (or Allardyce), opp. the Custom House; est. 1807; known as the Leith New Circulating Library; at 15 Tolbooth Wynd by 1813, probably same address; 2,000 vols.; succeeded by Robert Allardice by 1822; latter was involved in several partnerships and had other bookshop(s) in Edinburgh; cats. 1807 (Dalhousie UL), 1808*.
> *Edinburgh Advertiser* (9 Jun. 1807, 29 Jan. 1808); *Leith & Edinburgh Telegraph* (24 Mar. 1809).

James Burnet, 35 St. Bernard St.; est. 1816; at no. 16 by 1821.
> *Caledonian Mercury* (9 Mar. 1816).

James Whyte, 3 Morton St., by 1824; may have acquired some books of P. G. Buchanan of Edinburgh (see above); library at 13 George St. by 1828, though bookshop continued at previous address; also seems to have to have run bookshop at 14 South St. Andrews St., Edinburgh; dissolved by 1833.
> *Edinburgh Almanack* (1827) 361-2.

LIBERTON

Liberton Library: subscription library; est. 15 Feb. 1828, for working men; held at the parochial school; cat. 1830 (NLS).
> *NSA*, vol. 1 (1845) 26.

LOANHEAD

Loanhead Library: subscription library; est. 1818; minute book, 1818-53 (Midlothian AO).
> *NSA*, vol. 1 (1845) 337.

MUSSELBURGH

Subscription library

Musselburgh Library: subscription library; est. 1812; 1,300 vols. by 1846.
> Samuel Lewis, *A Topographical Dictionary of Scotland* (London, 1846), vol. 2, p. 295.

Circulating library

John Walker, High St.: circulating library, by 1825; later given as no. 33; still there in 1858, at least as bookseller.

Newton

Newton Parish Subscription Library: subscription library, by unknown date; NLS copy of John Main, *Sermons* (Edinburgh, 1797) belonged to this library.

Circulating (or subscription) library for colliery workers by ca. 1800; dissolved by 1830, though books remained in 1845.
NSA, vol. 1 (1845) 582.

Penicuik

Penicuik Village Library: subscription library; est. 1797; cost 11/6d. + 4s. p.a.; James Jackson was librarian from its inception until his death in 1854; 1,200 vols. and 50 members by 1837; held in Bank St. by 1876; dissolved 1879; cats. 1846 (NRS), supp. 1848*.
NSA, vol. 1 (1845) 47; John J. Wilson, *Annals of Penicuik* (Edinburgh, 1891) 21; M. H. Fisher, 'James Jackson of Planetree Shade', in: Penicuik Historical Society, *History of Penicuik*, vol. 3 (ca. 1982); also personal communication from the author and the local studies librarian, Midlothian Library, Roslin.

Portobello

William Nivison, 11 High St.: circulating library, by 1817; his main library was in Edinburgh (see above, 1815); cat. 1817*.
Caledonian Mercury (15 Nov. 1817).

William Fox, High St., foot of Brighton Place: circulating library, by 1820; still there in 1845.
Pigot (1820) 2nd edn.: *Addenda*.

Stow

Stow Congregational Library: subscription library; est. 1823; 300 vols. by 1843.
NSA, vol. 1 (1845) 426.

Wester Duddingston

Wester Duddingston Library: subscription library; est. 1821; 200 vols. by 1843; cost 6d. per quarter.
NSA, vol. 1 (1845) 395.

ELGINSHIRE

ELGIN

Subscription libraries

Elgin Literary Association: book club with permanent library; est. 1818; originally 20 members; 700 vols. by 1835.

Elgin Juvenile Literary Society; est. Jan. 1820; known as Elgin Reading Association by 1824.

Circulating library

Isaac Forsyth (1768-1859); est. 1789 with over 1,000 vols. in The Tower, High St.; known as Elgin Circulating Library; re-opened 1809 after purchasing another 1,000 vols. in London; 4,000 vols. by 1812; his books circulated throughout north-east Scotland, using carriers and packet-boats; took Alexander Young as partner, 1827; 6,000 vols. by 1830; may have dissolved by 1842, but bookshop acquired in 1844 by A. & Robert Ferguson (from Oliver & Boyd's, Edinburgh), who revived the library and moved to Roy Place, High St.; only 2,500 vols. when succeeded by George Wilson, 1846, who moved to 121 High St.; bought by Francis Russell in 1855; latter had run his own library since 1852, as well as the Elgin Literary Association (above); at 159 High St. by 1860, when partner with James Watson; Russell died 1861 and succeeded by James Watson, who still there in 1876; cats. 1789[1], supps. 1795[1] & 1798*, supps. 1803[2] & 1804[2], 1809*, supps. 1810-14* & 1821-3*, 1826*, supp. 1841*, 1844* ([1]NLS & Moray Local Heritage Centre, Elgin; [2]NRS); supp. 1830 printed in *Elgin & Forres Journal* (4 Nov. 1830).

> J. Thomas, "Forming the Literary Tastes of the Middle and Higher Classes': Elgin's Circulating Libraries and their Proprietors, 1789-1870', in: John Hinks & Catherine Armstrong (eds.), *Worlds of Print* (New Castle, Del., 2006), pp. 91-111; *Inverness Journal* (20 Oct. 1809, 4 May 1810, 23 Oct. 1812, 9 Dec. 1814, 13 Nov. 1818); *Aberdeen Journal* (11 Oct. 1809, 13 Nov. 1811, 2 Nov. 1814, 15 Nov. 1826); *Inverness Courier* (3 Oct. 1822, 16 Oct. 1823, 28 Oct. 1824, 15 Nov. 1826); *Elgin Courier* (19 Oct. 1827).

Edinburgh Almanack (1824-7): *Northern Counties Supp.*; *NSA*, vol. 13 (1845) 22; *Bibliotheck* 5 (1968) 132.

FOCHABERS

Fochabers Subscription Library: subscription library; est. 1826.
Edinburgh Almanack (1828): *Northern Counties Supp.*

FORRES

Forres Subscription Library: subscription library; est. 1805; still existed in 1842.
    J. Young & Co., *Supplement to the Almanacs for 1814*; *NSA*, vol. 13 (1845) 175-6; *Edinburgh Almanack* (1824-7): *Northern Counties Supp.*

GARMOUTH

Garmouth Subscription Library: subscription library; est. 1823.

Garmouth and Kingston Mechanics Library: subscription library; est. 1825.
    Edinburgh Almanack (1827-34): *Inverness Supp.*

FIFESHIRE

ANSTRUTHER

William Cockburn: circulating library, by 1812; bookseller here by 1792 until 1837.
    Fife & Kinross Register (1812).

AUCHTERTOOL

Auchtertool Library: subscription library; est. Mar. 1824; 215 vols. by 1836.
    NSA, vol. 9 (1845) 259.

BURNTISLAND (or WESTER KINGHORN)

Burntisland Library: subscription library, by 1820.
    Pigot (1820) 2nd edn.: *Addenda*.

CERES

Ceres Library: subscription library; est. 1828.
    NSA, vol. 9 (1845) 526.

CROSSGATES

Crossgates Library: subscription library; est. 1809; re-formed as an itinerating library for surrounding villages, 1837.
  J. W. Hudson, *History of Adult Education* (London, 1851) 198-9.

CUPAR

Cupar Library: subscription library; est. 1797; 148 members by 1813; held in St. Catherine St.; 4,000 vols. by 1836; at Guildahll in 1860; eventually merged with Cupar Public Library, and many books still survive there; cats. 1813, supps. 1818 & 1823, 1827* (Cupar Library; NLS); MS. cats. 1822-66 (Cupar PL).
  Pigot (1837); *NSA*, vol. 9 (1845) 16; Alexander Anderson, *Old Libraries of Fife* (privately printed, 1953) 6-7.

Fife Medico-Chirurgical Society: incl. subscription library; est. Nov. 1825.
  Fife & Kinross Register (1827).

DUNFERMLINE

Subscription libraries

Dunfermline Library; est. 26 Feb. 1789; originally 10s.6d. entry + 7s.6d. p.a.; 92 members by 1815; 3,000 vols. by 1844; at 15 High St.; merged with Trades Library (below) in 1870 and with Public (Municipal) Library in 1883; cats. 1796*, 1825, 1849[1], supp. 1861, 1863 (Dunfermline PL; [1]also in Edinburgh PL); minute book, 1789-1828 (Dunfermline PL).

Dunfermline Tradesmen's Library; est. Nov. 1808 by several weavers who pooled their own books; first kept in the house of the librarian's mother, then at many other addresses, incl. Broad St., Nethertown, and, from 1824, Dunfermline High St.; 95 members by 1826; merged with Mechanics' Institute in 1832 to become the United Tradesmen's and Mechanics' Library; in Kirkgate in 1834; moved back to High St. in 1843, then to Bridge St., 1853, and reached the County Buildings in 1858; merged with the Subscription Library (above) in 1870 and amalgamated with the Public (Municipal) Library in 1883; cats. before 1820?*, 1823, 1845, 1871 (Dunfermline PL); loans register, 1826-30 (Dunfermline PL).
  Andrew S. Robertson, *History of Dunfermline Tradesmen's and Mechanics' Library* (Dunfermline, 1914).

Circulating libraries

John Miller (1780-1852), Abbey Park Place; est. 1805; brother of George and James Miller of Dunbar (see below); to Bridge St. by 1807; 1,300 books by 1815; succeeded by son, John, 1852; dissolved 1866; label in JJ; cat. 1815*.
 W. J. Couper, *The Millers of Haddington, Dunbar & Dunfermline* (London, 1914), especially pp. 250-1.

Unidentified library for religious works by 1828.

Book club

Dunfermline Pamphlet Club: book club for periodicals and pamphlets, est. 12 Jun. 1810; 17 members at 12s. p.a.; minute book, 1810-11 (Dunfermline PL).
 John Fernie, *History ... of Dunfermline* (Dunfermline, 1815) 43; A. Mercer, *History of Dunfermline* (Dunfermline, 1828) 140; Alexander Anderson, *Old Libraries of Fife* (privately printed, 1953) 5, 10; Erskine Beveridge, *Bibliography of ... Dunfermline* (Dunfermline, 1901); *NSA*, vol. 9 (1845) 903.

Dysart

Dysart Subscription Library: subscription library, by 1815, when books kept in Coffee Room, according to Dysart Burgh Council minutes (Fife AO).
 Pigot (1820) 2nd edn.: *Addenda*.

Dysart Trades Library: subscription library; est. 1824.
 P. K. Livingstone, *Kirkcaldy and its Libraries* (Kirkcaldy, 1950) 7.

East Wemyss

East Wemyss Subscription Library: subscription library; est. 1817; 300 vols. by 1838; dissolved ca. 1900.
 NSA, vol. 9 (1845) 401; Alexander Anderson, *Old Libraries of Fife* (privately printed, 1953) 32.

Elie

Elie Library: subscription library; est. 1814; 5,000 vols. in 1953; moved to different building, 1958, and taken over by Fife County Libraries in 1968; minute books, 1841-1972 (Cupar PL).
 Alexander Anderson, *Old Libraries of Fife* (privately printed, 1953) 9; *NSA*, vol. 9 (1845) 292.

INVERKEITHING

Inverkeithing and Rosyth Subscription Library: subscription library; est. 1800; still existed in 1834.

Inverkeithing Evangelical Library: subscription library; est. 20 Jan. 1802; 1/6d. entry + 3d. per month; still existed in 1834; cat. 1822 (Dunfermline PL).

Alexander Anderson, *Old Libraries of Fife* (privately printed, 1953) 29; *Dunfermline Register* (1834).

KINGHORN

Kinghorn Library: subscription library; est. 1826.
: *Caledonian Mercury* (20 Mar. 1826); P. K. Livingstone, *Kirkcaldy and its Libraries* (Kirkcaldy, 1950) 7.

KINGSBARNS

Kingsbarns Library: subscription library; est. 1822, mainly by members of the Golf Club; dissolved 1840.
: *Caledonian Mercury* (14 Aug. 1824); *NSA*, vol. 9 (1845) 100.

KIRKCALDY

Kirkcaldy Library: subscription library; est. 5 Nov. 1800; kept in new Assembly Rooms, High St., from 1819; 6,000 titles by 1888; dissolved 1934; cats. 1867, 1888[1], supps. 1888-1925 (Kirkcaldy PL; [1]also in NLS); accounts, 1911-29 (Kirkcaldy PL).
: Alexander Anderson, *Old Libraries of Fife* (privately printed, 1953) 8.

George Bernard, 49 High St.: circulating library; est. 1827; may have been succeeded by John Crawford, the only library in High St. in 1837.
: *Kirkcaldy Directory* (1834); Pigot (1837).

P. K. Livingstone, *Kirkcaldy and its Libraries* (Kirkcaldy, 1950) 8-9.

LARGO

Largo Subscription Library: subscription library; est. 1820, according to letter by Sir John Leslie, 6 Sep. 1820 (in Edinburgh UL: ref. Phot. 1144/1); 500 vols. by 1837.
NSA, vol. 9 (1845) 444.

LETHAM (near Cupar)

Letham Library: subscription library, by 1825; minute books, 1825-83 (St. Andrews UL).

ROSYTH: see under INVERKEITHING

ST. ANDREWS

St. Andrews Subscription Library: subscription library; est. ca. 1822; 1,200 vols. and 100 members by 1837; 8s. p.a.
NSA, vol. 9 (1845) 493; *Fife & Kinross Register* (1834).

George Scott, South St.: circulating library, by 1820.
Pigot (1820) 2nd edn.: *Addenda*.

SCOONIE

Scoonie Library: subscription library; est. 'long before' 1836 when had 650 vols.
NSA, vol. 9 (1845) 275.

STRATHMIGLO

Strathmiglo Library: subscription library, by 1825.
Pigot (1825/6).

TORRYBURN

Torryburn Public Library: subscription library; est. 1827.
Dunfermline Register (1834).

WESTER KINGHORN: see BURNTISLAND

FORFARSHIRE

ARBROATH

Subscription libraries

Arbroath Subscription Library; est. 24 Aug. 1797; originally cost 1 gn. entry + ½ gn. p.a.; in various temporary rooms; in High St. by 1837; about 4,000 titles by 1859; books kept in Public Hall from 1868; merged with the Public (Municipal) Library, 1896; cats. 1799*, 1808*, supp. 1810*, 1813*, 1815*, 1825*, 1859, supp. 1875, 1892, 1896 (Arbroath PL); MS. cats. 1797-1872, and minute books, 1797-1896 (Angus AO, Montrose).

Arbroath Mechanics Library; est. 1824; kept at back of Town Hall by 1837.

Arbroath First United Associate Congregation (Antiburgher), North Grimsby Church, Library, by 1823; library cash book, 1823-59, and cat., n.d. (digital copy in NRS).

Circulating library

William Mudie, High St., by 1811.
   Montrose, Arbroath, & Brechin Review (11 Jan. 1811).

J. M. McBain, *History of the Arbroath Public Library* (Arbroath, 1894); Neil Craven, *Development of Public Libraries in Angus, 1870-1975* (unpublished MA thesis; Strathclyde University, 1976) chapter 18; *NSA*, vol. 11 (1845) 104; Pigot (1837).

BRECHIN

Subscription library

Brechin Library; est. 1804; 2,000 vols. by 1813, when cost 10s.6d. p.a.; part of stock sold to A. Black (see below) in 1823, but unclear if the subscription library continued.
   Angus & Mearns Register for 1813.

Circulating libraries

William Grim, Upper Wynd; est. 1803.

Alexander Black, by 1823, when added part of the Brechin Library, above, to his existing stock.
Montrose, Arbroath, & Brechin Review (24 Jul. 1823).

Neil Craven, *Development of Public Libraries in Angus, 1870-1975* (unpublished MA thesis; Strathclyde University, 1976) chapter 10.

Coupar Angus
(partly in Forfarshire): see under Perthshire

Dundee

Subscription libraries

Dundee Library; est. 1792; merged with Public Library, below, in 1815 (according to latter's minute books, 5 Apr. 1815).

Dundee Public Library; est. 1 Oct. 1796; originally 5s. entry + 1s. per quarter; a library belonging to the town's medical men was deposited in 1809; took over the Dundee Library, 1815; kept at 8 St. Clement's Lane from 1817; at 8 Vault St. by 1837 and 18 St. Clement's Lane by 1860; dissolved 1869 when books passed to the Public (Municipal) Library; cats. 1800, supps. to 1804, 1811, 1832 (Dundee PL); minute books, 1796-1825 (Dundee PL).
Scots Chronicle (27 Jan. 1797).

Westport Chapel Library, for dissenters, by 1824; cat. 1824 (Dundee PL).

Circulating libraries

Unidentified circulating library by ca. 1765, according to James Beattie; possibly Nicoll's, below.
Margaret Forbes, *Beattie and his Friends* (London, 1904) 276.

Robert Nicoll, High St., by 1782; began as a bookseller in 1767; died 1791 and succeeded by William Brown; for sale in 1794, when Brown moved to Edinburgh to publish the *Patriot Weekly Chronicle*; cat. 1782 (Dundee PL).
Caledonian Mercury (14 Jul. 1791, 4 Sep. 1794).

Robert T. Miller, High St., by 1804; bookseller here by 1797 until 1811; cat. n.d. (Dundee PL).
Dundee, Perth, & Cupar Advertiser (30 Nov. 1804, 22 Feb. 1805, 25 Dec. 1807).

William Chalmers, Castle St., by 1805, when succeeded by his brother, James; lent French books from 1808; moved to 4 Castle St., 1813; at no. 10 by 1840s; still there in 1850s; cats. by 1805*, supps. 1806* & 1808*, 1809*, 1818 (Dundee PL).

Dundee, Perth, & Cupar Advertiser (22 Feb., 29 Nov. & 27 Dec. 1805, 1 & 29 Jan. 1808, 17 Feb. 1809, 28 May 1813).

John Handyside Baxter, head of the Horse Wynd, Murraygate; est. 1806; known as the Minerva Circulating Library; by 1846 at 99 Murraygate, probably same address; died 1855.
Dundee, Perth, & Cupar Advertiser (6 Jun. 1806); *Dundee Courier* (5 Sep. 1855).

George Milne (1756-1839), front of the English Chapel, High St., by 1813.
Angus & Mearns Register for 1813.

Edward Lesslie, 83 Murraygate, by 1813; emigrated to USA in ca. 1830.
Angus & Mearns Register for 1813.

John Hamilton, Murdoch's Close, High St., by 1818; moved to 1 High St., 1819; at no. 2 by 1825; 700 titles in 1826; still there in 1834; cat. 1826 (Dundee PL).
Dundee, Perth, & Cupar Advertiser (1 Jan. & 23 Jul. 1819, 23 Jun. 1825).

William Straton, Hawkhill, by 1824; also a grocer.
Dundee Directory (1824).

James Jackson, 144 Overgate, by 1829; bookseller here by 1825; at no. 173 by 1846.
Dundee Directory (1829).

Forfar

Subscription library

Forfar Subscription Library; est. 21 Mar. 1795; only 860 vols. in 1821; merged with Public (Municipal) Library in 1892; cats. 1795[1], supps. to 1806, 1821, supps. 1837-47 (Forfar PL; [1]also in Dundee PL).
Neil Craven, *Development of Public Libraries in Angus, 1870-1975* (unpublished MA thesis; Strathclyde University, 1976) chapter 2.

Circulating libraries

John Small, High St., by 1825; bookseller by 1820.
Pigot (1825/6).

Peter Ranken, Castle St., before 1827, when for sale; 500 vols.
Dundee, Perth, & Cupar Advertiser (26 Jul. 1827).

Fowlis

Fowlis Library: subscription library, by 1815, when subscription raised from 6d. to 1s. per quarter; 600 vols. and 50 members by 1842; cats. 1815*, 1837*, 1854*; minute book, 1815-67 (Dundee AO).
 Neil Craven, *Development of Public Libraries in Angus, 1870-1975* (unpublished MA thesis; Strathclyde University, 1976) chapter 35; *NSA*, vol. 11 (1845) 467-8.

Glamis

Glammiss [sic] Library: subscription library; est. 1828.
 NSA, vol. 11 (1845) 349.

Montrose

Subscription libraries

Montrose Public Library; est. 1785; free to teachers and students; books kept in Academy until 1821 when moved to new Town Buildings; 100 members by 1835; 20,000 vols. by 1884; taken over by Montrose Natural History & Antiquarian Society and books moved to Museum; 27,000 vols. by 1910; taken over by Public (Municipal) Library, 1974 and moved books there in 1980; books later moved to County Library HQ, Forfar, where about 10,000 vols. survive; cats. 1813*, 1857*, supp. 1873*, 1880 (Glasgow UL; Aberdeen PL and UL; BL), 1896 (Montrose PL; Strathclyde UL); minute books, 1810-1957 (Angus AO, Montrose).
 OSA, vol. 5 (1793) 34; rules printed in *Gentleman's Magazine* 55 (1785), 535-6.

Montrose Reading Society; est. 1819; became Montrose Trades Library, 1855; kept at 41 John St.; dissolved 1904 and books transferred to Public (Municipal) Library, 1905; cats. 1858*, 1897 (Edinburgh PL); minute books, 1837-1904 (Angus AO, Montrose).

Circulating libraries

John Smith, High St., by 1811; bookseller here from 1808; died 1827.
 Montrose, Arbroath, & Brechin Review (11 Jan. 1811, 6 Jul. 1827).

David Petrie, High St.; est. 1823; cat. 1824*?
 Montrose, Arbroath, & Brechin Review (25 Dec. 1823).

Neil Craven, *Development of Public Libraries in Angus, 1870-1975* (unpublished MA thesis; Strathclyde University, 1976) chapter 27; *NSA*, vol. 11 (1845) 287.

Newtyle

Newtyle Library: subscription library; est. ca. 1822; chiefly religious books; still existed in 1842.
NSA, vol. 11 (1845) 566.

HADDINGTONSHIRE

Aberlady

Aberlady Subscription Library: subscription library, by 1821.
East Lothian Register for 1821; Haddingtonshire Register (1825).

Athelstaneford

Athelstaneford Subscription Library: subscription library, by ca. 1805?; still existed in 1835.
Haddingtonshire Register (1825); *NSA*, vol. 2 (1845) 52.

Dirleton

Dirleton Subscription Library: subscription library, by 1820; still existed in 1837.
East Lothian Register for 1820; Haddingtonshire Register (1825); Pigot (1837).

Dunbar

Subscription libraries

Dunbar Subscription Library; est. Dec. 1815, but did not last long; the Dunbar Subscription Library is recorded in 1820, but unclear whether refers to this or following library.
East Lothian Register for 1820.

Dunbar Library, by 1825; presumably a different library from the preceding; held in High St.; dissolved by 1860 when remnants of stock for sale.
Haddingtonshire Register (1825); Pigot (1825/6); *Aberdeen Journal* (12 Dec. 1860).

Circulating library

George and James Miller; est. Nov. 1789; their brother was John Miller of Dunfermline (see above); partnership dissolved in 1791; James continued as bookseller and ran a juvenile circulating library for a time; George (1771-1835) moved to new shop in High St. in 1792 and continued the library; known as Dunbar and County Circulating Library; 3,500 titles by 1809; lost business when local garrison withdrawn, so moved library to Haddington in 1814 (see below); cats. 1789*, 1790*, 1791*, 1792*, 1806*, supp. 1807*, 1808*, 1809*, 1811*, supp. 1812*.

W. J. Couper, *The Millers of Haddington, Dunbar & Dunfermline* (London, 1914); James Miller, *History of Dunbar* (Dunbar, 1859) 307-8.

East Linton

Linton Subscription Library: subscription library, by 1820.
East Lothian Register for 1820; *Haddingtonshire Register* (1825); Pigot (1825/6-37).

Garvald

Garvald Subscription Library: subscription library, by 1820; not recorded in 1825.
East Lothian Register for 1820.

Gifford

Gifford Subscription Library: subscription library, by 1820; not recorded in 1825.
East Lothian Register for 1820.

Haddington

Subscription libraries

Haddington Subscription Library: subscription library, by 1820; in Hardgate by 1837; may have dissolved by 1850; the Haddington Town and Country Library was est. in 1853 and unclear whether took over stock of former library; the new library in Church St. by 1860 and had 1,000 vols. when taken over by the (Sir John) Gray Library (est. 1717) in 1869; books of latter now in NLS;

cats. 1840 & supps. 1841-5 (NLS), 1862+ (Haddington PL), 1881+ (BL) [+Town and Country Library].
  Pigot (1820); *NSA*, vol. 2 (1845) 16-17; *Leeds Mercury* (23 Oct. 1869).

Theological library for students of divinity, run by Rev. John Brown, who served as Burgher minister from 1758 to 1787; transferred to Selkirk (see below).

Circulating libraries

Charles Herriot, Allan's New Land, by 1778; previously bookseller in Edinburgh.
  Ruddiman's Weekly Mercury (?? Jun. 1778) [according to cutting in Glasgow UL].

George Neill's Haddington & County Circulating Library, High St., before 1807, when the business was re-est.; still there in 1852 as Neill & Son.
  Edinburgh Advertiser (27 Oct. 1807).

George Miller, foot of the High St.; est. 1814 with 2,500 vols.; his library was originally in Dunbar (see above); bankrupt 1816; library continued by his son, James, but dissolved 1819; blamed the introduction of Samuel Brown's itinerating libraries in 1817; cat. 1814*.

George Tait, High St., by 1826.

W. J. Couper, *The Millers of Haddington, Dunbar & Dunfermline* (London, 1914), especially pp. 109, 132-3; Pigot (1825/6-37); Thomas Mackay (ed.), *Autobiography of Samuel Smiles* (London, 1905) 30.

Innerwick

Innerwick Library: subscription library, by 1824; used by Alexander Somerville, the journalist.
  Alexander Somerville, *The Autobiography of a Working Man* (London, 1951) 47.

North Berwick

North Berwick Library: subscription library, by 1816, when had 155 vols.; unsuccessful, and books handed over to Rev. Samuel Brown for one of his first itinerating libraries, which commenced in 1817.
  [Thomas Mason], *Free Libraries of Scotland* (Glasgow, 1880) 2-3; W. R. Aitken, *History of the Public Library Movement in Scotland to 1955* (Glasgow, 1971) 32.

North Berwick Subscription Library: subscription library, by 1821; this may have dissolved soon afterwards, since another North Berwick Subscription

Library was est. in 1826; latter began with books from the recently dissolved School of Arts; 500 vols. by 1835; held in Westgate by 1837; still existed in 1876; later merged with Public Library, which taken over by East Lothian County Libraries; inventory (East Lothian Council).
East Lothian Register for 1821; Haddingtonshire Register (1825); *Caledonian Mercury* (30 Dec. 1826); Pigot (1837); *NSA*, vol. 2 (1845) 341.

Ormiston

Ormiston Friendly Association for the Protection of Property: subscription library; benefit society, est. 1784, incl. a library; 100 vols. by 1835.
Haddingtonshire Register (1825); *NSA*, vol. 2 (1845) 150.

Two unspecified subscription libraries by 1825; they are probably the library above as well as one of Samuel Brown's itinerating libraries.
Pigot (1825/6-37).

Prestonpans

Prestonpans Subscription Library: subscription library, by 1820; still there in 1837.
Pigot (1820) 2nd edn.: *Addenda*, & (1825/6-37); *Haddingtonshire Register* (1825).

Tranent

Tranent Parish Library: subscription library: est. 1792 by kirk minister; anyone in parish could join for 1s. p.a., raised in 1800 to 4s. entry + 2s. p.a.; 200 vols. by 1813.
Cheap Magazine (1813) 376.

Tranent Library: subscription library; est. 1820; still existed in 1837.
East Lothian Register for 1820 and 1821; OSA, vol. 10 (1794) 99; Pigot (1837); *Haddingtonshire Register* (1825).

INVERNESSSHIRE

Campbelltown

Campbelltown Subscription Library: subscription library; est. 1820.
　Pigot (1825/6); *Edinburgh Almanack* (1827-34): *Inverness supp.*

Fort William

Fort William Subscription Library: subscription library; est. 16 Jul. 1819; still there in 1837; cat. ca. 1821 (Bodleian Library; Glasgow UL); minute book, 1819-35 (West Highland Museum, Fort William).
　Pigot (1820) 2nd edn.: *Addenda*, & (1825/6-37); *Edinburgh Almanack* (1827): *Inverness Supp.*

Inverness

Subscription libraries

Inverness Subscription Library; est. 1820; held in New St.; in the Academy Hall by 1824; cat. 1828 (Inverness PL).
　Inverness Journal (10 Aug. 1821).

Raining School Library: library of mainly religious works issued free to children attending school; est. Nov. 1821; adults could use the library for a small subscription; still existed in 1847.
　Inverness Journal (16 Nov. 1821).

Medical Society of the North; est. 1817: subscription library for medical practioners; held in Castle St.
　Inverness Courier (30 Apr. 1818, 6 Jun. 1822); *Aberdeen Journal* (31 Jan. 1821).

Inverness Literary Club Library; est. Aug. 1822; held at Raining School by 1847.

Circulating libraries

Alexander Davidson, opp. the Exchange, by 1782; became known as Inverness Circulating Library and almost certainly succeeded by Donald McDonald who began business in 1797 and was using the same designation by 1804; R. Dick took over Donaldson's shop, and presumably library, 1808; an unidentified circulating library, opp. the Exchange, was for sale in 1809 and was probably Dick's, who is not heard of again; succeeded by James Smith and G. Clark by 1811; label of Smith & Clerk's [sic] Inverness Circulating Library in BL copy of Mary Charlton's *Rosella* (London, 1799); their partnership dissolved in 1813 and Smith continued on own, moving to Bridge St.; G. Clark may also have run library in Peterhead (see above); Smith was in Church St. by 1820, and still known as Inverness Circulating Library; succeeded by Robert Baillie Lusk, 1824, and moved to High St.; in East St. by 1825; succeeded by Kenneth Douglas, 1826, who in High St. by 1827; 6,000 vols. by 1847; he died in 1860; cats. 1782 & supp. 1783, 1804[1], 1811, 1824, 1828, 1832 (Inverness PL; [1]only in Library Co. of Philadelphia).

Bibliotheck 5 (1968) 132; William Simpson, *Old Inverness booksellers* (Inverness, 1931) 9; *Aberdeen Journal* (2 Jan. 1798); *Edinburgh Advertiser* (13 Oct. 1797, 21 Aug. 1798); *Inverness Journal* (23 Jun. 1809, 1 Jan., 7 & 28 May 1813, 7 Jan. 1820); *Inverness Courier* (28 Oct. & 25 Nov. 1824, 16 Nov. 1825, 28 Jun. 1826); Pigot (1820) 2nd edn.: *Addenda*.

Donald Morrison, 1 Church St.; est. 1826; bookseller here by 1820; library still here in 1852; see also under Perth; cat. 1826*.

Inverness Courier (1 Feb. 1826).

Edinburgh Almanack (1824-34): *Northern Counties Supp.*; *History ... of Inverness* (Inverness, 1847) 85-86; Pigot (1825/6).

KINCARDINESHIRE

BANCHORY DEVINICK

Banchory Devinick Library: subscription or parish library?, by ca. 1810?; cost 1s. p.a.; under parish schoolmaster; taken over by the Free Church; still existed in 1898; probably the same as the Banchory Devinick Reading Society; cats. ca. 1850, 1864 (Aberdeen UL), 1898 (NLS).

NSA, vol. 11 (1845) 187.

LAURENCEKIRK

'Public Library' next to inn, presented and owned by Lord Gardenstone, and available for local inhabitants and travellers, by 1770s; surviving books now in University of Dundee Library; cat. 1780 (Aberdeen UL).

OSA, vol. 5 (1793) 178; *NSA*, vol. 11 (1845) 150; *Times* (16 Nov. 1787); J. R. Barker, 'Lord Gardenstone's Library at Laurencekirk', *Bibliotheck* 6 (1971), 41-51; George Birkbeck Hill, *The Footsteps of Dr. Johnson* (London, 1890) 109-10.

MARYCULTER

Maryculter Library: subscription or parish library?, est. 1822.
   NSA, vol. 11 (1845) 194.

STONEHAVEN

John Beattie's Stonehaven Circulating Library, Barclay St.: circulating library; est. 1816; bookseller here by 1810; label in G. K. Scott clln.; library still here in 1860; cat. by 1818*.
   Angus & Mearns Register for 1813; *Aberdeen Journal* (1 May 1816, 24 Jun. 1818); Pigot (1825/6).

John Wood, Evans St.: circulating library, by 1820; for sale in 1821 when had 600 vols.
   Pigot (1820) 2nd edn.: *Addenda*; *Aberdeen Journal* (5 Dec. 1821).

KINROSSSHIRE

KINROSS

Kinross Tradesmen's Library: subscription library; est. 1824; in Main St. by 1876; moved to Mackintosh Memorial Institute, 1885/6; 2,400 vols. by 1910; still existed in 1930s; cats. 1841 (NLS), 1898*; minute books, 1874-98 (Perth AO) and 1898-1905 (Perth Museum).

MILNATHORT

Milnathort Library: subscription library; est. 1797; 1,270 vols. by 1839; dissolved ca. 1930.
   NSA, vol. 9 (1845) 66.

Stewartry of Kirkcudbright

Balmaghie

Balmaghie Library: subscription library, possibly by 1825; existed 'many years' before 1844.
NSA, vol. 4 (1845) 188.

Borgue

Subscription library for religious books, possibly by 1825; existed 'some years' before 1841.
NSA, vol. 4 (1845) 62.

Castle Douglas

Castle Douglas Library: subscription library, by 1812.
Dumfries & Galloway Courier (28 Dec. 1813).

A. Macmillan & Co.: circulating library; est. 1817; they were also ironmongers and grocers.
Dumfries & Galloway Courier (28 Jan. 1817).

Dalbeattie

James Murray, draper: circulating library by 1825, according to SBTI; cousin to Allan Anderson of Dumfries (see above).

Gatehouse-of-Fleet

Gatehouse-of-Fleet Subscription Library: subscription library, by 1793; apparently dissolved soon afterwards.
Robert Heron, *Observations Made in a Journey through the Western Counties of Scotland*, vol. 2 (Perth, 1793) 221.

Gatehouse-of-Fleet Subscription Library: subscription library, by 1820; apparently a new library.
Pigot (1820) 2nd edn.: *Addenda*, & (1821-25/6).

Kirkcudbright

Subscription library

Kirkcudbright Subscription Library; est. 1 May 1777; originally 40 members; books kept in various places, incl. the Grammar School; 400 titles by 1824; merged with another, newly-established, subscription library in 1842, but disused by 1846; books transferred to Mechanics' Institute in 1854 and still kept in Town Hall in 1950s; cats. 1780*, 1802*, 1813*, 1824 (Hornel Library, Broughton House, Kirkcudbright); minute books, 1777-1842 (Hornel Library), 1842-54 (Dumfries & Galloway Museums).

Robert Heron, *Observations Made in a Journey through the Western Counties of Scotland*, vol. 2 (Perth, 1793) 194; *NSA*, vol. 4 (1845) 34.

Circulating libraries

John Nicholson, High St., by 1819, when had 479 titles; previously in Horse Guards; in 1827 a number of books from the library were sent to Thomas Fowler of Gatehouse-of-Fleet to be given out; Nicholson in Castle St. by 1837; John and James Nicholson still here in 1850s, and moved to High St. in 1860s, but unknown if library still carried on; cat. 1819 (Stewartry Museum, Kirkcudbright).

John Cannon, High St., by 1825; still there in 1852.

Pigot (1820-37).

Lanarkshire

Airdrie

Airdrie Library: subscription library; est. 10 Dec. 1792; 10s. entry + 2s. p.a.; £1 entry from 1896; max. 40 members, later 50; merged with Mechanics' Institute, 1837, which taken over by the Public (Municipal) Library in 1854; cat. 1818*; minute book, 1792-1833 (formerly in Airdrie PL).

J. Gardner, 'An Airdrie Library in the Eighteenth Century', *Airdrie Advertiser* (30 Jul. 1921); Airdrie Public Library, *A Century of Reading* (Airdrie, 1953) 4.

BIGGAR

Biggar Public Library: subscription library; est. 17 Dec. 1797; merged with the Parish Library (below) in 1863; many books apparently ended up on a hogmanay bonfire in 1921.

Biggar Parish Library: subscription library; est. 1800 by the working classes.

Biggar Evangelical Library: subscription library for religious books; est. 1807.

> Some books from the above libraries are now in Gladstone Court Museum, Biggar, where the Roberton Village Library (see Roberton, Dumfriesshire) is now located, incl. various archives and catalogues.

William Hunter, *Biggar & the House of Fleming* (Edinburgh, 1867) 371-2; *NSA*, vol. 6 (1845) 369; *Library History* 3 (1974) 160.

BOTHWELL

Bothwell Parish Library: probably a subscription library; est. 1798; frequented by supporters of Tom Paine; dissolved, possibly some time, before 1836.
NSA, vol. 6 (1845) 802.

CAMBUSLANG

Cambuslang Public Library: subscription library, by 1828; still existed in 1850s.

James A. Wilson, *History of Cambuslang* (Glasgow, 1929) 172-4.

CAMBUSNETHAN

Two subscription libraries est. by 1790.
OSA, vol. 12 (1794) 574.

CARLUKE

Carluke Library: subscription or parish library?, est. 1827; 600 vols. by 1839.
NSA, vol. 6 (1845) 594.

COATBRIDGE: see LANGLOAN

Covington

Covington Library: subscription library; est. ca. 1800; still flourishing in 1815; two books in Biggar Museum.
'An English Commercial Traveller', *Letters from Scotland* (London, 1817) 149-51.

Dalserf

Dalserf Library: subscription library; est. 1822; disused by 1840, when books in parish schoolroom.
NSA, vol. 6 (1845) 759.

East Kilbride

East Kilbride Subscription Library: subscription library, by 1790.
Thomas E. Niven, *East Kilbride* (Glasgow, ca. 1965) 293.

Glasgow

Subscription libraries

By 1796 there were said to be at least three subscription libraries for the working classes in Glasgow, as well as one in Anderston, two in Gorbals, one in Brownfield, three in Bridgeton, one in Tradeston, and one at Mr Gillespie's cotton mill at Woodside.
Scots Chronicle (30 Dec. 1796, 20 Jan. & 10 Feb. 1797).

Stirling's Public Library: not a proprietary subscription library, but bequeathed to the city by Walter Stirling; est. Jan. 1791 in St. Enoch's Square; users paid 5 gns. entry from 1793, raised to 10 gns. in 1816, but was 5 gns. from 1833; moved in 1805 to Hutcheson's Hospital at 52 Ingram St., and to Miller St., 1844; admitted annual members from 1848; new building erected in 1864 on same site, 48 Miller St.; merged with the Glasgow Public (i.e. Subscription) Library, 1871 (see below); 830 members by 1888, and had 50,000 vols. by 1907; taken over by Glasgow City Libraries, 1912, and moved to former Mitchell Library building in Miller St.; moved to Royal Exchange, Queen St., 1954, and became for many years a branch lending library of the City Libraries; removed to 62 Miller St., 1994, then back to Royal Exchange, 2002, as the 'Library at the Gallery of Modern Art'; cats. 1792*, 1795 (University of Cape Town Library), 1801 (Watt Library, Greenock), 1805[1,2], supp. 1819[1], 1833[2], 1852[2], 1870[2], 1888[1,2,3], supps. to 1903[2] (Mitchell Library; [1]also in

NLS; [2]also in Glasgow UL; [3]also in CUL & London Library); minute books & other papers, 1791-1912 (Mitchell Library).

Thomas Mason, *Public and Private Libraries of Glasgow* (Glasgow, 1985) 31-100; W. J. S. Paterson, *Stirling's and Glasgow Public Library, 1791-1907* (Glasgow, 1907); *Glasgow Mercury* (26 Mar. 1793); *Glasgow Courier* (10 Mar. 1792, 13 Apr. 1805).

Glasgow Friendly Library Society; est. May 1802; mainly for religious books; at 1 Antigua Place by 1825; cat. 1802, supp. ca. 1805 (Mitchell Library).

Glasgow Public Library; est. Dec. 1804; moved to Millar's School, George St., 1805; incl. a Juvenile Library of 100 titles by 1810; 550 members by 1818; at 151 George St., 1847; to 15 Bath St. in 1856; took over Stirling's Library (see above) in 1871, and books transferred to latter's building; known as Stirling and Glasgow Public Library; cats. 1810[1,2,3], supps. to 1819, 1821[1], supps. to 1840[1], 1846[2], supp. 1848[2], 1859, 1865 (Mitchell Library; [1]also in Glasgow UL and State Library of N.S.W., Sydney; [2]BL; [3]Watt Library, Greenock); minute book, 1814-46 (Mitchell Library).

Glasgow Courier (16 Feb. 1805); *Glasgow Herald* (20 Jun. 1856).

Glasgow Theological Library; est. 1808; rules in Mitchell Library.

Robertsonian Theological Library; est. 1814; kept in Mitchell St.; at John St. by 1821; shares cost £5 in 1824 (max. 200), but annual subscribers admitted at 10s.6d. p.a.; 165 members by 1816, and 4,000 vols. by 1818; taken over by the United Secession Synod in 1824/5 for the benefit of students at Divinity Hall; in 1847 the Synod became the United Presbyterian Church and used Divinity Hall in Edinburgh, though unclear whether library transferred there; cat. 1815 (Glasgow UL).

Caledonian Mercury (2 Nov. 1821, 18 Sep. 1824, 24 Sep. 1825, 14 May 1827).

Barony of Gorbals Public Library; est. 1817; held at 34 Crown St.; at 69 Crown St. by 1828; still existed in 1852; cat. 1822 (Glasgow UL).

Glasgow North Quarter Library, by 1819; 400 vols. by 1820; held in a schoolroom; intended for mechanics; at 3 Weaver St. by 1837 and still recorded there in 1843; but a Glasgow North Quarter Public Library was est. in 1842 for moral and religious reading (according to 1843 cat. in Mitchell Library), which possibly a re-foundation but might be a different library.

Glasgow Herald (17 Jul. 1820).

Glasgow Foreign Library; est. 1820; held at 169 Trongate, then at 81 Hutcheson St.; run by a committee with bookseller John Wylie (see below) as librarian; cost 1 gn. + 12s. p.a.; 67 subscribers in 1823; at 56 Argyle St. by end 1823, and at 97 Argyle St. with Wylie's circulating library by 1828; dissolved 1832 when Wylie bankrupt; another, probably unconnected, Glasgow Foreign

Library was est. in 1834 for annual subscribers; latter still existed in 1849 when had 813 vols.; cat. 1823 (Edinburgh PL).
Glasgow Herald (20 Oct. 1820, 9 Nov. 1849, 13 Apr. 1855).

Glasgow Gas Workmen's Library: general subscription library for workers at the gas works, Kirk St.; est. 29 Oct. 1821 by the manager, James Beaumont Neilson (1792-1865); cost 7s.6d. + 1½d. per week; only weekend borrowing allowed; 300 vols. by 1825; rules (1822) in NLS.
Caledonian Mercury (17 Jan. 1825); Timothy Claxton, *Hints to Mechanics* (London, 1839) 208-11.

Barrowfield Printfield and Dyework Library: general subscription library for workers; est. 23 Mar. 1824; cat. 1825 (Glasgow UL).

Glasgow Mechanics' Library, by 1825; originally at 18 Incle Factory Lane, Hutchesontown; at no. 31 by 1828; at 57 North Hanover St. by 1843 and no. 61 by 1847.

Calton Public Library, by 1825; originally at 12 Struther St.; at 4 James St. by 1828, 7 James St. by 1837, and 46 Canning St. by 1860; still there in 1876.

Bridgeton Public Library; est. 1824; held in John St.; at 2 Muslin St. by 1843, 9 John St. in 1847, and 53 Main St. by 1860; cat. 1824 & poster (Glasgow UL).

Circulating libraries

John Smith of Finnieston (1724-1814), Trongate; est. 1753; moved to King, or New, St. by 1757 and to 72 Trongate in 1763, and later at no. 111; died 1814 but run by son of same name, 'the younger' (1753-1833), from 1781; at 75 Hutcheson St. by 1796, and no. 85 from 1798; grandson, also John Smith (1784-1849), 'the youngest', became partner in 1803; known as the Glasgow Circulating Library; 20,000 vols. by 1816; moved to 40 High St. by 1828, when the library was discontinued and offered for sale; bookshop moved to other addresses before 70 St. Vincent St. in 1835; at latter address started a 'Select reading club', whose books sold annually until 1892 (lists of books, 1836-46, in Glasgow UL); bookshop existed until 2000; cats. 1762*, 1769*, 1772*, supp. 1778*, 1783*, ca. 1784^1, supp. 1786^1, 1796^1, supps. 1797-1805^1, 1805^2, supps. 1806-8^2, ca. 1815^1, supp. 1821^1 (^{1}Mitchell Library; University of Minnesota, Minneapolis; ^{2}Glasgow UL).
John Smith & Son Ltd., *A Short Note on a Long History* (Glasgow, 1925); *Glasgow Journal* (22 Jul. 1762, 23 Jun. 1763, 29 Dec. Jan. 1769, 24 Sep. 1772, 8 Mar. 1781); *Glasgow Mercury* (29 Oct. 1778, 11 Sep. 1783, 7 Sep. 1786, 25 Jun. 1793); *Glasgow Courier* (23 Aug. 1796, 21 Dec. 1797, 30 Nov. 1805); *Glasgow Advertiser* (26 Jan. 1798, 4 Sep. 1801); *Glasgow Herald* (16 Mar. & 13 Jul. 1810); cf. *ODNB* for the youngest Smith.

David Home, Exchange Walk; est. 1759; dissolved 1766; cat. 1759*, supp. 1760*.
: *Glasgow Journal* (2 Jul. 1759, 27 Nov. 1766); *Edinburgh Evening Courant* (16 Feb. 1760).

James Knox, Donald's Land, Trongate, by 1767; label in NLS; died 1776 and succeeded by John Robb; cat. 1767 (Glasgow UL).
: *Glasgow Chronicle* (13 Jun. 1776).

Archibald Coubrough, 17 High St.; est. 1778, when claimed 4,000 vols.; 5,000 vols. by 1779; known as the Town & Country Circulating Library; run by John Coubrough by 1793, and by Archibald Coubrough by 1799; at 24 High St. by 1803 (where Robert Galloway, see below, had been); still there in 1809; label in NLS; cats. 1778*, 1779*, 1784*, ca. 1785*, supp. 1786*, 1788*, 1792*.
: *Glasgow Mercury* (29 Oct. 1778, 4 Nov. 1779, 25 Nov. 1784, 9 Nov. 1786); *Glasgow Courier* (17 Apr. 1792).

John Liddell (or Liddle), by 1779 until ca. 1782, according to SBTI.

David Montgomerie and John McNair, near Blackfriars Wynd; est. 23 Nov. 1779; in Buchanan's Land, Trongate, by 1781 when partnership ended; former at Gibson's Wynd in 1782; partner with Archibald McGown from June 1784 and moved to head of the Stockwell; McGown proposed to open a musical circulating library as well; in 1797 Archibald McGoun [sic], jun., announced that he was moving his father's music shop from Hutcheson St. to Stockwell St., but no reference to any library; cats. 1779*, 1782*, supp. 1784*.
: *Glasgow Mercury* (11 Nov. 1779, 22 Nov. 1781, 10 Oct. 1782, 27 May 1784); *Glasgow Courier* (13 Jun. 1797).

Robert Galloway (1752-94), by ca. 1788; originally a shoemaker; at 24 ?? High St.; library continued, presumably by widow; Mrs Galloway ran library at 279 High St. by 1799; at 408 Gallowgate by 1804.
: Alexander Campbell, *An Introduction to the History of Poetry in Scotland* (Edinburgh, 1798) 309; *Glasgow Advertiser* (10 Mar. 1794).

James Spence ?, above 113 Trongate, by 1790; see following.

James Spencer, Gallowgate Bridge, by 1790; same person as Spence, above?; succeeded by Joshua Noble, 1791, and moved to opp. Tron Church; 4,000 vols.

William Pinkerton, 10 Saltmarket, by 1791.

William Glen, Saltmarket, by 1792; bankrupt, 1795.

John McFadyen's musical circulating library; est. 1798; he was a book and music seller in Hutcheson St. by 1796; at 30 Wilson St. by 1799, and at no. 63 from 1826 to 1837.
> *Select Collection of Psalm & Hymn Tunes* (Glasgow, ca. 1800?) imprint; *Glasgow Courier* (16 Jun. 1796, 8 Jun. 1799); *Caledonian Mercury* (5 Jan. 1805); *Glasgow Herald* (23 Mar. 1810).

John & James Scrymgeour, 1 Glassford St., by 1800; James moved to Edinburgh and died in 1805; succeeded by William Stark; John Scrymgeour decided to re-commence at 2 Hutcheson St., to Stark's annoyance; Scrymgeour's library for sale in 1810 after his death; Stark at 99 Glassford St. by 1809; cats. 1802*, supp. 1803*, and 1805* for both Scrymgeour and Stark.
> *Glasgow Advertiser* (27 Oct. 1800); *[Glasgow] Herald & Advertiser* (17 Jan. & 21 Oct. 1803); *Glasgow Courier* (11 Apr., 14, 17, & 21 Sep., 1 & 5 Oct. 1805); *Glasgow Herald* (16 Feb. 1810).

Archibald Murdoch's Anderston Circulating Library, by 1807; for sale in 1808; presumably the same person as the A. Murdoch who started a library at 2 Brunswick Place in 1807; at no. 42 in 1808; succeeded in 1811 by David Potter; moved to 31 Wilson St. and became partner with Archibald McCallum (or McCullum?) by 1815; latter took over in 1817 and re-issued Potter's 1811 cat. under his own name; see below for Potter; at 65 & 67 Wilson St. by 1826, when claimed 24,000 vols; at 9 Exchange Place by 1840, and at 88 St. Vincent St. by 1843; for sale in 1845, when only had 3,000 vols; cats. 1808*, supp. 1810*, 1811, 1817, supps. to 1836 (Mitchell Library), 1826*, supps. 1829 & 1832/3 (Cambridge UL).
> *Glasgow Herald* (8 Jan. & 24 Oct. 1808, 18 May 1810, 16 Oct. 1826, 12 May 1845).

Alexander Molleson's 'Traveller's Library', 19 Glassford St.; est. 1808; intended to encourage people to buy books after reading them; dissolved at unknown date; in 1820 he opened a new library at Antigua Place, Newton St., until at least 1825.
> *Glasgow Herald* (4 Jul. 1808, 19 May 1820).

John Boyd & son, 6 Hutcheson St.; est. 1809; as (John) Wylie & Boyd by 1811 (see below for Wylie); run by Boyd & son again by 1817, and by David Boyd on own by 1820; at 48 Glassford St. by 1825, then at no. 95 and other addresses.

D. Macintyre's musical circulating library, 598 Argyll St.; est. 1809; cat. 1809*.
> *Clyde Commercial Advertiser* (13 Dec. 1809).

John Gardner, 103 King St., by 1813; at no. 107 by 1815, then to Finnieston Rd., Anderston, by 1817 until 1820.

Archibald McFeat, 105 Trongate, by 1817, with father, Walter McFeat, who had been a bookseller (and possibly librarian?) at 84 Trongate by 1798 (with Margaret Bogle); at 25 Glassford St. by 1828.

David Potter, 98 Glassford St., by 1819; presumably a new business started by the same Potter as above; bankrupt 1822 when library of 1,500 vols. for sale.
   Glasgow Herald (14 Jun. 1822); *Edinburgh Gazette* (17 May 1822).

John Jones, 11 Nelson St., by 1820.

Duncan Campbell Macarthur, address unknown, by 1821, when bankrupt.
   Glasgow Herald (18 May 1821).

Richard Griffin & Co., 75 Hutcheson St.; est. 1 Jan. 1821; at no. 64 by 1826 and at 115 Buchanan St. by 1837, possibly only as booksellers; advert. in Glasgow UL; cat. 1821*, supps. 1822* & 1826*.
   Glasgow Herald (18 Jan. 1822, 21 Aug. & 20 Oct. 1826).

John Carmichael, 85 Hospital St., Hutchesonton, by 1823.

John Wylie, 48 Argyle St., by 1825 (presumably same as the Wylie mentioned above under Boyd); he also ran the Glasgow Foreign Library (see above); both libraries at 97 Argyle St. by 1828; bankrupt 1832; died 1833; inventory in NRS.

John Smith, 25 Gallowgate, by 1825; this was different to the library run by John Smith, above; may be same as the library run by a John Smith at 64 Nelson St. and 30 London St. in 1828.

James Cameron, 54 Gallowgate, by 1825; may have been succeeded by Hugh Cameron, who ran library at 97 Gallowgate by 1828.

Thomas Peat, 35 Shuttle St., by 1825.

Matthew Paul, 2 North St., Anderston, by 1828; he was also a tailor.

John Robertson, 6 Main St., Gorbals, by 1828; succeeded by John Burton by 1835, by when a John Robertson is running the Western Public Library at 144 Argyle St.; cat. supp. 1837 of the latter library (Glasgow UL).

Robert Laurie, 28 Commerce St., by 1828?; at 8 King St., Tradeston, by 1832, and no. 3 by 1840; at 52 Bridge St., Tradeston, by 1843; died in 1847 when library of 650 vols. for sale.
   Glasgow Herald (30 Apr. 1847).

Book clubs

Several book societies for the working classes est. by 1816, according to Cleland (see reference below), but some could be small subscription libraries.

Book club at Calton, by ca. 1825; members were mostly weavers; John McAdam, future promoter of Italian unity, was a member.
    Janet Fyfe (ed.), *Autobiography of John McAdam (1806-1883)*, Scottish History Society 4th ser. 16 (Edinburgh, 1980) 3; cf. *ODNB*.

James Cleland, *Annals of Glasgow*, vol. 2 (Glasgow, 1816) 433-4, 444-7; *Glasgow Delineated* (Glasgow, 1812) 62-63; John Strang, *Glasgow and its Clubs* 3rd edn. (Glasgow, 1864) 129; Robert Chapman, *Picture of Glasgow* 3rd edn. (Glasgow, 1818) 227-31; local guides and directories; Holden (1805-11); Pigot (1820-37).

Govan

Mrs Thom, a minister's widow, est. a library in 1818; originally cost 5s. p.a.; 6d. per quarter by 1842; 1,100 vols. by 1849, according to Select Committee Report; still existed in 1896 when proposed to hand it over to the parish; cats. 1818, 1842[1] (Strathclyde AO; [1]also in BL & Glasgow UL); misc. papers (Strathclyde AO).

Hamilton

Hamilton Library: subscription library; est. 1807 or 1808; 3,000 vols. by 1835; held in Grammar School Square; dissolved at unknown date before 1873; list of members (1824) in Hamilton PL.
    NSA, vol. 6 (1845) 290-1; Pigot (1837); *Glasgow Herald* (13 Mar. 1873).

Lanark

Subscription libraries

Lanark Subscription Library, by 1824; cost 10s. + 6s. p.a.

New Lanark Reading Society, by unknown date, but probably existed in 1820s; still existed in 1860; later known as New Lanark Library; may have been founded by Robert Owen; many of the books are in the Lindsay Institute, Lanark.

Circulating libraries

William Robertson, Castlegate St., by 1820; in High St. by 1837.
    Pigot (1820-37).

Two circulating libraries by 1828.

Edinburgh Almanack (1824): *West Country Lists*; W. Davidson, *History of Lanark* (Lanark, 1828) 77-78; *Upperward Almanack for Lanarkshire* (1860) 33.

Langloan

Langloan Library: subscription library; est. 1794 by local weavers; moved to Old Monkland, Coatbridge; two original members still belonged in 1844; 500 vols. by 1844; still existed in 1864.
 Janet Hamilton, *Poems, Sketches & Essays* rev. edn. (Glasgow, 1885) 16-17; *Scots Chronicle* (25 Oct. 1796); *Glasgow Herald* (5 Jul. 1844); Andrew Miller, *Rise & Progress of Coatbridge* (Glasgow, 1864) 81-82.

Larkhall

Larkhall Library: subscription library; est. 1809; 500 vols. by 1840.
 NSA, vol. 6 (1845) 759.

Leadhills

Leadhills Reading Society: subscription library; est. 23 Nov. 1741 for the local miners, and encouraged by James Stirling; cost 2s.6d. entry + 4s. p.a.; new building in 1791; 500 vols. in 1767 and almost 4,000 vols. by 1904; still exists; rules (1761) in Hornel Library, Broughton House, Kirkcudbright; cats. 1767 (MS. owned by Marquis of Linlithgow), 1800 (owned by Stirling of Garden), 1904 (NLS; Wanlockhead Museum Trust), 1985 (published); catalogue records to be made available on the SCRAN website; membership list in NLS; misc. papers and minute books, 1821-date (Wanlockhead Museum Trust).
 P. Kaufman, 'Leadhills: Library of Diggers', in: Paul Kaufman, *Libraries and their Users* (London, 1969) 163-70; P. Jackaman, 'The Company, the Conmon Man, and the Library', *Library Review* 29 (1980) 27-32; W. S. Harvey, 'Local History from a Library's Shelves', *Local Historian* 19 (1989) 58-62; J. C. Crawford, 'The Ideology of Mutual Improvement in Scottish Working Class Libraries', *Library History* 12 (1996) 49-61; J. C. Crawford, 'The Leadhills Library and a Wider World', *Library Review* 46 (1997) 539-53; *OSA*, vol. 4 (1792) 511-2.

New Lanark: see Lanark

Rutherglen

Rutherglen Library: subscription library; est. 1813; at 77 Main St. by 1876; 3,000 vols. and 76 members by 1897; dissolved by ca. 1920.
 Pigot (1820) 2nd edn.: *Addenda*.

Strathaven

Subscription library; est. 1809; ca. 1,200 vols. by 1835.
 NSA, vol. 6 (1845) 312.

LINLITHGOWSHIRE

Bathgate

Subscription Library, by 1825.
 Pigot (1825/6).

Borrowstowness (Bo'ness)

Bo'ness Library: subscription library, by ca. 1810; 1,250 vols. by 1843.
 Pigot (1820) 2nd edn.: *Addenda*; *NSA*, vol. 2 (1845) 147.

South Queensferry

Queensferry Evangelical Library: subscription library, by 1825 when had 31 members; cat. 1827*; minute book, 1825-56 (NLS).

Queensferry Library: subscription library, by unknown date; 600 vols. by 1843; cat. n.d. (Blackburn Library, West Lothian).
 NSA, vol. 2 (1845) 14.

Whitburn

Whitburn Library: subscription library, by 1816; 1,000 vols. by 1825.

Another subscription library here by 1816, probably a religious library organized by local minister, Rev. J. Brown, who planned similar libraries in

the area: see 'A loud cry from the Highlands', in his *Brief Account of a Tour in the Highlands of Perthshire* (Edinburgh, 1818).
Caledonian Mercury (22 Apr. 1816); *Inverness Journal* (14 Jan. 1820); Pigot (1820) 2nd edn.: *Addenda*, & (1825/6-37).

MIDLOTHIAN: see EDINBURGHSHIRE

MORAYSHIRE: see ELGINSHIRE

NAIRNSHIRE

NAIRN

Nairn Subscription Library: subscription library; est. 1816.
Inverness Courier (9 Feb. 1816); Pigot (1820) 2nd edn.: *Addenda*; *Edinburgh Almanack* (1824): *Northern Counties Supp.*

PEEBLESSHIRE

LINTON

Linton Library: subscription library or parish library?, by ca. 1800; 500 vols. by 1834.
NSA, vol. 3 (1845) 163-4.

PEEBLES

Second United Associate Congregation Library: subscription library, by 1829 and probably a few years before; cat. 1829 (NLS).

Alexander Elder, High St.: circulating library, by 1790s; still there in 1825.
William Chambers, *Memoir of Robert Chambers* 8th edn. (Edinburgh, 1874) 54-59, 321-2; Pigot (1825/6); C. H. Layman (ed.), *Man of Letters: the Early Life and Love Letters of Robert Chambers* (Edinburgh, 1990) 57-60.

Perthshire

Alyth

Mrs. Elizabeth Mackenzie: circulating library, by 1814; run with son, William Lyon Mackenzie (1795-1861); dissolved 1817; the latter ran circulating library in Dundas, Canada, 1820-3, subsequently becoming a newspaper owner and then politican.
Dictionary of Canadian Biography, vol. 9 (Toronto, 1976) 497.

Auchterarder

Auchterarder Public Library: subscription library; est. 1809.
Perth & Perthshire Register (1819, etc.).

Bankfoot

Bankfoot Library: subscription library; est. 1822, according to *NSA*; other sources say that the library was est. in Jan. 1827, but this may be a refoundation; 300 vols. by 1838.
NSA, vol. 10 (1845) 447; P. R. Drummond, *The Life of Robert Nicoll, Poet* (Paisley, 1884) 37-38.

Birnam: see Little Dunkeld

Bridge of Earn

Mrs - Wilson: circulating library, by 1819; may be same person who previously at Perth (see below).
Aberdeen Journal (16 Jun. 1819).

Comrie

Comrie Parochial Library: subscription library, but probably not proprietary; est. 26 Jan. 1820; held in the school; moved to the Reading Room in 1880; new building opened in Drummond St. in 1901 and named Dundas Library after late Lady Lucy Dundas; taken over by County Council, 1962; cats.

1824*, 1853*, 1885*, 1896*; cash book, 1820-1923, & minute book, 1912-53 (Perth AO); press-cuttings (Bell Library, Perth).
    Pigot (1820) 2nd edn.: *Addenda*.

COUPAR ANGUS (partly in Forfarshire)

Subscription library

Coupar Angus Public Library, by 1811; in Commercial St. by 1825; still existed in 1837.

Circulating libraries

William Tainsh (or Tavish?), St. John St., by 1825.

Thomas Miller, George's St.; est. 1825.
    Dundee, Perth, & Cupar Advertiser (29 Sep. 1825).

Perth & Perthshire Register (1812, etc.). Pigot (1820) 2nd edn.: *Addenda*, & (1825/6-37).

CRIEFF

Agricultural library by 1774, acc. to NLS MS. 430900, letter from Charles Elliot, 2 Dec. 1774.

Crieff Public Library: subscription library; est. 1818; the library of the Strathearn Agricultural Society (est. 1809) deposited in 1819; 900 vols. by 1838.
    Caledonian Mercury (23 Nov. 1809); Alexander Porteous, *History of Crieff* (London, 1912) 354; *Perth & Perthshire Register* (1824, etc.); *NSA*, vol. 10 (1845) 522.

DEANSTON

Subscription Library at Deanston Works, by 1825.
    Pigot (1825/6); *NSA*, vol. 10 (1845) 1242.

DUNBLANE

Leightonian Library, The Cross: not a proprietary subscription library, but opened to the public on payment of a subscription in 1734, so similar to Dumfries Presbytery Library, above; originally est. as a diocesan library by Archbishop Robert Leighton and opened in 1688; made available to visitors to

nearby mineral wells in early 19th century; still exists; books now administered by Stirling University Library; cats. 1793+[1,2], supp. 1809, 1843[1,3], supp. 1855, 1940 (all in Stirling UL or at Dunblane; [1]also in NLS; [2]also in BL and Lambeth Palace Library; [3]also in Bodleian Library; +available online); cat. & receipts of loans, 1700-45 (Stirling AO); MS. cat., ca. 1843 (Aberdeen UL).
 G. Willis, 'The Leighton Library, Dunblane: its History and Contents', *Bibliotheck* 10 (1981) 139-57.

Dunkeld (see also Little Dunkeld)

Dunkeld Library: subscription library; est. 1809; refers to the McIntosh Library, bequeathed by Rev. Donald McIntosh; cost £1.5s. entry + 12s. p.a.; 2,000 vols.; deposited in the Bell [formerly Sandeman] Library, Perth, in 1933; cats. 1823[1], 1839, 1852 (Bell Library, Perth; [1]also in NLS and Glasgow UL).
 Pigot (1825/6) & Perthshire Registers.

Errol

Errol Library: subscription library; est. 1824.
 NSA, vol. 10 (1845) 399.

Gask

Gask Library: subscription or parish library?, est. 1824.
 NSA, vol. 10 (1845) 284.

Inchewan: see Little Dunkeld

Kilspindie

Kilspindie Library: subscription library, by ca. 1815; 300 vols. by 1843 when had been est. 'upwards of 30 years'.
 NSA, vol. 10 (1845) 1166.

Kincardine

Unidentified circulating library by 1825, used by Peter Mackenzie, gardener at Tulliallan Castle.
Chambers' Edinburgh Journal (11 May 1850) 300.

Little Dunkeld

Several book clubs by 1793, according to *OSA*, vol. 6 (1793) 369.

Inshewan Reading Society: book club, with permanent library; proposed Sep. 1796, but earliest rules date from 1810; seems to have been moribund for most of its existence; met at Middle Inchewan; moved to Wester Inchewan, 1824; dissolved 1854; minute book, 1810-54 (Bell Library, Perth).
 W. R. Aitken, *History of the Public Library Movement in Scotland to 1955* (Glasgow, 1971) 311-5.

Longforgan

Longforgan Library: subscription library; est. 1823; chiefly religious books; still existed in 1838.
 NSA, vol. 10 (1845) 420.

Methven

Methven Reading Society: subscription library; est. 14 Mar. 1797; 120 members by 1819; 1,100 vols. by 1837; still existed in 1920s.
 Perth & Perthshire Register (1812, etc.); *NSA*, vol. 10 (1845) 156.

Perth

Subscription libraries

Perth Public Library; est. 27 Dec. 1784; opened 1786; although it was a subscription library, the property was vested in the burgh council, not the subscribers; took over former burgh library, 1786; originally kept in Academy, then in Sessions House from 1792; 54 members by 1789; at South Kirkside by 1817, when had 3,000 vols. and cost 10s. entry + 15s. p.a.; moved to new Provost Marshall memorial building, (no. 78) George St., in Jan. 1824; merged with Perth Literary & Antiquarian Society in 1890s; rules (1786) in Bell Library, Perth; cats. 1788*, 1793*, 1801*, supp. 1806[1], 1813[1], supp.

1817*, 1819², 1824²,³, supps. 1826-7*, 1830², 1836²,⁴, ca. 1846⁴, 1849²,⁵, supps. to 1856² (¹Perth AO; ²Bell Library, Perth; ³Glasgow UL; ⁴BL; ⁵NLS); minute books and other records, 1784-1874 (Perth AO).

    D. Allan, 'Provincial Readers and Book Culture in the Scottish Enlightenment: the Perth Library, 1784-c.1800', *The Library* 7th ser. 3 (2002) 367-89; *Perth Courier* (25 Dec. 1817, 21 Dec. 1820); *Perthshire Courier* (28 Dec. 1826).

Perth Reading Society; est. 1797; 10s. entry + 1/6d. per quarter; held in Edwards Close, High St.; in Kirk Wynd, High St., by 1837; dissolved 1849; books bought by the Perth Anderson Institution, thence passed to the Mechanics' Library and finally to the Sandeman Library [now the Bell, or Perth Public, Library] in 1898; cat. 1829, supps. to 1835 (Bell Library, Perth).

Perth Mechanics' Library; est. 24 Nov. 1823; held in High St.; at 28 South Methven St. by 1840 and in Kirk Close by 1847; moved to the Hall of the Hammermen Incorporation at 175 High St. in 1856; at 238 High St. by 1862; most books were destroyed by fire in 1869, but a new library was opened in same year in South St. John's Place, with 400 members and 7,000 vols.; 11,000 vols. by 1897; dissolved 1900 and the books passed to the Sandeman Library; cats. 1832, supp. 1850*, 1859, 1863, 1864, supps. 1870-89 (Bell Library, Perth); cash books, 1824-49, 1870-96, MS. cat. 1875-97, & minute books, 1850-56, 1889-1900 (Perth AO).

    W. R. Aitken, *History of the Public Library Movement in Scotland to 1955* (Glasgow, 1971) 303-11.

North United Presbyterian Congregation Library; est. 29 Apr. 1824; cat. ca. 1824 (Bell Library, Perth).

Circulating libraries

Robert Morison (1722-91), High St.; est. 1752; he was also a 'glasier'; a 'new' library was est. by R. Morison and son, Robert (1764-1853), on 1 July 1790; see David Morison, below, and also Inverness; cat. 1752*.

    R. H. Carnie, *Publishing in Perth before 1807*, Abertay Historical Society 6 (Dundee, 1960) 9; *Caledonian Mercury* (19 May 1752; 21 Jun. 1790); D. C. Smith, *The Historians of Perth* (Perth, 1906) 76-109; *ODNB*.

Thomas Hill, George St., [later no. 23] by 1792 when had 1,800 vols.; for sale in 1824, with 1,200 vols., when moved to Edinburgh; John R. Norrie ran library here by 1876, but no continuity known; cats. 1792*, 1796*, by 1807*, 1813*.

    Edinburgh Advertiser (23 Mar. 1792, 12 Jan. 1796); *Perth Courier* (8 May 1807, 25 Feb. 1813, 11 May 1820, 26 Mar. 1824).

Minerva Library, by 1805, when had 2,400 vols.; might be Hill's library, above; cat. 1805 (Beinecke Library, Yale).

David Morison (1792-1855), began to lend periodicals in 1810 and was lending books in 1819; he was also librarian to the Perth Library, and grandson and nephew of the Morisons, above.
Perth Courier (22 Feb. 1810, 13 May 1819).

Mrs - Wilson, above the grocer, High St.; est. 1816; may be same person who later at Bridge of Earn (see above); cat. 1816*.
Perth Courier (24 Oct. 1816).

David Peat, by 1816; bookseller for many years previously; at 24 High St. in 1830s and presumably before; library still there in 1850s; cat. n.d. but post-1848 (Bell Library, Perth).
Perth Courier (28 Nov. 1816, 26 Oct. 1820).

John Balmain, 47 High St., by 1825, when moved to 78 St. John St.; cat. 1825*.
Perthshire Courier (3 Jun. 1825).

Alexander Wilson, 37 George St., by 1825.

Perth & Perthshire Register (1806-); Pigot (1825/6-37); A. R. Thompson, 'The Use of Libraries by the Working Class in Scotland in the Early 19th Century', *Scottish Historical Review* 42 (1963) 21-29.

RAIT

Village library: est. ca. 1812 by the horticulturist, Archibald Gorrie (1778-1857) of Annat Gardens; still existed in late 1830s, with 300 vols.
J. C. Loudun, *Manual of Cottage Gardening* (London, 1830) 63; *NSA*, vol. 10 (1845) 1166.

TYNDRUM

Miners' Library: subscription library for miners at the lead mines of the Earl of Breadalbane, by 1785; 7-800 vols. by 1786.
Times (4 Jan. 1786).

RENFREWSHIRE

BARRHEAD

Subscription library for the working classes by 1796, according to *Scots Chronicle* (30 Dec. 1796).

Barrhead Book Club: book club, est. 1819; met every 2 weeks in Stewart's Academy.
Renfrewshire Directory (1832).

GREENOCK

Subscription libraries

Greenock Library; est. 1 Jan. 1783, with 82 members; held in the Grammar School by 1792 and in the English School from 1794; 75 members by 1793; a Juvenile Library was set up in 1812; see below for the Foreign Library; incl. a bequest of 300 mathematical works; in Market St. by 1815; moved to Masons' Hall, Charles St., 1831, and finally to the new Watt Monument building, Union St., in 1837; 10,000 vols. by 1840; 682 members by 1966; dissolved 1972; building re-opened 1974 as the local history library of the Public Library, incorporating the Subscription Library's older stock; cats. 1787, 1792, 1796*, 1800*, 1803*, supp. 1806*, 1808, supps. 1812-21, 1826, 1832, 1844[1], supp. 1850, 1873[2], supps. 1894-5, 1897[2,3,4] & supps. to 1903 (Watt Library; NLS; [1]also in Manchester PL; [2]also in BL; [3]also in Strathclyde UL; [4]also in NLW); index to cats. to 1832 (printed 1852) in NLS; minute books, 1794- (Watt Library).

    James T. Hamilton, *Greenock Libraries* (Greenock, [1969]); George Williamson, *Old Greenock* (London, 1888), vol. 2, 256-60; *OSA*, vol. 5 (1793) 583; *NSA*, vol. 7 (1845) 470; *Library History* 3 (1974) 160.

Greenock Foreign Library; est. 19 Feb. 1807; met in room next door to the Subscription Library; originally 57 members paying 10s.6d. p.a.; although this library was run independently of the Subscription Library, members of the former had to belong to the latter; amalgamated with the main library in 1834; cats. 1808, 1812, etc. (Watt Library); minute book, 1807-33 (Watt Library).

Eclectic Library Society, by 1811; dissolved Oct. 1822.
    Greenock Advertiser (10 Apr. 1811, 10 Jan. 1815, 22 Oct. 1822).

Greenock Relief Congregational Library, presumably for church members; est. 1816; still existed in 1840s.
    Renfrewshire Directory (1832); *Greenock Directory* (1841).

Greenock Trades' Library, by unknown date; held in Bank St.; dissolved 1832 and merged with Greenock Mechanics' Library (est. 1829).
   Robert Murray Smith, *A Page of Local History* (Greenock, 1904) 10, 16.

Circulating libraries

Unidentified circulating library before 1783, when for sale; described as belonging to a late bookseller; probably refers to William McAlpine, who was bookseller here from 1765; in Cathcart St., but last heard of in New St. in 1783 (SBTI).
   Glasgow Mercury (20 Nov. 1783).

Robert Paton, Jamieson's Land, William St., by 1805; cat. by 1805*.
   Greenock Advertiser (1 Feb. 1805); *Greenock & Port Glasgow Directory* (1805); Holden (1809-11).

John Lang, 45 Cathcart St.; est. 1810; at no. 50 by 1831; died and books for sale, 1833; 1,300 vols.
   Greenock Advertiser (7 Sep. 1810, 11 Jun. 1833).

James Kerr, jun., Cathcart St., by 1825; at 10 Hamilton St. by 1837, and other addresses after 1845; James Kerr, sen., presumably his father, was bookseller at 103 Hamilton St. by 1820 and ran library at no. 22 by 1831.

James Morison, or Morrison, Cathcart St., by 1825; person of same name ran library in Largs (see above).

Pigot (1825/6-37).

Houston

Houston and Killallan Book Club: probably a permanent subscription library; est. 1824.
   Renfrewshire Directory (1832).

Johnstone

Subscription libraries

Subscription library for the working classes at Bridge of Johnstone by 1796, according to *Scots Chronicle* (30 Dec. 1796).

Johnstone Library, by 1820; held in William St.

Circulating library

John Johnstone, William St.: circulating library, by 1820; he was also a teacher; it is possible he was librarian to the subscription library rather than a circulating librarian.

Pigot (1820) 2nd edn.: *Addenda*, & (1825/6-37).

KILBARCHAN

Kilbarchan Subscription Library: subscription library; est. 1808; dissolved in 1846? (petition to Lord Advocate, NRS AD58/184).

Kilbarchan Relief Library: subscription library; est. 1823.

Renfrewshire Directory (1830).

LOCHWINNOCH

Lochwinnoch Library: subscription library; est. 1823; held in High St.; 600 vols. by 1830; cost 6s. entry + 6s. p.a.; probably same as the 'Public Library', revived in 1856.
Renfrewshire Directory (1830); *Glasgow Herald* (22 Aug. 1856).

Several book clubs said to have existed long before 1820.
NSA, vol. 7 (1845) 108.

PAISLEY

Subscription libraries

Ten subscription libraries for the working classes by 1796, according to *Scots Chronicle* (30 Dec. 1796). These may be the clubs referred to by Semple, below, who claimed that a number of workers' book clubs existed from 1770 for about 30 years which interchanged books amongst themselves.
David Semple, *Poems and Songs and Correspondence of Robert Tannahill* (Paisley, 1876), p.xxxvii.

Paisley Library Society; est. 14 May 1802; 4,500 vols. and 200 members by 1837; held at 51 Moss St. by 1831, no. 22 by 1834, and 109 High St. by 1856; merged with Paisley Athenæum, 1848, and with Public (Municipal) Library in 1870/1 when had 15,000 vols.; cats. 1822[1], 1830, 1858 (Paisley PL; [1]also in Watt Library, Greenock); rules (1802) in BL.

[T. Crichton], *The Library: a Poem* (Paisley, 1804); *Glasgow Herald* (7 Mar. 1867, 29 Sep. 1870).

Paisley Trades Library; est. 1 Jan. 1806; cost 6s. p.a.; kept at 45 High St. by 1820, and at the Lyceum, High St., by 1825; 1,000 vols. by 1823; at 42 New St. by 1837; dissolved 1846 when 2,000 vols. for sale; many books preserved in case revived; cats. 1823*, 1831, supp. ca. 1835 (Paisley PL); sale cat. 1846*.
Paisley Advertiser (25 Dec. 1824); *Glasgow Herald* (7 Dec. 1846); *Freeman's Journal* (31 Dec. 1846).

Paisley Theological Library; est. 18 May 1808; originally 54 members, mostly from the Associate Burgher Congregation; held at Session House, then at 25 or 22 Moss St.; cost 1s. p.a.; 700 vols. by 1825; still existed in 1850; cats. 1815, 1825[1] (Paisley PL; [1]also in Bodleian Library); accounts, 1808-50 (Paisley PL).

Paisley Juvenile Library; est. 1814; based in Low Church; rules & cat. (1814) in Paisley PL.

Canal Street Relief Library, for dissenters; est. 25 Jan. 1815 with 500 titles; kept in Session House; cost 2s. entry + 1s. per quarter; incl. a juvenile library; cats. 1815 (Paisley PL), 1817 (Cambridge UL).

Renfield Street Associate Congregation Library, for dissenters; est. 3 Oct. 1825; cat. 1828 (Paisley PL).

Circulating libraries

George Caldwell's Paisley Circulating Library, St. Mirren St.; est. 1769; began as his private library; also a weaver; in 1774 moved to larger premises in Causeyside; to 1 Dyer's Wynd, Moss St., near the Cross, by 1789; still there in 1825, but long retired; cat. 1789 (Paisley PL).
Robert Brown, *Paisley Poets, with Brief Memoirs of Them* (Paisley, 1889), vol. 1, p. 369.

Robert Aitken, Buchanan's Head, by 1769, according to label in Allegheny College Library; he subsequently moved to Philadelphia.

John Brown, 'midst of the East side of the Water Wynd', by 1794; wrote and published *Six Original Essays* (Paisley, 1794).

Thomas Auld, near the Cross, by 1809; at 8 Moss St. by 1820 and 240 High St. by 1825; cat. 1809, supp. 1811 (Paisley PL; NLS).

Robert Dick, 3 Old Bridge, by 1812; run by Thomas Dick by 1820; at 3 High St. by 1823; Joseph Murray ran library here by 1837.

Book clubs

Paisley Encyclopaedia Club, by 1771; bought successive editions of the *Encyclopaedia Britannica*; still existed in 1830s.

David Semple, *Poems and Songs and Correspondence of Robert Tannahill* (Paisley, 1876) xxxvii.

'Numerous' book clubs by 1820s, according to John Urie, *Reminiscences of 80 years* (Paisley, 1908) 27.

W. M. Metcalfe, *History of Paisley* (Paisley, 1909) 405-7; J. C. Crawford, 'The High State of Culture to Which this Part of the Country has Attained': Libraries, Reading and Society in Paisley, 1760-1830', *Scottish Historical Review*, forthcoming; *NSA*, vol. 7 (1845) 299-300; *NSA*, vol. 7 (1845) 299-300; Pigot (1825/6-37); local directories.

Pollokshaws

Subscription library for the working classes by 1796, according to *Scots Chronicle* (30 Dec. 1796).

Pollokshaws Public Library: subscription library; est. 1818; held at Town Buildings.

Renfrewshire Directory (1830).

Port Glasgow

Subscription libraries

Port Glasgow Library; est. 1798; held in Fore St.; 1,500 vols. & 50 members by 1832; still existed in 1876, when in Princes St.
Renfrewshire Directory (1832); *Edinburgh Almanack* (1834): *Western Supp.*

Port Glasgow Book Society; est. 1814; cat. 1815 (Mitchell Library).

Circulating library

Robert Gemmell, Fore St., by unknown date; bookseller by 1820; still here in 1834.

Renfrew

Renfrew Social Book Club: might be subscription library; est. 1802; possibly same as the following.
Renfrewshire Directory (1832).

Renfrew Library: subscription library; est. 'long before' 1836.
NSA, vol. 7 (1845) 31.

Tollcross

Subscription library for the working classes by 1796, according to *Scots Chronicle* (30 Dec. 1796).

ROSSSHIRE

Dingwall

Subscription libraries

Dingwall Library: est. 1820; 400 vols. by 1831; diss. ca. 1835.
    I. Mowat, 'Literacy, Libraries and Literature in 18th and 19th Century Easter Ross', *Library History* 5 (1979) 1-10 (p.6).

Wester Ross Subscription Library: subscription library, proposed 1826, according to letter by H. Bethune in Seaforth papers (NRS), and in business in 1827; may have taken over the Dingwall Library, above, and become the Dingwall and Wester Ross Subscription Library; printed label of the latter, dated Mar. 1856 (when had 800 vols.), and an undated printed label of the Dingwall Library are both inside the NLS copy of *Two Letters ... on the Proposals for Peace with the Regicide Directory of France* (London, 1793); Dingwall Library in High St. in 1876.
    Caledonian Mercury (23 Apr. 1827).

Invergordon

Invergordon Library: subscription library; est. 1816.
    Edinburgh Almanack (1824): *Northern Counties Supp.*

Tain

Tain Library: subscription library, by 1820.
    Pigot (1820) 2nd edn.: *Addenda*; *Inverness Courier* (10 Apr. 1823); *Edinburgh Almanack* (1824): *Northern Counties Supp.*

ROXBURGHSHIRE

DENHOLM

Denholm Library: subscription library; est. 19 Jan. 1805; originally 5s. entry + 1s. per quarter; 30 members in 1808; open on Wednesday and Saturday afternoons only; kept at librarian's house; 880 vols. by 1839; moved to the Old Ha', 1865; A. Carnegie gave money to convert the birthplace of John Leyden, the poet, into home for library; dissolved 1903; stock passed to the Crown but was transferred to the Denholm Reading & Recreation Club in 1913 and moved to Comrades' Hall where it still existed in 1933; cats. 1808*, 1817*, 1880 (Bodleian Library).

W. F. Cuthbertson, 'An Old Denholm Book', *Hawick Archaeological Society Transactions* (1933) 19-24; *NSA*, vol. 3 (1845) 437.

Woodside Library: subscription library/free library; est. 1825; belonged to James Douglas of Cavers and intended for children attending Denholm Sabbath School; 1,000 vols.; still existed in 1839.

NSA, vol. 3 (1845) 437.

HAWICK

Subscription libraries

Hawick Public Library; est. 1762; 56 members and 3,500 vols. by 1838; probably held in various premises, but at 5 Silver St. by 1837, at 6 Sandbed from 1869, and 6 Buccleuch St. by 1874; dissolved 1893; cats. 1772*, 1779*?, 1786*, ca. 1792+, 1841, 1872[1], supp. 1876 (Hawick PL & NLS; [1]also in Edinburgh PL; info. on non-extant catalogues from Charles Elliot's letterbooks in NLS; +wrongly catalogued as 'ca. 1810').

H. K. Mackay, 'Hawick Subscription Library', *Hawick Archaeological Society Transactions* (1992) 33-41.

Hawick Trades Library; est. 1802; held in Drumlanrig St.; in High St. by 1837; 4s. p.a.; 135 members by 1838; 1,400 vols. by 1850; cat. 1833 (Hawick PL; NLS).

Circulating libraries

William Ainslie, High St., by 1825.

Robert Armstrong, Silver St., by unknown date; bookseller here by 1820 and still here in 1852.

NSA, vol. 3 (1845) 414; Pigot (1825/6-37); James Wilson, *Annals of Hawick* (Edinburgh, 1850) 179.

JEDBURGH

Subscription libraries

Jedburgh Company Library; est. ca. 1777; another source suggests ca. 1760, which probably too early; cost 5 gns. + 9s. p.a. by 1800, and had 60 members; held in Old Gaol by 1837; dissolved 1856.
   A. E. Hall, 'Disputes in Book Societies', *Monthly Magazine* 10 (Dec. 1800) 402-3.

Waugh's Library, by ca. 1785??; kept at Old Bridge End by 1837; dissolved by 1840?

Jedburgh Library; est. in 1790s; mainly for religious books; held at Old Bridge End; dissolved 1843.

Circulating library

Circulating library not known before 1834.

Book club

Book society by 1834, and presumably earlier.

Alexander Jeffrey, *History & Antiquities of Roxburghshire*, vol. 2 (Edinburgh, [1857]) 114-6; *NSA*, vol. 3 (1845) 20; Pigot (1821-37).

KELSO

Subscription libraries

Kelso Library; est. Nov. 1750; 5,000 vols. by 1789; kept in Council House from 1759; moved to new building in Chalkheugh, 1795; 2,500 titles by 1838; 65 members in 1857; dissolved 1907, though not finally wound up until 1927; cats. 1761*, 1773*, ca. 1793 (Bodleian Library), 1802 (Glasgow UL), 1814 (NLS; Birmingham UL), 1838 (Edinburgh UL; NRS; Borders Library HQ, Selkirk), 1857 (BL; NRS; Davis, California, UL); rules (1830) in Edinburgh PL & UL; minute books & other papers, 1849-1942 (NRS).
   Sir James B. Paul (ed.), *Diary of George Ridpath, 1755-61*, Scottish History Society 3rd ser. 2 (Edinburgh, 1922); *OSA*, vol. 10 (1794) 597; P. Kaufman, 'Library News from Kelso', *Library Review* 17 (1960) 486-9.

Kelso New Library; est. 1778; held in Over Wynd by 1837; 2,000 vols. by 1838; merged with Modern Library (below) in 1858, when together had 4,000 vols.

Kelso Modern Library; est. 1800; held in Churchyard by 1837; 1,500 vols. by 1838; merged with New Library (see above).

Circulating libraries

Ebenezer Hardie, by 1808??; bleaching receipts were available from 'Ebenezer Hardie, library', but unclear whether he ran his own circulating library or was librarian to one of the subscription libraries, above.
Caledonian Mercury (24 Mar. 1808).

Archibald Rutherfurd, Bridge St., by 1816; see following.
Kelso Mail (13 Jun. 1816).

John Rutherfurd, Bridge St.; est. 1823; unclear whether he took over the previous library, run by his father; in Market Place by 1837; died 1855; cats. 1816*, 1831 (Borders Library HQ, Selkirk).
Kelso Mail (17 Jul. 1823).

Walter Grieve, Market Place, by 1826.
Kelso Mail (2 Mar. 1826).

Book club

Book club existed 'for many years' before 1838, when had 24 members; still existed in 1860.

James Haig, *Topographical & Historical Account of... Kelso* (Edinburgh, 1825) 125-6; Holden (1811); Pigot (1825/6-37); Alexander Jeffrey, *History ... of Roxburghshire*, vol. 3 (Edinburgh, 1859) 37-38; *NSA*, vol. 3 (1845) 342-3.

LILLIESLEAF

Lilliesleaf Library: subscription library; est. ca. 1818 and possibly many years before; new building, ca. 1857; dissolved ca. 1935; the books pulped in 1942; cats. 1824*, 1844*, supp. 1857*; minute book, 1824-69 (Borders AO, Hawick).
NSA, vol. 3 (1845) 31-2.

Melrose

Subscription libraries

St. Mary's Library: subscription library; est. 1798; 2,500 vols. by 1864.

Two subscription libraries by 1825; a cat. of the parish library (1828) is in NLS, but unclear which library is meant.

Circulating library

Unidentified circulating library, by 1802.
> Francis Paget Hett (ed.), *Memoirs of Susan Sibbald (1783-1812)* (London, 1926), pp. 166-8, 176, 197-8, 200.

Alexander Jeffrey, *History & Antiquities of Roxburghshire*, vol. 3 (Edinburgh, 1864) 46; *NSA*, vol. 3 (1845) 71; Pigot (1825).

Morebattle

Morebattle Library: subscription library; est. ca. 1800; over 600 vols. by 1839, when cost 1 gn. entry + 3s.6d. p.a.
> *NSA*, vol. 3 (1845) 455-6.

New Castleton
(also known as Castletown or Liddiesdale)

Two subscription libraries by 1825.
> Pigot (1825/6).

St. Boswells

St. Boswells Library: subscription library; est. 1799; 1,000 vols. by 1834.
> *NSA*, vol. 3 (1845) 112.

SELKIRKSHIRE

ETTRICK

Ettrick Library: subscription or parish library?, by ca. 1810; over 30 members and 600 vols. by 1833; cat. 1824*.
 NSA, vol. 3 (1845) 75.

ETTRICK BRIDGE

Ettrick Bridge Library: subscription library?, by 1812; subscribed to W. Scott, *Border Exploits* (Hawick, 1812).

GALASHIELS

Galashiels Subscription Library: subscription library; est. 1797; kept in Overhaugh by 1837; 153 members by 1843; dissolved 1859; many books acquired by the Mechanics' Institute.

William Gill: circulating library, by 1825.

Alan Carter, *History & Development of the Library Services of Galashiels and Selkirkshire* (unpublished MA thesis; Strathclyde University, 1975); Pigot (1825/6-37).

SELKIRK

Selkirk Subscription Library: subscription library; est. 1772; originally 2 gns. + 7s.6d. p.a.; 55 members in 1775; held at various rooms, incl. Town House from 1806; moved to new building in New Rd., now Tower St., in 1829; dissolved 1901; cats. 1775*, 1840, 1856, 1875 (Borders Library HQ, Selkirk); registers, 1800-14 (Borders AO, Hawick; info. on non-extant catalogue from Charles Elliot's letterbooks in NLS).

Theological Library, for students of divinity of the Associate Synod Theological Hall (the Burghers); est. 1787 by Rev. George Lawson, but had originated in Haddington; similar to the Theological Library in Alloa (see above); 624 titles in 1817; MS. cat., 1789-1823 (Borders AO); cats. ca. 1803, 1817[1] (Glasgow UL; [1]also in Borders Library HQ).
 John MacFarlane, *The Life and Times of George Lawson, D.D.* (Edinburgh, 1862), pp. 292-3 and ff.

Selkirk New Library: subscription library, by 1826; cat. 1826 (Borders Library HQ, Selkirk).

Alan Carter, *History & Development of the Library Services of Galashiels and Selkirkshire* (unpublished MA thesis; Strathclyde University, 1975); *Southern Reporter* (23 May 1901); *Library Association Record* 3 (1901) 264.

STIRLINGSHIRE

BANNOCKBURN

Bannockburn Colliery Library: subscription library for workers, est. June 1828.
Stirling Journal (28 Aug. 1828).

Bannockburn Subscription Library: subscription library; est. 1828.
Stirling Journal (14 Aug. 1828).

BOTHKENNAR

Bothkennar Library: subscription library; est. 1824; a religious library for youths; cat. 1824 (NLS).

CAMPSIE

Subscription library for the working classes by 1796, according to *Scots Chronicle* (30 Dec. 1796).

DENNY

Denny Library: subscription or parish library?, est. 1806; 1,100 vols. by 1840; cost 1 gn. entry + 2s. p.a.
NSA, vol. 8 (1845) 135.

FALKIRK

Falkirk Library: subscription library; est. 1792; 102 members by 1818; 3,000 vols. by 1840; held in Wilson's Buildings; stock advertized for sale over 9

nights in 1855 and almost wound up in 1856, but re-established in 1857 as a new library with books from School of Arts; many books sold off in 1864; cats. 1810 & supp. 1812 (NRS), 1818 (Mitchell Library), 1864 (Falkirk PL).
Falkirk Herald (31 Jan., 7 Feb., & 6 Nov. 1856, 1 Apr. 1858, 21 Jan. 1864).

Subscription library for the working classes by 1796, according to *Scots Chronicle* (30 Dec. 1796); unclear whether the previous library is meant.

Relief Church Library: subscription library; est. 1823; 2,000 vols. by 1836; still existed in the 1880s.

William Nimmo, *History of Stirlingshire*, 2nd edn. by William MacG. Stirling (Stirling, 1817) 758; *NSA*, vol. 8 (1845) 35; James Love, *Local Antiquarian Notes and Queries*, vol. 4 (Falkirk, 1928), pt. 2, p. 63.

Kilsyth

Kilsyth Reading Society: subscription library, by 1818, when had 200 titles; 5s. entry + 1s. per quarter; still existed in 1841; cat. 1818 (NLS).
NSA, vol. 8 (1845) 166.

Polmont

Polmont Library: subscription or parish library?, est. 1820; still existed in 1841.
NSA, vol. 8 (1845) 199.

Stirling

Subscription libraries

Stirling Society for Promoting the Knowledge and Practice of Christianity: not a subscription library as such, but incl. a library for members and those recommended by them; 90 vols. by 1798; books lent on Wednesday afternoons; cat. 1798 (NLS).

Stirling Subscription Library; est. 1 Jan. 1805; originally kept in Bow St.; moved to new building in Quality St., 1817, when had 130 members; in the Athenaeum, 8 King St., by 1837; 2,000 vols. by 1841; dissolved 1881; cats. 1844, 1855, 1869 (Stirling PL).

William Nimmo, *History of Stirlingshire*, 2nd edn. by William MacG. Stirling (Stirling, 1817) 381-2; *NSA*, vol. 8 (1845) 443; Pigot (1837); *Stirling Journal* (8 Apr. 1881).

Circulating library

Charles Randall (1749-1812), Baxter's Wynd, before 1798 when for sale with 3,000 vols.; bookseller by 1793; bookshop continued by widow, Mary, who at some time may have re-started circulating library; in Baker's Wynd by 1813, later Vennell Close; succeeded by William Macnie, 1820, but library does not appear to have been continued.
Glasgow Courier (29 Mar. 1798).

STRATHBLANE

Strathblane Library: subscription or parish library?, est. 1817; 700 vols. by 1841.
NSA, vol. 8 (1845) 88.

WEST LOTHIAN: SEE LINLITHGOWSHIRE

WIGTOWNSHIRE

STRANRAER

Subscription libraries

Stranraer Library; est. 1771; books sold in 1856; cat. 1774 (NRS).
Galloway Advertiser (8 May 1856).

Stranraer Theological Library; est. 1820; moved premises in 1847 and continued until 1863.
Galloway Advertiser (30 Sep. 1847, 5 Mar. 1863).

Stranraer Sabbath School Library, by 1825; cat. 1825 (NRS).

Circulating libraries

Robert Dick, Charlotte St., by 1820; he was also a shoemaker; given as George St. by 1825, but back in Charlotte St. by 1852 when still running library.

Two other circulating libraries by 1820; one was probably run by Peter Walker, who was in High St by 1820, certainly as a bookseller; later in George St.; still ran library in 1852.

Pigot (1820-37); *NSA*, vol. 4 (1845) 100; *Edinburgh Almanack* (1845): *Western Supp.*

Whithorn

Whithorn Library: subscription library, by 1825.
   Pigot (1825/6-37).

Wigtown

Wigtown Subscription Library: subscription library; est. 8 Sep. 1795; originally cost 1 gn. + 6s. p.a., increased to 2 gns. + 7s.6d. p.a. in 1807; in 1828 only open two hours per week; minute book & other papers, 1795-1832 (Hornel Library, Broughton House, Kirkcudbright).
   M. Towsey, 'First Steps in Associational Reading: Book Use and Sociability at the Wigtown Subscription Library, 1795-9', *Papers of the Bibliographical Society of America* 103:4 (2009) 455-95.

Isle of Arran (Buteshire)

Lamlash

Kilbride Library: subscription library; est. 1824; 80 members and 300 vols. by 1840; cost 1s. p.a.; Kilbride was the parish, also including Brodick; known from the 1850s as Lamlash Library; 418 vols. still survived in 1974, but have since disappeared.
   J. C. Crawford, 'Books, Libraries and the Decline of Gaelic on the Island of Arran', *Library Review* 36 (1987) 83-94 (cf. pp. 89-90, 92); *NSA*, vol. 5 (1845) 36.

Isle of Bute (Buteshire)

Rothesay

Subscription libraries

Rothesay Library; est. 1792; held in Watergate St., then in Bishop St. by 1834, and in Montague St. by 1860; 1,400 vols. by 1840; merger suggested with Mechanics' Institute, 1862; cat. 1820 (Glasgow UL).
   Glasgow Herald (19 Apr. & 13 Aug. 1862).

Rothesay Cotton Mills: subscription library for the workers by 1796.
Scots Chronicle (25 Oct. 1796).

Rothesay Youths Library; est. 1818; 1,200 vols. by 1840.

Circulating library

David Condie, Watergate: circulating library, by 1825; may have been succeeded by William Glass, who in this street by 1837.

NSA, vol. 5 (1845) 115; Pigot (1825/6-37).

Isle of Lewis

Stornoway

Stornoway Library: subscription library, by 1822, according to letter by John MacKenzie, librarian, in Seaforth papers (NRS); still existed in 1830s.
NSA, vol. 14 (1845) 139.

Isle of Mull

Tobermory

Tobermory Library: subscription library, by 1824; receipt for 3 guineas in privately-owned papers of Maclean-Clephane of Torloisk (NRAS 3283/Bundle 300).
Caledonian Mercury (23 Apr. 1827).

Isle of Skye

Kyleakin

Kyleakin Library: subscription library; est. 1820.
Inverness Journal (14 Jul. 1820).

ORKNEY

KIRKWALL

Orkney Library Society: subscription library; est. Aug. 1815; originally 58 members paying ½ gn. p.a.; incorporated the old 'bibliotheck' of Kirkwall; merged with Public (Municipal) Library, 1890; the old 'bibliotheck' books were sold in 1891 but eventually reached Aberdeen UL; cats. 1816[1], 1844[2] (Kirkwall PL; [1]also in Glasgow UL; [2]also in Aberdeen UL & Wellcome Institute, London); misc. papers, 1817-90, and MS. cat. ca. 1830 (Tankerness House Museum, Kirkwall).

W. R. Aitken, *History of the Public Library Movement in Scotland to 1955* (Glasgow, 1971) 2-4.

STROMNESS

Stromness Library: subscription library; est. ca. 1825 and certainly by 1827; still existed in 1841 when cost 7s. p.a.; cat. 1829 (Kirkwall PL).

Caledonian Mercury (23 Apr. 1827); *NSA*, vol. 15 (1845) 38.

SHETLAND

LERWICK

Lerwick Library: subscription library; est. Jan. 1809; still existed in 1875; minute book, 1857-1875 (Shetland AO); cats. n.d., 1875 (Lerwick PL).

Index of Locations in Listing

Aberdeen, Aberdeenshire	139	Berwickshire	153
Aberdeenshire	139	Biggar, Lanarkshire	197
Aberlady, Haddingtonshire	188	Birnam: see Little Dunkeld	
Airdrie, Lanarkshire	196	Bo'ness: see Borrowstowness	
Alexandria, Dunbartonshire	162	Bonnyrigg, Edinburghshire	164
Alloa, Clackmannanshire	156	Borgue, Stewartry of Kirkcudbright	195
Alva, Clackmannanshire	157	Borrowstowness, Linlithgowshire	206
Alyth, Perthshire	208	Bothkennar, Stirlingshire	225
Angus: see Forfarshire		Bothwell, Lanarkshire	197
Annan, Dumfriesshire	157	Brechin, Forfarshire	184
Anstruther, Fifeshire	179	Bridge of Earn, Perthshire	208
Arbroath, Forfarshire	184	Burntisland, Fifeshire	179
Ardrossan, Ayrshire	145	Bute (Isle of)	228
Argyllshire	144	Cabrach, Banffshire	152
Arran (Isle of)	228	Caithnessshire	155
Athelstaneford, Haddingtonshire	188	Cambuslang, Lanarkshire	197
Auchterarder, Perthshire	208	Cambusnethan, Lanarkshire	197
Auchtertool, Fifeshire	179	Campbelltown, Invernessshire	192
Ayr, Ayrshire	145	Campbeltown, Argyllshire	144
Ayrshire	145	Campsie, Stirlingshire	225
Ayton, Berwickshire	153	Canonbie, Dumfriesshire	157
Balmaghie, Stewartry of Kirkcudbright	195	Cardno, Aberdeenshire	141
Banchory Devinick, Kincardineshire	193	Carluke, Lanarkshire	197
Banff, Banffshire	151	Castle Douglas, Stewartry of Kirkcudbright	195
Banffshire	151	Castletown: see New Castleton	
Bankfoot, Perthshire	208	Catrine, Ayrshire	146
Bannockburn, Stirlingshire	225	Ceres, Fifeshire	179
Barrhead, Renfrewshire	214	Chirnside, Berwickshire	154
Bathgate, Linlithgowshire	206	Clackmannanshire	156
Beith, Ayrshire	146	Closeburn, Dumfriesshire	158

Coatbridge: see Langloan	
Cockburnspath, Berwickshire	154
Coldingham, Berwickshire	154
Coldstream, Berwickshire	154
Comrie, Perthshire	208
Coupar Angus, Forfarshire/Perthshire	209
Covington, Lanarkshire	198
Craigdam, Aberdeenshire	142
Cramond, Edinburghshire	164
Crieff, Perthshire	209
Crossgates, Fifeshire	180
Cumbernauld, Dunbartonshire	163
Cupar, Fifeshire	180
Dalbeattie, Stewartry of Kirkcudbright	195
Dalkeith, Edinburghshire	164
Dalmally, Argyllshire	144
Dalmellington, Ayrshire	147
Dalry, Ayrshire	147
Dalserf, Lanarkshire	198
Darvel, Ayrshire	147
Deanston, Perthshire	209
Denholm, Roxburghshire	220
Denny, Stirlingshire	225
Dingwall, Rossshire	219
Dirleton, Haddingtonshire	188
Dufftown, Banffshire	152
Dumbarton, Dunbartonshire	163
Dumbartonshire: see Dunbartonshire	
Dumfries, Dumfriesshire	158
Dumfriesshire	157
Dunbar, Haddingtonshire	188
Dunbartonshire	162
Dunblane, Perthshire	209
Dundee, Forfarshire	185
Dunfermline, Fifeshire	180
Dunkeld, Perthshire (see also Little Dunkeld)	210
Dunlop, Ayrshire	147
Duns, Berwickshire	154
Dunscore, Dumfriesshire	159
Dysart, Fifeshire	181
East Kilbride, Lanarkshire	198
East Linton, Haddingtonshire	189
East Lothian: see Haddingtonshire	
East Wemyss, Fifeshire	181
Edinburgh, Edinburghshire	164
Edinburghshire	164
Elgin, Elginshire	178
Elginshire	178
Elie, Fifeshire	181
Errol, Perthshire	210
Ettrick, Selkirkshire	224
Ettrick Bridge, Selkirkshire	224
Eyemouth, Berwickshire	155
Fala, Edinburghshire	174
Falkirk, Stirlingshire	225
Fenwick, Ayrshire	147
Fifeshire	179
Fochabers, Elginshire	178
Forfar, Forfarshire	186
Forfarshire	184
Forres, Elginshire	179
Fort William, Invernessshire	192
Fountainhall, Edinburghshire	174
Fowlis, Forfarshire	187
Fraserburgh: see Cardno	
Galashiels, Selkirkshire	224

INDEX OF LOCATIONS IN LISTING

Galston, Ayrshire	148
Garmouth, Elginshire	179
Garvald, Haddingtonshire	189
Gask, Perthshire	210
Gatehouse-of-Fleet, Stewartry of Kirkcudbright	195
Gifford, Haddingtonshire	189
Girvan, Ayrshire	148
Glamis, Forfarshire	187
Glasgow, Lanarkshire	198
Gorebridge, Edinburghshire	175
Govan, Lanarkshire	204
Grange, Banffshire	153
Greenlaw, Berwickshire	155
Greenock, Renfrewshire	214
Haddington, Haddingtonshire	189
Haddingtonshire	188
Hamilton, Lanarkshire	204
Hawick, Roxburghshire	220
Helensburgh, Dunbartonshire	163
Houston, Renfrewshire	215
Huntly, Aberdeenshire	142
Inchewan: see Little Dunkeld	
Innerwick, Haddingtonshire	190
Inveresk, Edinburghshire	175
Invergordon, Rossshire	219
Inverkeithing, Fifeshire	182
Inverness, Invernessshire	192
Invernessshire	192
Irvine, Ayrshire	148
Jedburgh, Roxburghshire	221
Johnstone, Dumfriesshire	160
Johnstone, Renfrewshire	215
Keith, Banffshire	153
Kelso, Roxburghshire	221
Kilbarchan, Renfrewshire	216
Kilbirnie, Ayrshire	148
Kilmarnock, Ayrshire	148
Kilspindie, Perthshire	210
Kilsyth, Stirlingshire	226
Kilwinning, Ayrshire	149
Kincardine, Perthshire	211
Kincardineshire	193
Kinghorn, Fifeshire	182
Kingsbarns, Fifeshire	182
Kinross, Kinrossshire	194
Kinrossshire	194
Kirkcaldy, Fifeshire	182
Kirkcudbright (Stewartry of)	195
Kirkcudbright, Stewartry of Kirkcudbright	196
Kirkintilloch, Dunbartonshire	163
Kirkwall, Orkney	230
Kyleakin, Isle of Skye	229
Lamlash, Isle of Arran	228
Lanark, Lanarkshire	204
Lanarkshire	196
Langholm, Dumfriesshire	160
Langloan, Lanarkshire	205
Largo, Fifeshire	183
Largs, Ayrshire	150
Larkhall, Lanarkshire	205
Laurencekirk, Kincardineshire	193
Leadhills, Lanarkshire	205
Leith, Edinburghshire	175
Lerwick, Shetland	230
Letham, Fifeshire	183
Lewis (Isle of)	229
Liberton, Edinburghshire	176
Liddiesdale: see New Castleton	

Lilliesleaf, Roxburghshire	222
Linlithgowshire	206
Linton, Peeblesshire	207
Little Dunkeld, Perthshire	211
Loanhead, Edinburghshire	176
Lochgilphead, Argyllshire	145
Lochmaben, Dumfriesshire	160
Lochwinnoch, Renfrewshire	216
Lockerbie, Dumfriesshire	160
Longforgan, Perthshire	211
Maryculter, Kincardineshire	194
Mauchline, Ayrshire	150
Maybole, Ayrshire	150
Melrose, Roxburghshire	223
Methven, Perthshire	211
Midlothian: see Edinburghshire	
Milnathort, Kinrosshshire	194
Moffat, Dumfriesshire	161
Moniaive, Dumfriesshire	161
Monkland: see Dunscore	
Montrose, Forfarshire	187
Moray: see Elginshire	
Morebattle, Roxburghshire	223
Muirkirk, Ayrshire	150
Mull (Isle of)	229
Musselburgh, Edinburghshire	176
Nairn, Nairnshire	207
Nairnshire	207
New Castleton, Roxburghshire	223
New Cumnock, Ayrshire	150
New Deer, Aberdeenshire	142
New Lanark: see Lanark	
New Machar, Aberdeenshire	142
Newmilns, Ayrshire	151
Newton, Edinburghshire	177
Newton-Upon-Ayr, Ayrshire: see under Ayr	
Newtyle, Forfarshire	188
North Berwick, Haddingtonshire	190
Oldmeldrum, Aberdeenshire	142
Orkney	230
Ormiston, Haddingtonshire	191
Paisley, Renfrewshire	216
Peebles, Peeblesshire	207
Peeblesshire	207
Penicuik, Edinburghshire	177
Perth, Perthshire	211
Perthshire	208
Peterhead, Aberdeenshire	143
Pollokshaws, Renfrewshire	218
Polmont, Stirlingshire	226
Port Glasgow, Renfrewshire	218
Portobello, Edinburghshire	177
Preshome, Banffshire	153
Prestonpans, Haddingtonshire	191
Rait, Perthshire	213
Renfrew, Renfrewshire	218
Renfrewshire	214
Renton, Dunbartonshire	163
Roberton, Dumfriesshire	161
Rossshire	219
Rosyth: see under Inverkeithing	
Rothesay, Isle of Bute	228
Roxburghshire	220
Rutherglen, Lanarkshire	206
St Andrews, Fifeshire	183
St. Boswells, Roxburghshire	223
Saltcoats, Ayrshire	151
Sanquhar, Dumfriesshire	161

INDEX OF LOCATIONS IN LISTING

Scoonie, Fifeshire	183
Selkirk, Selkirkshire	224
Selkirkshire	224
Shetland	230
Skye (Isle of)	229
South Queensferry, Linlithgowshire	206
Stewarton, Ayrshire	151
Stirling, Stirlingshire	226
Stirlingshire	225
Stonehaven, Kincardineshire	194
Stornoway, Isle of Lewis	229
Stow, Edinburghshire	177
Stranraer, Wigtownshire	227
Strathaven, Lanarkshire	206
Strathblane, Stirlingshire	227
Strathmiglo, Fifeshire	183
Stromness, Orkney	230
Tain, Rossshire	219
Tarbolton, Ayrshire	151
Thornhill, Dumfriesshire	161
Thurso, Caithnessshire	155
Tillicoultry, Clackmannanshire	157
Tillyching, Aberdeenshire	144
Tobermory, Isle of Mull	229
Tollcross, Renfrewshire	219
Torryburn, Fifeshire	183
Towie, Aberdeenshire	144
Tranent, Haddingtonshire	191
Turriff, Aberdeenshire	144
Tyndrum, Perthshire	218
Wanlockhead, Dumfriesshire	161
West Lothian: see Linlithgowshire	
Wester Duddingston, Edinburghshire	177
Wester Kinghorn: see Burntisland	
Westerkirk, Dumfriesshire	162
Whitburn, Linlithgowshire	206
Whithorn, Wigtownshire	228
Wick, Caithnessshire	156
Wigtown, Wigtownshire	228
Wigtownshire	227

Index to Survey

This is an index to selected personal names, place-names, and broad subjects. Individual libraries are not indexed, only places.

Aberdeen, 6-7, 55-6, 114, 115, 116-17, 118-19
Aikman, William, 64
Airdrie, 72-3
Aitken, Robert, 64
Alloa, 111-12, 129
Alnwick, 28
Alyth, 64
Angus, Alexander, 55, 107
Annan, 67
Annapolis, 64
Arbroath, 38, 42-3, 85, 86, 88, 91-2, 106, 129
Archbald, Mary, 17
Ayr, 34, 37, 41, 43, 56, 77, 106, 110, 128
Banff, 57, 80-1, 120-1
Bannockburn, 27
Bath, 10-11
Bathurst, N.S.W., 65
Baxter, John, 66
Beattie, James, 2-3, 56
Beith, 56, 67, 76
Belfast, 65, 69
Bell, Robert, 64
Ben Cruachan, 25
Bertram, James, 50-1
Berwick-upon-Tweed, 28
Biggar, 114, 128
Boats, libraries on, 11

Book clubs, general, 2, 119-23
    proposed, 89-90
Boston, Mass., 64
Boswell, James, 13
Bothkennar, 115
Bowman, Walter, 12
Brash & Reid, 17
Bray, Thomas, 7, 28-9
Brodie family, 17
Brougham, Lord, 83
Brown, Alexander, of Aberdeen, 55, 118
    of Edinburgh, 50
Brown, John, of Whitburn, 126
Brown, Samuel, 63, 83, 114-15, 125-6
Brown, William, of Aberdeenshire, 126
    of Dundee, 86-7
Burns, Robert, 21-2, 48, 70, 95-7, 119-20
Burrell, William, Sir, 29
Cabrach, 39-40, 70
Caldwell, George, 57
Cambusnethan, 70
Campbeltown, 70, 114
Canada, 64
Carlile, Richard, 103
Carlyle, Thomas, 67
Carnegie, Andrew, 79

Carruthers, Willy, 4, 107
Castle Douglas, 67
Chambers, Robert, 52-3, 60-1, 92
Chambers, William, 51-2, 61-2
Charleston, S.C., 19-20, 29, 65
Charters, Samuel, 69
Children's libraries, 115, 124
Circulating libraries, general, 2-4, 9-11, 65-9, 86-9, 125, 135-6
    abroad, 64-5
    for foreign books, 117
Clark, George, 106
Clennell, John, 43
Coke, William, 46
Coldstream, 36, 43
Colman, George, 13
Comrie, 124
Covington, 76-7
Creech, William, 3
Crichton, Thomas, 40
Crieff, 116
Cumbernauld, 127
Cupar, 38, 42, 97, 116, 129
Dalbeattie, 67
Dalkeith, 6, 73-6, 108
Davidson, Alexander, 57
Denholm, 89, 113
Dick, Robert, 67-8
Drawings, lending of, 118-19
Drummond, Peter R., 68
Dumfries, 7-9, 28, 38, 67, 96-7
Dunbar, 62-3, 115
Dunblane, 8
Dundee, 36-7, 43, 66-8, 85, 86-7, 110-11, 116

Dunfermline, 41, 62, 77-9, 88, 122
Dunkeld, 113, 121
Duns, 29-30, 36-8, 42-7, 85, 88-91, 94, 106-7, 110
Dunscore, 95-6
Edinburgh, circulating libraries, 3, 9-10, 33, 46-53, 65, 67-8, 87-9, 115, 117-8
    newspaper club, 121
    subscription libraries, 5, 30, 39, 44, 84, 90, 98, 103-5
    theological libraries, 112-13
Elder, Alexander, 60-2
Elgin, 58, 92
Elliot, Charles, 46, 92-3, 116
Eyemouth, 67
Falkirk, 85
Fancourt, Samuel, 2
Farquhar, William, 59-60
Fenwick, 25, 39
Findlater, Mary, 43, 108
Forbes, John, 50-1
Forbes, Peter, 6, 74-6, 108
Forsyth, Isaac, 13, 58-9, 91-2
Fort William, 33
Fowlis, 111
Franklin, Benjamin, 28
Galashiels, 33, 44, 128
Galloway, Robert, 67
Galt, John, 101
Gardenstone, Francis, Lord, 13-14
Geddes, William, 11
Gilfillan, Samuel, 124-5
Glasgow, book club, 114
    circulating libraries, 54, 67, 117-18

subscription libraries, 41, 45, 71, 83, 86, 107, 109, 114, 115, 117
Gorrie, Archibald, 13
Govan, 16
Grant, James, Sir, 17
Gray, John, 12
Greenock, 34, 37-9, 43, 85-6, 101, 105-6, 111, 115, 128
Haddington, 12, 63
Hall, Agnes E., 102
Hall, James, 5, 44
Hamilton, Janet, 63-4, 71
Hawick, 29, 33-4, 36, 37, 92-4, 107, 127, 129
Hill, John, 67, 107
Hill, Peter, 95-6
Hopetoun, earls of, James, 3rd earl, 16, 23
    John, 2nd earl, 19, 23
    John, 6th earl, 24
Hume, David, 121
Hunter, William, 65, 87
Imlach, James, 57, 81
Innerpeffray, 11-12
Innerwick, 124
Inns, libraries in, 13-15
Inshewan, 40, 100
Inverkeithing, 114
Inverness, 57-8, 66, 116
Irvine, 56
Itinerating libraries, 125-6
Jamestown, 26, 88, 95
Jedburgh, 12, 28, 35-6, 102
Johnson, Samuel, 13
Juvenile libraries, 115, 124
Kelso, 28-36, 43, 102-3, 126-7

Kendal, 72, 120
Kennedy, James, 107
Kilmarnock, 37-8, 43, 56, 85-6, 103
Kincaid & Donaldson, 31, 94
Kincardine, 122
Kingston, Jamaica, 64
Kinloch Rannoch, 15
Kinnear, Robert, 33, 65
Kinross, 79
Kirkcudbright, 33, 39-41, 44, 79, 85-6, 108, 110
Kirkintilloch, 121
Kirkwood, James, 7
Lamlash, 128
Lanark, 15-16, 67, 122
Lane, William, 66
Langholm, 110-11
Langloan, 63, 70-1
Lauder, John, Sir, 9
Laurencekirk, 13-14
Law libraries, 116
Lawrie, Alexander, 49
Lawson, George, 112
Leadhills, 17-24
Leake, James, 10-11
Leith, 46
Lilliesleaf, 41, 128-9
Locke, John, 28
Logie, 12
Loudon, Samuel, 64
MacCulloch, John, 14-15
McIntosh, Donald, 113
Mackay, Alexander, 50, 59, 87, 88-9
Mackenzie, William Lyon, 64-5
McLeish, James, 87

Macmillan, A., 67
Maconachie, John, 67
Mauchline, 119-20
Medical libraries, 116
Mein, John, 64
Mein, Susan, 4
Melrose, 4, 36, 108, 115
Meuros, James, 56
Military libraries, 42
Millar, James, 81-2
Millar, John, 70-2
Miller, George, 62-3, 73
Miners' libraries, 17-27
Moir, George, 56
Molleson, Alexander, 54
Montgomery, John, 67
Montrose, 9, 38, 45, 85, 89, 90-2 105, 110, 131-2
Morison, David, 53-4
Morison, Robert, 53
Muir, Thomas, 121
Murray, James, 67
Murray, John, 49
Music, lending of, 54-5, 117-8
New Lanark, 82
New York, 29, 64
Newman, A. K., 66, 69
Newspapers, lending of, 9, 50-1, 122
   for use in library, 105
Newton, 27
Niagara-on-the-Lake, 65
Nicoll, Robert, 68-9
North Berwick, 125
Oldmeldrum, 67
Orkney, 84-5, 97

Ormiston, 16
Otto, William, 22
Owen, Robert, 82
Paine, Thomas, 100-1, 103, 112, 121
Paisley, 39-40, 42-3, 56-7, 64, 77, 92, 112, 115, 122-3
Pate, James, 88, 98
Paul, Matthew, 68
Peat, David, 68
Peddie, James, 5, 44, 113
Peebles, 60-2
Perth, 28, 41, 43, 53-4, 68, 84, 89, 90, 92, 97-8, 109, 128
Peterhead, 39, 43-44, 59-60, 77, 90-1, 98-9, 106, 108, 128
Philadelphia, 28-9, 64
Pocklington, 5
Preshome, 114
Prints, lending of, 49, 118-19
Prisoners-of-war, 42
Private libraries, lending from, 16-17
Rait, 13
Ramsay, Allan, 9-11, 19, 50
Ramsay, John, 13-14
Renton, 39, 86, 91
Ridpath, George, 30-2
Robertson, William, 67
Rothesay, 71, 115
Rutherford, Archibald, 35
Saltoun, 8
Scott, Walter, Sir, 3, 32-3, 47-8, 51, 79
Selkirk, 36, 42, 44, 91, 92-3, 101, 105, 112-13, 120
Sibbald, James, 46-50, 94
Smellie, William, 15

Smiles, Samuel, 126
Smith, James, 66
Smith, John, I, II, III, 54, 65
Smith, Mary, 108
Society for Promoting Christian Knowledge, 7, 119
Somerville, Alexander, 62, 108-9, 124
Stirling, 41, 113-14, 116
Stirling, James, 18-19
Stirling, Walter, 45
Stirling, William, 39
Stranraer, 67-8, 113
Struthers, Gavin, 5
Struthers, John, 17
Subscription libraries, general, 1-2, 5-6, 28-9, 84-6, 98-9, 123-5, 127-30, 133-4
   librarians, 106-9
   shares & borrowing rights, 36-42, 73
   stock, 90-105
   workers', 69-84
Sutherland, John, 51
Symington, James, 49
Tansh, Joannah, 33, 51, 115
Taylor, William, 109
Telford, Thomas, 26-27, 110
Theological libraries, 111-3
Thom, Agnes, 16
Tillicoultry, 73
Tranent, 124
Tyndrum, 26
Wanlockhead, 24-5, 95
Watt, James, 111
Wells, Robert, 19-20

Westerkirk, 26-7
White, William, 56
Wigtown, 34, 79, 85-6
Wilson, Matthew, 22
Wilson, William, 33, 50-2
Wodrow, Robert, 9-10
Women, as library members, 33-5, 39-40, 73
Wordsworth, Dorothy, 23-4
Workers' libraries, 69-84
Yair, John, 10
Zetetical societies, 103-5